INQUIRY JOURNAL

DISCOVERING OUR PAST
A HISTORY OF THE
WORLD
EARLY AGES

Cover: (l to r) Christina, Queen of Sweden; Confucius; West African griot; Alaric; Omar Khayyam

Cover Credits: McGraw-Hill Education

mheducation.com/prek-12

Send all queries to:
McGraw-Hill Education
8787 Orion Place
Columbus, OH 43240

ISBN: 978-0-07-692755-5
MHID: 0-07-692755-5

Printed in the United States of America.

5 6 7 8 9 LWI 23 22 21

Table of Contents

Dear Student,

Most of us are curious, and we have questions about many things. We have the more personal questions, such as, "Will my favorite book be made into a movie?" or "Why does my former best friend not want to hang out with me anymore?" to questions of a larger nature about the world around us. These might include questions such as, "What does being treated like an adult mean?" "Why can't people share?" "Why do we have to go to war?" "How do I understand what I see or read about in history, online, or in the news?" and "Why is the peace process so difficult?"

Asking good questions helps us take charge of our own learning. Learning to ask good questions is a process, as "yes" and "no" types of questions do not get us very far in discovering why events happened or why people feel as they do. Once we master this process, however, we become better thinkers and researchers and can find out more about subjects that interest us. Asking good questions is also important if we want to understand and affect the world around us.

In this book, as in other parts of this program, there will be "Essential Questions" that you will research. These types of questions concern all people – those who have lived, those who are living now, and those who will live in the future. Examples of these questions include: "How do new ideas change the way people live?" "What makes a culture unique?" "What characteristics make a good leader?" and "Why does conflict develop?" You will choose some of your own supporting questions to help you answer the Essential Question.

As you move through the study of history, you will be reading primary and secondary sources about a specific time period. Primary sources—whether they are diaries, poetry, letters, or artwork—were created by people who saw or experienced the event they are describing. Secondary sources—whether they are biographies, or history books, or your student text—are created after an event by people who were not part of the original event.

Once you have completed the readings and the text notes, there is a "Report Your Findings" project in which you answer the Essential Question. You will work on some parts of the project by yourself, and you will work on other parts of the project with your classmates. You will be given many opportunities to take informed action. This means that you will use what you have learned and apply it to a current issue in a way that interests you. You will share this information with other students or with people outside of the classroom.

What Does a Historian Do?

ESSENTIAL QUESTIONS

- ## Why is history important?
- ## How do we learn about the past?
- ## How do you research history?

Think about what you know about history. How do you learn about historical events? How do you know that the facts are correct?

TALK ABOUT IT COLLABORATE

With a partner, discuss the information you would need to answer these questions. For example, one question might be: *How do historians decide which events are important?*

DIRECTIONS: Now write three additional questions that will help you explain why history is important.

MY RESEARCH QUESTIONS

Supporting Question 1:

_____

_____

Supporting Question 2:

_____

_____

Supporting Question 3:

_____

_____

What Is History?

DIRECTIONS: Search for evidence in the lesson to help you answer the following questions.

1 DETERMINING CENTRAL IDEAS Why do people study history?

_____

_____

_____

2 DESCRIBING How do historians measure time using labels?

_____

_____

3 COMPARING What are some similar features of the different calendars that were developed?

_____

_____

_____

4 DRAWING CONCLUSIONS Why might a historian use a time line instead of a calendar to show when events occurred?

_____

_____

_____

_____

_____

ESSENTIAL QUESTION

Why is history important?

As you gather evidence to answer the Essential Question, think about:

- what history is.
- what history can explain.
- how historians measure and describe time.

My Notes

_____

_____

_____

_____

_____

_____

5 **IDENTIFYING CONNECTIONS** How did the Gregorian calendar improve upon the Julian calendar?

_____
_____
_____
_____
_____
_____
_____
_____
_____

6 HISTORY How is studying prehistory different from studying events that were recorded in writing?

_____
_____
_____
_____
_____
_____
_____
_____
_____
_____

The History of Herodotus

ESSENTIAL QUESTION

Why is history important?

DIRECTIONS: Study the excerpt below. Then respond to the questions that follow.

EXPLORE THE CONTEXT: *The History of Herodotus* was written by Greek historian and geographer Herodotus in about 400 B.C.E. Herodotus traveled extensively and spent his lifetime compiling information about the Greco-Persian Wars. This book represents the first time a historian attempted to write about history in an organized, factual manner including a cause-and-effect explanation of events. After his death, his writing was divided into nine books.

PRIMARY SOURCE: BOOK

66 This is the Showing forth of the Inquiry of Herodotus of Halicarnassos, to the end that neither the deeds of men may be forgotten by lapse of time, nor the works great and marvellous, which have been produced some by Hellenes and some by Barbarians, may lose their renown; and especially that the causes may be remembered for which these waged war with one another. 99

— from *The History of Herodotus, Herodotus, 440* B.C.E.

VOCABULARY

deeds: actions
lapse: passage
Hellenes: Greeks and other members of the Greek Empire
Barbarians: people who were not part of the Greek Empire
renown: fame
waged: carried on

1 DESCRIBING Who is the audience for this book?

_____

_____

_____

2 IDENTIFYING PERSPECTIVES What was Herodotus's purpose for writing the book?

_____

_____

_____

_____

_____

3 **DETERMINING POINT OF VIEW** Why did Herodotus think people might forget about the events he wrote about?

_____

_____

_____

_____

_____

4 **DRAWING CONCLUSIONS** Based on this excerpt, what kinds of events can the reader predict will be described in the book?

_____

_____

_____

_____

_____

_____

5 **HISTORY** Herodotus was the first historian to write in a narrative form. What does Herodotus have in common with modern historians?

_____

_____

_____

_____

_____

_____

_____

Understanding the Past

ESSENTIAL QUESTION

Why is history important?

DIRECTIONS: Study the excerpt below. Then respond to the questions that follow.

EXPLORE THE CONTEXT: The Society for American Archaeology produced a series of articles to guide teachers in teaching history called "Archaeology for Educators." The following excerpt appears in one of the articles.

PRIMARY SOURCE: ARTICLE

❝This thirst for knowledge reaches into the past, even when one is focused on solving contemporary problems. The search for solutions often requires an understanding of how problems developed or how our elders might have approached analogous problems in the past. We study both our collective pasts and our individual pasts to gain a better understanding of who we are today and where we are going in the future. Lessons learned from the past can influence—hopefully for the better—the social, political, and environmental actions we take today.

By studying the past we learn how and why people lived as they did throughout the world and the changes and causes of such changes, that occurred within these cultures. We study the past to acquire a broader and richer understanding of our world today and our place in it. ❞

— from *Understanding the Past,* Society for American Archaeology, 2018

VOCABULARY

contemporary: current or modern
elders: people who are older or who lived in the past
analogous: similar
collective: shared
acquire: gain

1 **DETERMINING CENTRAL IDEAS** What is the main idea of this excerpt?

_____

_____

_____

_____

_____

2 IDENTIFYING PERSPECTIVES Why did the author write this article?

_____

_____

_____

_____

3 `HISTORY` According to the author, why do we study history?

_____

_____

_____

_____

_____

4 SUMMARIZING What does the author say is needed to solve current problems?

_____

_____

_____

_____

_____

5 INFERRING Think of a problem that your community faces. Based on the excerpt, what kind of advice do you think the author would give on how to solve that problem?

_____

_____

_____

_____

_____

ESSENTIAL QUESTION

How do we learn about the past?

As you gather evidence to answer the Essential Question, think about:

- what types of evidence historians use to understand the past.
- how historians write about evidence.
- how a person's experiences can affect how that person interprets the past.

My Notes

How Does a Historian Work?

DIRECTIONS: Search for evidence in the lesson to help you answer the following questions.

1 **DETERMINING CENTRAL IDEAS** How do historians answer questions they have about the past?

2A **CONTRASTING** What is the difference between a primary source and a secondary source?

2B **DESCRIBING** Fill in the chart below with examples of primary and secondary sources.

Primary Sources	Secondary Sources

3 DRAWING CONCLUSIONS Why is it important for historians to determine if a source is reliable?

_____

_____

_____

4 IDENTIFYING STEPS Describe the steps historians take to draw conclusions and make inferences about historical events.

_____

_____

_____

_____

_____

_____

5 DRAWING CONCLUSIONS Why is it important that scholars review each other's work?

_____

_____

_____

6 HISTORY What are some reasons that historians might have different interpretations of events in history?

_____

_____

_____

_____

Why Study History?

ESSENTIAL QUESTION
How do we learn about the past?

DIRECTIONS: Study the excerpt below. Then respond to the questions that follow.

EXPLORE THE CONTEXT: Historians can predict certain outcomes based on their previous study of cause-and-effect relationships. The following is an excerpt from an article on the Web site for the American Historical Association.

PRIMARY SOURCE: ARTICLE

" . . . Historians do not perform heart transplants, improve highway design, or arrest criminals. . . . History is in fact very useful, actually indispensable, but the products of historical study are less tangible, sometimes less immediate, than those that stem from some other disciplines.

. . . [H]istory offers a storehouse of information about how people and societies behave. . . . [H]istory is inescapable as a subject of serious study follows closely on the first. The past causes the present, and so the future. Any time we try to know why something happened—whether a shift in political party dominance in the American Congress, a major change in the teenage suicide rate, or a war in the Balkans or the Middle East—we have to look for factors that took shape earlier. . . . Only through studying history can we grasp how things change; only through history can we begin to comprehend the factors that cause change; and only through history can we understand what elements of an institution or a society persist despite change. "

—from *Why Study History*, Peter N. Stearns, 1998

VOCABULARY

indispensable: necessary
tangible: able to be held
inescapable: unavoidable
dominance: the state of being superior
comprehend: to understand
persist: stay the same

1 ANALYZING STRUCTURE Why does the author begin this excerpt with a list of things that historians do not do?

_____

_____

_____

_____

2 **IDENTIFYING CONNECTIONS** How does the author argue that events that have taken place in the past are connected to events that will take place in the future?

_____

_____

_____

_____

3 **ANALYZING CENTRAL IDEAS** What is the central idea of this article?

_____

_____

_____

_____

_____

4 HISTORY The author mentions that we might want to understand the causes of a war in the Balkans. Why might it be important to understand why wars start?

_____

_____

_____

_____

5 **INTEGRATING INFORMATION** What can you infer the author wants the readers of this article to do?

_____

_____

_____

_____

The Historical Point of View

ESSENTIAL QUESTION

How do we learn about the past?

VOCABULARY

conditions: the circumstances in which people live

convenient: easy

urged: suggested or stated

DIRECTIONS: Study the excerpt below. Then respond to the questions that follow.

EXPLORE THE CONTEXT: This excerpt was written by American historian James Harvey Robinson in 1904. Robinson focused on more than the technicalities of what occurred in history in his studies. He sought to put historical events in the context of the times in which they occurred. In this excerpt, Robinson discusses primary and secondary sources.

PRIMARY SOURCE: BOOK

❝ It is clear that all our information in regard to past events and conditions must be derived from evidence of some kind. This evidence is called the *source*. Sometimes there are a number of good and reliable sources for an event. . . . Sometimes there is but a single, unreliable source . . . For a great many important matters about which we should like to know there are, unfortunately, no written sources at all, and we can only guess how things were. . . .

Few, however, of those who read and study history ever come in contact with the *primary*, or first-hand sources; they get their information at second hand. It is much more convenient to read what Gibbon has to say of Constantine than to refer to Eusebius, Eutropius, and other ancient writers from whom he gained his knowledge. Moreover, Gibbon carefully studied and compared all the primary sources, and it may be urged that he has given a truer, fuller, and more attractive account of the period than can be found in any one of them. His *Decline and Fall of the Roman Empire* is certainly a work of the highest rank; but, nevertheless, it is only a report of others' reports. It is therefore not a *primary* but a *secondary* source. ❞

—from *Readings in European History*, James Harvey Robinson, 1904

1 **DETERMINING CENTRAL IDEAS** What is the main idea of this excerpt?

_____

_____

_____

2 **ANALYZING TEXT** Who is the audience for this article?

_____

_____

_____

3 **INFERRING** What can the reader infer about Eusebius and Eutropius based on the excerpt?

_____

_____

_____

_____

4 **ANALYZING POINTS OF VIEW** What argument does the author present for using a secondary source?

_____

_____

_____

_____

5 HISTORY The author describes the difference between a primary and a secondary source. Based on what you know about studying history, why is understanding this difference important?

_____

_____

_____

_____

_____

ESSENTIAL QUESTION

How do you research history?

As you gather evidence to answer the Essential Question, think about:

- how to conduct research.
- how to use the Internet safely.
- how to tell fact from opinion.

My Notes

Researching History

DIRECTIONS: Search for evidence in the lesson to help you answer the following questions.

1A EVALUATING INFORMATION Why is it important to have a topic that is not too broad or too narrow?

1B ANALYZING IDEAS How can a researcher narrow a topic that is too broad? Give an example.

2A DISTINGUISHING FACT FROM OPINION What is the difference between a fact and an opinion?

2B DISTINGUISHING FACT FROM OPINION Give at least one example of a fact and one example of an opinion.

Fact	Opinion

3 ANALYZING SOURCES What can a researcher conclude about a source that contains many opinions?

_____

_____

4 EVALUATING EVIDENCE What are two things a researcher can do to determine if an article on the Internet is a reliable source?

_____

_____

_____

_____

_____

5 EVALUATING Why are there laws against plagiarism, and how can a researcher avoid plagiarizing?

_____

_____

_____

_____

_____

6 EVALUATING EVIDENCE Why should researchers avoid evaluating and drawing conclusions about historical events based on modern attitudes?

_____

_____

_____

_____

_____

Library or Archive?

ESSENTIAL QUESTION

How do you research history?

DIRECTIONS: Read the excerpt below. Then respond to the questions that follow.

EXPLORE THE CONTEXT: This excerpt discusses the similarities and differences between a library and an archive. The excerpt describes how each resource can be valuable to historians.

PRIMARY SOURCE: ARTICLE

66Which is a better resource to help you find the information you need, a library or an archives? Libraries and archives are different from one another in many ways. Here are some of the differences you can expect:

. . . A library contains published books and periodicals that usually can be checked out and replaced if lost or stolen. When using a library, you would:

- Use a card- or online-catalog that lists every item in the library's collections.

- Identify each item that you would like to use by its call number, which is a code used to categorize and organize items in libraries by subject.

- Walk directly to a shelf in the library and retrieve an item (self-service).

Questions relating to general historical or factual information, biographical information, and compiled, statistical information are usually better answered in a library. . . .

An archives provides access to original records that were created and/or accumulated by a person, family, organization, or government institution in the course of its "life" or daily business. Because these records usually cannot be replaced, security and preservation of the records play an important role in making them available to the public. 99

— from *Gather Information About Your Topic*. National Archives and Records Administration, National Archives, 2018

VOCABULARY

archives: a collection of original records that contain historical information and data

periodicals: publications that are put out at regular intervals, such as newspapers and magazines

accumulated: gathered

1 **COMPARING** What is one way that archives and libraries are alike?

_____

_____

_____

2 **CONTRASTING** What is one way that materials in a library are different from materials in an archive?

_____

_____

_____

3 **HISTORY** Should a researcher looking for the transcript of a speech given at a city council meeting in her town 20 years ago look in her local library or the city's archives? Why?

_____

_____

_____

_____

4 **DESCRIBING** What is a disadvantage of making archives available to the public?

_____

_____

_____

5 **ANALYZING INFORMATION** What is one way that archivists could make archives more accessible to the public?

_____

_____

_____

_____

Evaluating Sources

Shanahan, Timothy and Shanahan, Cynthia. "Teaching Disciplinary Literacy to Adolescents: Rethinking Content-Area Literacy." Harvard Educational Review 78, no. 1, Spring 2008.

ESSENTIAL QUESTION

How do you research history?

DIRECTIONS: Study the excerpt below. Then respond to the questions that follow.

EXPLORE THE CONTEXT: The following excerpt is from an article in the *Harvard Educational Review*, a scholarly journal about education. The article discusses the ways that experts in different subject areas analyze the material they are reading. The following excerpt focuses on the way that historians interpret sources.

PRIMARY SOURCE: ARTICLE

"The historians . . . emphasized paying attention to the author or source when reading any text. That is, before reading, they would consider who the authors of the texts were and what their biases might be. Their purpose during the reading seemed to be to figure out what story a particular author wanted to tell; in other words, they were keenly aware that they were reading an interpretation of historical events and not 'Truth.'

. . . [T]he historian is revealing that he does not read the text as truth, but rather as an interpretation that has to be judged based on its credibility. He attempts to evaluate its credibility through an examination of the author's biases. . . . [H]e also knows that he, as a reader, has his own biases, and that . . . he could miss important insights. The point is that he reads with a view in which both author and reader are fallible and positioned."

— from *Teaching Disciplinary Literacy to Adolescents: Rethinking Content-Area Literacy*, Timothy Shanahan and Cynthia Shanahan, 2008

VOCABULARY

biases: opinions or prejudices that affect a person's viewpoint
keenly: intensely
credibility: likelihood of being true
insights: deep understandings
fallible: capable of being wrong

1 ANALYZING CENTRAL IDEAS According to the author, what do historians pay attention to as they read a text?

_____

_____

_____

2 DETERMINING POINT OF VIEW Why does the author place the word _Truth_ in quotation marks?

_____

_____

_____

_____

3 HISTORY Why do historians need to be aware of the biases held by authors of texts they are reading?

_____

_____

_____

_____

4 EVALUATING EVIDENCE Based on the article, how might a historian's personal biases affect how he or she interprets a source?

_____

_____

_____

_____

5 IDENTIFYING PERSPECTIVES What do the author of a text and the reader have in common based on the information in the article?

_____

_____

_____

ESSENTIAL QUESTIONS

Why is history important?

How do we learn about the past?

How do you research history?

1 Think About It

Think back to the Supporting Questions you wrote at the beginning of the chapter. Review the evidence that you gathered in this chapter. Do you have the evidence you need to answer your questions? What else do you need to know?

_____

_____

_____

_____

_____

2 Organize Your Evidence

Fill in the chart with the information you learned about why it is important to study history and how history is studied. Use the information in the chart to develop a position statement about what historians do.

The Importance of Studying History	How History Is Studied

3 Talk About It

With a partner or in a small group, discuss your Supporting Questions and the evidence you gathered in the chart. Think about any evidence you still need to gather to answer your questions. Take notes on the discussion, writing down the main points your peers make and any questions that come up.

_____

_____

_____

_____

_____

4 Write About It

On a separate piece of paper, write one paragraph to answer each Essential Question in this chapter. Use your Supporting Questions, the evidence you gathered in the chart, and your position statement to write your answers.

5 Connect to the Essential Questions

Working with a partner, diagram or create a plan for a game that would help students understand the study of history. Make sure your game addresses the Essential Questions from this chapter: _Why is history important? How do we learn about the past? How do you research history?_

TAKE ACTION

MAKE CONNECTIONS Historians help people understand their place in the world by interpreting and writing about the historical events that led to where we are now. Understanding a shared history can help people feel connected to one another and their communities.

DIRECTIONS: Think about something that is special about your community. Is there a park that everyone enjoys? Do you have an amazing theater group? Is there an attraction that people travel to see? Choose something about your town that you think is special. Research the history of the place or thing that you chose. Create a slide show that shows your audience the history of your subject. Your slide show should include images and details that illustrate the history and show how this place or thing came to be associated with your community. Share your slide show with the class, with a historical group in your community, or at a senior center.

_____

_____

_____

_____

_____

_____

_____

_____

_____

_____

Studying Geography, Economics, and Citizenship

ESSENTIAL QUESTIONS

- ## How does geography influence the way people live?
- ## Why do people trade?
- ## Why do people form governments?

Think about how these three questions explain where and how people live.

TALK ABOUT IT COLLABORATE

Discuss with a partner what information you would need to know to answer these questions. For example, one question might be: *What types of governments do people form?*

DIRECTIONS: Now write three additional questions that will help you explain how geography affects people's lives, why people trade, and why people form governments.

MY RESEARCH QUESTIONS

Supporting Question 1:

_____

_____

Supporting Question 2:

_____

_____

Supporting Question 3:

_____

_____

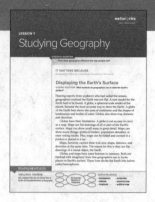

ESSENTIAL QUESTION

How does geography influence the way people live?

As you gather evidence to answer the Essential Question, think about:

- the different types of maps and how they help us understand where and how people live.

- the Six Essential Elements of Geography and how they can be used to discuss where and how people live.

- how charts, graphs, diagrams, and tables can be used to study human populations.

My Notes

Studying Geography

DIRECTIONS: Search for evidence in the lesson to help you answer the following questions.

1 **DETERMINING CENTRAL IDEAS** How can a geographer identify a place's absolute location?

_____

_____

_____

_____

2 **CONTRASTING** Contrast the advantages of maps using Goode's Interrupted Equal-Area projection, the Mercator projection, the Robinson projection, and the Winkel Tripel projection.

_____

_____

_____

_____

_____

_____

_____

_____

_____

_____

_____

_____

_____

3 GEOGRAPHY Use the following chart to give examples of the five themes of geography.

FIVE THEMES OF GEOGRAPHY	
Theme	**Example**
Location	
Place	
Human-environment interaction	
Movement	
Regions	

4 **CONTRASTING** How are general-purpose maps different from special-purpose maps?

_____

_____

_____

_____

_____

5 **ANALYZING IDEAS** Why would a geographer be interested in studying culture?

_____

_____

_____

_____

_____

Report on Human Impacts on Oceans

DIRECTIONS: Study the excerpt below and answer the accompanying questions.

EXPLORE THE CONTEXT: Scientists studying the oceans and other natural systems often account for human influences on those systems. In this article, a group of marine scientists presents its findings from a study of marine ecosystems.

VOCABULARY

cumulative: including or adding everything that came before
quantitative: relating to how much there is of something
temporal: relating to time
proactive: controlling a situation by preparing for problems
trajectories: processes of change

PRIMARY SOURCE: ARTICLE

66 The ocean is crowded with human uses. As human populations continue to grow and migrate to the coasts, demand for ocean space and resources is expanding, increasing the individual and cumulative pressures from a range of human activities.

. . . Quantitative methods to map cumulative human impacts were recently developed and initially applied to marine ecosystems globally. . . . Missing from these studies is an assessment of the location and intensity of change in cumulative impacts over time. Such temporal assessments would illuminate where and to what degree stressors are increasing or decreasing in intensity and impact, thus providing a means to assess management efficacy and adaptively respond to change. They can also support proactive management by informing our expectation of future states by tracking current trajectories. . . . 99

—from *Nature Communications* by Benjamin S. Halpern, Melanie Frazier, et al., 2015

1 INTERPRETING What problem have the authors of the article been studying?

_____

_____

2 INTEGRATING INFORMATION Which of the Six Essential Elements of Geography does this article address? Explain.

_____

_____

_____

_____

3 EVALUATING ARGUMENTS What argument do the authors make about the problem? How do they support this argument?

_____

_____

_____

_____

_____

_____

4 PREDICTING If the authors persuade others successfully, what might be the outcome?

_____

_____

_____

5 GEOGRAPHY The authors describe a problem in the environment. If this problem is not addressed, how might it affect human populations?

_____

_____

_____

Population Projections

ESSENTIAL QUESTION

How does geography influence the way people live?

VOCABULARY

native: born in a place

DIRECTIONS: Study the table below and answer the accompanying questions.

EXPLORE THE CONTEXT: Beginning in 1790, the U.S. Census Bureau has collected data about the American people and economy. In addition to counting the country's population, the agency analyzes data in several categories. The data is available to the public to study.

PRIMARY SOURCE: TABLE

	Projected Size of the Native and Foreign-Born Population 2016–2060						
	Native			**Foreign Born**			**Percent Foreign Born**
	Population	**Numeric Change**	**Percent Change**	**Population**	**Numeric Change**	**Percent Change**	
2016	279,283,000	—	—	43,845,000	—	—	13.57
2020	285,852,000	1,634,000	0.58	46,703,000	716,000	1.56	14.04
2025	293,786,000	1,542,000	0.53	50,270,000	711,000	1.43	14.61
2030	301,057,000	1,387,000	0.46	53,783,000	690,000	1.30	15.16
2035	307,425,000	1,200,000	0.39	57,104,000	645,000	1.14	15.67
2040	312,965,000	1,055,000	0.34	60,156,000	586,000	0.98	16.12
2045	318,006,000	990,000	0.31	62,894,000	521,000	0.84	16.51
2050	323,025,000	1,025,000	0.32	65,310,000	458,000	0.71	16.82
2055	328,434,000	1,124,000	0.34	67,434,000	404,000	0.60	17.03
2060	334,364,000	1,224,000	0.37	69,333,000	366,000	0.53	17.17

Note: Data on population change refers to differences in population between July 1 of the preceding year and June 30 of the indicated year. 2016 base population. Nativity is determined based on country of birth. Those born in the United States or in U.S. territories are considered native born while those born elsewhere are considered foreign born.

Source: U.S. Census Bureau, Population Division: Washington, D.C. March, 2018

1. **INTERPRETING CHARTS** What information is presented in this table?

2. **DETERMINING MEANING** Why does the data for the year 2016 appear different from the data in the other rows?

3. **INTERPRETING TABLES** What conclusion can you reach about the Census Bureau's predictions?

4. **CONSTRUCTING HYPOTHESES** Looking at these predictions, what hypothesis do you have about the data in the years before 2016? Explain.

5. **GEOGRAPHY** What geographic factors might explain the Census Bureau's predictions about the foreign-born population?

ESSENTIAL QUESTION

Why do people trade?

As you gather evidence to answer the Essential Question, think about:

- what economics is.
- the role of trade among countries.
- the advantages and disadvantages of world trade.

My Notes

Exploring Economics

DIRECTIONS: Search for evidence in the lesson to help you answer the following questions.

1 **DESCRIBING** Why is capital necessary for people to make goods and offer services?

_____

_____

_____

2A **DETERMINING CENTRAL IDEAS** How do supply and demand interact in a free market economy?

_____

_____

_____

_____

_____

2B **IDENTIFYING EFFECTS** How does scarcity affect supply and demand?

_____

_____

_____

3 **DESCRIBING** What happens when an economy expands and contracts?

_____

_____

_____

4 **EVALUATING INFORMATION** A country produces more grain than its population needs. At the same time, the country has very few trees to produce lumber. How might the country manage its exports and imports?

_____

_____

_____

_____

5 ECONOMICS Use the chart below to contrast the advantages and disadvantages of global trade.

ADVANTAGES AND DISADVANTAGES OF GLOBAL TRADE	
Advantages	**Disadvantages**

A Debate on Free Trade

DIRECTIONS: Study the excerpt below and answer the accompanying questions.

EXPLORE THE CONTEXT: The issue of free trade versus the protection of home industries has long inspired debate. French economist Frédéric Bastiat outlined arguments related to economic restrictions in his book *Economic Sophisms*. A sophism is an argument built on a false belief. This type of argument can be deliberately made in order to trick an opponent.

PRIMARY SOURCE: BOOK

❝ You enter the legislative precincts. The subject of debate is whether the law should prohibit international exchanges, or proclaim freedom.

A deputy rises, and says:—
If you tolerate these exchanges the foreigner will inundate you with his products: England with her textile fabrics, Belgium with coals, Spain with wools, Italy with silks, Switzerland with cattle . . . so that home industry will no longer be possible.

Another replies: —

If you prohibit international exchanges the various bounties which nature has lavished on different climates will be for you as if they did not exist. You cannot participate in the mechanical skill of the English, in the wealth of the Belgian mines, in the fertility of the Polish soil, in the luxuriance of the Swiss pastures, in the cheapness of Spanish labour, in the warmth of the Italian climate; and you must obtain from an unprofitable and misdirected production those commodities which, through exchange, would have been furnished to you by an easy production.

Assuredly, one of these deputies must be wrong. But which? . . . You have to choose between two roads, and one of them leads necessarily to poverty. **❞**

—from *Economic Sophisms* by Frédéric Bastiat, 1909

VOCABULARY

inundate: to overwhelm or flood
bounties: things given in great amounts
lavished: gave generously
commodities: materials or products that can be bought or sold

1 **ANALYZING TEXT** How does the author present two sides of a debate?

_____

_____

2 **DETERMINING POINT OF VIEW** What do you think the author's opinion is about the two sides of the debate? Support your answer with evidence from the text.

_____

_____

_____

_____

_____

3 **ECONOMICS** In your own words, write a statement about what the author might say about free trade.

_____

_____

_____

4 **CITING TEXT EVIDENCE** What descriptive language does the author use to appeal to the reader's emotions?

_____

_____

_____

_____

5 **EVALUATING ARGUMENTS** How could the author have structured the argument differently to make the sides equal?

_____

_____

_____

Tariffs After World War I

ESSENTIAL QUESTION

Why do people trade?

DIRECTIONS: Study the excerpt below and answer the accompanying questions.

EXPLORE THE CONTEXT: After World War I, most of Europe needed to rebuild and recover economically. Soon, Europe's agricultural production had rebounded, which meant that American agricultural products were no longer in high demand there. American industries were also concerned about decreasing demand for their products in Europe.

VOCABULARY

tariff: a tax on imports or exports
entrenched: established and unlikely to change
protectionism: the practice of shielding a country's home industries from foreign competition
foster: to encourage or promote
perilous: dangerous

SECONDARY SOURCE: ARTICLE

❝To provide protection for American farmers, whose wartime markets in Europe were disappearing with the recovery of European agricultural production, as well as U.S. industries that had been stimulated by the war, Congress passed the temporary Emergency Tariff Act in 1921, followed a year later by the Fordney-McCumber Tariff Act of 1922.

. . . Calls for increased protection flooded in from industrial sector special interest groups and soon a bill meant to provide relief for farmers became a means to raise tariffs in all sectors of the economy. When the dust had settled, Congress had produced a piece of legislation, the Tariff Act of 1930, more commonly known as the Smoot-Hawley tariff, that entrenched the protectionism of the Fordney-McCumber tariff.

. . . Smoot-Hawley did nothing to foster cooperation among nations in either the economic or political realm during a perilous era in international relations.

. . . To this day, the phrase "Smoot-Hawley" remains a watchword for the perils of protectionism.❞

—from "Protectionism in the Interwar Period" by the U.S. Department of State, Office of the Historian

1 **UNDERSTANDING CONTEXT** What historical context led to the passage of the Fordney-McCumber Tariff Act of 1922?

_____

_____

_____

_____

2 **ECONOMICS** Would a tariff allow for free trade or create a barrier to it? Explain.

_____

_____

_____

3 **ANALYZING INFORMATION** The tariff was meant to protect farmers. How did its influence spread?

_____

_____

_____

_____

4 **IDENTIFYING EFFECTS** What effect did the tariff have on relationships among countries?

_____

_____

_____

5 **ANALYZING IDEAS** Reread the last sentence of the excerpt. What is the author saying about the significance of the phrase "Smoot-Hawley"?

_____

_____

_____

_____

ESSENTIAL QUESTION

Why do people form governments?

As you gather evidence to answer the Essential Question, think about:

- how governments represent people.
- the responsibilities of citizens.

My Notes

Practicing Citizenship

DIRECTIONS: Search for evidence in the lesson to help you answer the following questions.

1 **DESCRIBING** What makes the U.S. government a representative government?

_____

_____

_____

_____

2 **IDENTIFYING CONNECTIONS** Complete the chart to name a check each branch of the U.S. government has on the other branches.

		Example of Check
Executive branch checks the	legislative branch by	
Executive branch checks the	judicial branch by	
Legislative branch checks the	executive branch by	
Legislative branch checks the	judicial branch by	
Judicial branch checks the	executive branch by	
Judicial branch checks the	legislative branch by	

3 **EXPLAINING ISSUES** Why could it be a problem for society if citizens did not stay informed about important issues?

_____

_____

_____

_____

_____

4 **IDENTIFYING EFFECTS** Why is civic participation necessary in a society?

_____

_____

_____

_____

_____

_____

5 GEOGRAPHY How does increased globalization affect people's responsibilities as citizens?

_____

_____

_____

_____

_____

_____

Preamble to the Constitution of the United States

ESSENTIAL QUESTION
Why do people form governments?

DIRECTIONS: Study the excerpt below and answer the accompanying questions.

EXPLORE THE CONTEXT: After the American Revolution, as the United States began to define itself as an independent country, people were divided over the role of the new government. Delegates from the states met to draft a constitution that would become the highest law of the land. After much debate, a final draft was completed in 1787.

VOCABULARY

tranquility: the state of being calm and peaceful
posterity: future generations of people
ordain: to order something officially

PRIMARY SOURCE: DOCUMENT

❝ We the People of the United States, in Order to form a more perfect Union, establish Justice, insure domestic Tranquility, provide for the common defence, promote the general Welfare, and secure the Blessings of Liberty to ourselves and our Posterity, do ordain and establish this Constitution for the United States of America. ❞

—from the Constitution of the United States, 1787

1A INFERRING What does a government need to do to "establish justice"?

_____

_____

_____

_____

1B **INFERRING** What does a government need to do to "insure domestic Tranquility"?

_____

_____

_____

_____

1C **INFERRING** What does a government need to do to "provide for the common defence"?

_____

_____

_____

_____

2 **INFERRING** Why do you think those people who wrote the Constitution were concerned about "our Posterity"?

_____

_____

_____

_____

_____

3 CIVICS How does this Preamble to the Constitution explain the reasons for the formation of the U.S. federal government?

_____

_____

_____

_____

_____

Speech Before the Virginia Ratifying Committee

ESSENTIAL QUESTION

Why do people form governments?

DIRECTIONS: Study the excerpt below and answer the accompanying questions.

EXPLORE THE CONTEXT: Before the U.S. Constitution became the law of the United States, it had to be ratified, or formally agreed to, by the states. Each state set up a committee to debate the document. Patrick Henry, who had previously served as Virginia's governor, was a state delegate in 1788 when he gave this speech to the state's ratifying committee.

PRIMARY SOURCE: SPEECH

66 Where are your checks in this government? . . . It is on a supposition that your American governors shall be honest, that all the good qualities of this government are founded; but its defective and imperfect construction puts it in their power to perpetrate the worst of mischiefs, should they be bad men; and, sir, would not all the world, from the Eastern to the Western Hemisphere, blame our distracted folly in resting our rights upon the contingency of our rulers being good or bad? Show me that age and country where the rights and liberties of the people were placed on the sole chance of their rulers being good men, without a consequent loss of liberty! I say that the loss of that dearest privilege has ever followed, with absolute certainty, every such mad attempt. 99

—from "Speech Before the Virginia Ratifying Committee" by Patrick Henry, 1788

VOCABULARY

supposition: a belief that is not fully proved; an assumption
defective: imperfect
perpetrate: to carry out a harmful action
folly: a foolish act
contingency: a future circumstance that cannot be predicted

1 **CITING TEXT EVIDENCE** Is Henry arguing for ratification at this time? Cite evidence from the text to support your answer.

_____

_____

_____

2 **DETERMINING POINT OF VIEW** What concern does Henry have? How would he solve the problem that he points out?

_____

_____

_____

3 **HISTORY** How does Henry use examples from history to support his argument?

_____

_____

_____

4 **EVALUATING ARGUMENTS** Point out descriptive language that Henry uses to appeal to his audience. What else does he do to get his audience's attention?

_____

_____

_____

_____

5 **EVALUATING ARGUMENTS** Delegates disagreed about the Constitution. What might someone state as a counterargument to Henry?

_____

_____

_____

_____

1 Think About It

ESSENTIAL QUESTIONS

How does geography influence the way people live?

Why do people trade?

Why do people form governments?

Review the Supporting Questions you developed at the beginning of the chapter. Review the evidence that you gathered in this chapter. Were you able to answer each Supporting Question?

If there was not enough evidence to answer your Supporting Questions, what additional evidence do you think you need to consider?

_____

_____

_____

2 Organize Your Evidence

Use a chart to organize the evidence you will use to support your findings about how geography, the economy, and the government affect how people live.

	How It Affects How People Live	Evidence From the Text
Geography		
Economy		
Government		

③ Talk About It

Work in small groups. Talk with your group about the effects of geography, the economy, and the government on people in the United States. Specifically discuss each category. On the lines below, take notes from the group discussion.

_____

_____

_____

④ Write About It

You will be reading about world history in future chapters. How do you think your understanding of geography, the economy, and government will relate to your understanding of historical events? Write your predictions.

_____

_____

_____

⑤ Connect to the Essential Questions

Choose a community—either yours or one that interests you. Using a mix of primary and secondary sources and your notes from the group discussion, determine how geography, the economy, and the government affect the lives of people in the community. Create a visual essay showing some of the effects these factors have on the people. Keep in mind the three ESSENTIAL QUESTIONS: _How does geography influence the way people live? Why do people trade? Why do people form governments?_

1. Identify the effects that each factor—geography, the economy, and the government—has on the people in your community. Write a paragraph for each.

2. Find images to illustrate some of the effects. Print them out to accompany your paragraphs or create a digital essay on the computer.

3. Write captions to accompany the images, explaining why you have chosen them to illustrate your points.

TAKE ACTION

MAKE CONNECTIONS The U.S. Constitution does not allow the government to make laws limiting people's freedom of speech, but that doesn't mean that people can say whatever they want without experiencing consequences. Now that people are connected online and information spreads quickly, people's speech often negatively affects the feelings and perspectives of others. Online platforms such as Twitter and Facebook have banned people who broke their rules by, for example, spreading hateful speech or harassing others. Since these organizations are companies—not the government—they have the right to limit what people can say on their sites. People often debate the limits people put on others' speech. How should companies handle speech that others find offensive?

DIRECTIONS: Think about a Web site that you are familiar with. How does it regulate what people can post? Read the terms of service if you aren't sure. How do you feel about the site's rules? Write an e-mail to the company, stating your point of view about its posting policies. Explain whether you think its policies are or are not effective and why. If you find fault with its policies, provide suggestions about how the company could improve its site.

_____

_____

_____

_____

_____

_____

Early Humans and the Agricultural Revolution

ESSENTIAL QUESTION

How do people adapt to their environment?

Think about how this question might connect the earliest human societies and civilizations to civilization today.

TALK ABOUT IT COLLABORATE

Discuss with a partner what type of information you would need to know to answer this question. For example, one question might be: How does understanding early human survival relate to people's struggles to survive today?

DIRECTIONS: Now write three additional questions that would help you to explain how the development of early humans led the way to civilization and to humans' continuing efforts to sustain a viable civilization.

MY RESEARCH QUESTIONS

Supporting Question 1:

_____

_____

Supporting Question 2:

_____

_____

Supporting Question 3:

_____

_____

ESSENTIAL QUESTION

How do people adapt to their environment?

As you gather evidence to answer the Essential Question, think about:

- how technology changed ways in which Paleolithic people existed in their environments.
- the effects of the Ice Ages on human migration.

My Notes

Hunter-Gatherers

DIRECTIONS: Search for evidence in Lesson 1 to help you complete the following items.

1 **DESCRIBING** During the Paleolithic Age, what roles did men and women play within each group to contribute to the survival of the group?

2 **HISTORY** How did the Ice Ages lead to the spread of humans from Europe and Asia into North and South America?

3 **SUMMARIZING** Answer the questions in each box. Then use your answers to summarize how Paleolithic people adapted for survival.

A. What kinds of tools and weapons did Paleolithic people make? How did they use them?

B. What kinds of shelters did Paleolithic people build or use, and why did they differ among groups?

C. How did use of fire change the lives of Paleolithic people?

D. In what ways did Paleolithic people communicate?

E. Write a summary explaining how Paleolithic people adapted.

The Role of Caves

ESSENTIAL QUESTION

How do people adapt to their environment?

DIRECTIONS: Read the following excerpt written by an anthropological archaeologist and answer the accompanying questions.

EXPLORE THE CONTEXT: Many archaeologists study caves because of the wealth of information they hold in artifacts and paintings. Archaeologist Holley Moyes explores caves as mysterious and sacred places. She has found many skeletons in the darkest parts of caves and became interested in why ancient people offered their sacrifices in these dark spaces.

VOCABULARY

anthropology: the study of human society and culture

archaeologist: a person who studies material remains to learn about the past

seminal: an important part of a work that influences other parts of the work

antiquity: the long-ago past

Pleistocene: the geological period from about 2,588,000 to 11,700 years ago

SECONDARY SOURCE: BOOK

"For over a century, the idea of living in caves has gripped the imagination of scholars and the general public to the point that, in popular culture, the term cave man has become synonymous with early humans. This is not surprising when we consider that European caves produced some of archaeology's seminal finds. . . . Much of the earliest evidence for the antiquity of man came from European caves in which Pleistocene mammal bones co-occurred with stone tools."

—Holley Moyes, *Sacred Darkness: A Global Perspective on the Ritual Use of Caves,* 2012 C.E.

1 ANALYZING Why do you think the author establishes the geographic location of the caves in this excerpt?

_____

_____

_____

_____

2 **CITING TEXT EVIDENCE** What does the author mean by saying caves have "gripped the imagination of scholars and the general public"?

_____

_____

_____

_____

3 **EXPLAINING** How does the author provide clues to the meaning of the word _seminal_?

_____

_____

_____

_____

4 **ANALYZING** Based on this excerpt, what is the author's purpose for writing this book?

_____

_____

_____

_____

5 **HISTORY** How does this excerpt help the reader know more about human ancestors?

_____

_____

_____

_____

Early Tools

DIRECTIONS Examine the image and then answer the accompanying questions.

EXPLORE THE CONTEXT: This photo shows two axe heads at left and other stone tools from the Paleolithic era. The Paleolithic era lasted from about 40,000 B.C.E. to 20,000 B.C.E.

PRIMARY SOURCE: ARTIFACTS

1 **DESCRIBING** How did early humans use these tools?

_____

_____

_____

_____

2 EXPLAINING EFFECTS How did these tools help early humans survive their environment?

_____

_____

_____

_____

_____

3 EXPLAINING Explain how stone and fire helped early humans become a social group.

_____

_____

_____

_____

_____

_____

_____

4 HISTORY What is one important way stones contributed to early humans' survival? Support your answer using information from the photograph.

_____

_____

_____

_____

_____

ESSENTIAL QUESTION

How do people adapt to their environment?

As you gather evidence to answer the Essential Question, think about:

- how farming changed the ways in which people lived.

- how peoples' communities changed as their way of life changed.

My Notes

The Agricultural Revolution

DIRECTIONS: Search for evidence in Lesson 2 to help you complete the following items.

1 **HISTORY** Use the web organizer below to show changes and advances in people's way of life during Neolithic times.

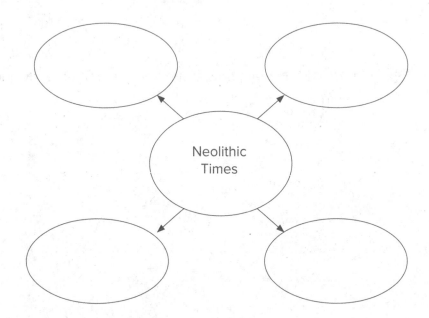

1A **CITING TEXT EVIDENCE** People in various parts of the world began planting different kinds of food crops. Complete the chart with examples of food grown in each region.

Region	Foods Grown
Southwest Asia	
Nile Valley	
Central Africa	
India	
China and Southeast Asia	
Mexico and Central America	

2 INFERRING Why did people in Neolithic communities build permanent homes?

_____

_____

3 `CIVICS` How did permanent settlements lead to job specialization among community members?

_____

_____

_____

4 DESCRIBING During the Bronze Age, civilizations began to develop, and all of these civilizations shared characteristics. Complete the chart below with details to illustrate each characteristic.

Characteristic	Details
Cities and Government	
Religions	
Social Structure	
Culture and Technology	
Writing and Art	

Agriculture and Trade

ESSENTIAL QUESTION

How do people adapt to their environment?

DIRECTIONS: Read the excerpt and answer the accompanying questions.

EXPLORE THE CONTEXT: Geographer Lydia Mihelic Pulsipher is a cultural-historical geographer. She studies how people and geography affect each other in the present and the past. In this excerpt, she discusses the development of farming.

VOCABULARY

husbandry: care of plants and animals

secure: reliable

"day job": familiar term for work that a person needs to pay everyday bills

sustenance: food needed for survival

SECONDARY SOURCE: BOOK

❝Why did agriculture and animal husbandry develop in the first place? Certainly the desire for more secure food resources played a role, but the opportunity to trade may have been just as important. Many of the known locations of agricultural innovation lie near early trade centers. There, people would have had access to new information and new plants and animals brought by traders, and would have needed products to trade. Perhaps, then, agriculture was at first a profitable hobby for hunters and gatherers that eventually, because of the desire for food security and market demands, grew into a "day job" for some—their primary source of sustenance.❞

— Lydia Milhelic Pulsipher, *World Regional Geography: Global Patterns, Local Lives,* 2006 C.E.

Copyright © McGraw-Hill Education · Pulsipher, Lydia Mihelic and Alex Pulsipher. 2011. World Regional Geography: Global Patterns, Local Lives. 5th ed. New York: W.H. Freeman and Company.

1 IDENTIFYING CAUSES According to the author, why did early humans develop agriculture and animal husbandry?

_____

_____

2 `ECONOMICS` According to the excerpt, how did the Agricultural Revolution affect trade?

_____

_____

_____

3 ANALYZING How did the excerpt show that the Agricultural Revolution affected even the early humans' thinking?

_____

_____

_____

4 INFERRING Based on this excerpt, how did early humans adapt to their environment?

_____

_____

_____

Tools in the Bronze Age

DIRECTIONS: Examine the following image and answer the accompanying questions.

EXPLORE THE CONTEXT: In the Bronze Age, early humans learned to mix copper with bronze. This mixture of metals made it easier for people to make very specialized objects—tools, weapons, and household goods—that were stronger and more durable. Bronze tools like these in the photo were used between 3000 and 1200 B.C.E.

PRIMARY SOURCE: ARTIFACTS

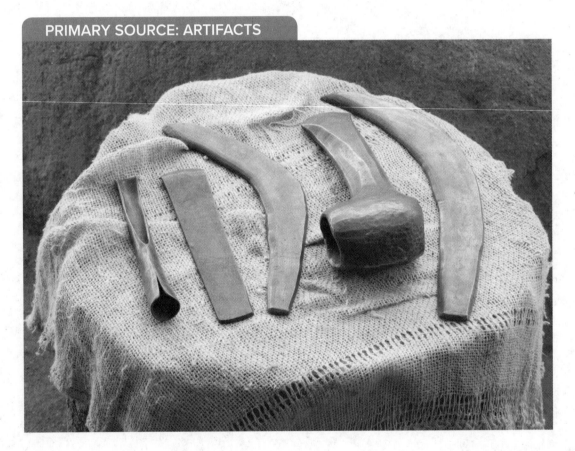

1 **DESCRIBING** What are these tools? How do you think they were used?

_____

_____

2 **COMPARING AND CONTRASTING** How are these tools similar to and different from the tools you analyzed in Lesson 1?

_____

_____

_____

3 **EVALUATING EVIDENCE** Why are these artifacts so important for the study of history?

_____

_____

_____

_____

4 **INFERRING** How might these tools have changed the way early humans interacted with their environment?

_____

_____

_____

1 Think About It

ESSENTIAL QUESTION

How did people adapt to their environment?

Review the supporting questions that you developed at the beginning of the chapter. Review the evidence that you gathered in this chapter. Were you able to answer each Supporting Question?

If there was not enough evidence to answer your Supporting Questions, what additional evidence do you think you need to consider?

_____

_____

_____

_____

2 Organize Your Evidence

Use a chart to organize the evidence you will use to support your position statement. Think about the most basic ideas you had about early humans. Use the topics of the lessons to describe how your original ideas (column 1) changed into new ideas (column 3).

1	2	3
What I thought before lesson	Topics in lessons	What I know after lesson
	Making and using tools	
	Paleolithic hunters and gatherers	
	Nomadic lifestyle	
	Participation	
	Agricultural Revolution	
	System of farming	
	Trade increases	
	Growth of religion and art	

③ Write About It

Create a position statement focused on the ESSENTIAL QUESTION: *How did people adapt to their environment?* Use the evidence you gathered above to guide you in developing the statement.

_____

_____

_____

_____

_____

_____

_____

_____

④ Talk About It

Work in small groups to present your position statement and evidence. Gather feedback from your classmates before you write your final conclusion. You may choose to refine your position statement after you have discussed it with your classmates. Group members should listen to each other's arguments, ask questions, and offer constructive advice.

⑤ Connect to the Essential Question

Develop a visual essay to present your position statement and the evidence you will use to support your position. Draw or choose photos and art from appropriate Web sites to illustrate the evidence. Include captions or short paragraphs explaining the evidence you present and how it helps support your position statement.

CITIZENSHIP
TAKING ACTION

MAKE CONNECTIONS For early humans, chances for survival improved when people lived in groups. Cooperation became a key part of everyday existence. Today, working together as a community is also important, both to push for change and to improve people's quality of life.

DIRECTIONS: Create a poster to hang in a public space. In your poster, use a combination of text and images to educate the public about the benefits of community involvement and cooperation.

Mesopotamia

ESSENTIAL QUESTION

How does geography influence the way people live?

Think about how this question might relate to the Sumerian city-states.

TALK ABOUT IT

Discuss with a partner what type of information you would need to answer this question. For example, one question might be: Why did the geography of Mesopotamia encourage rivalries among the Sumerian city-states?

DIRECTIONS: Now write down three additional questions that would help you explain why the Sumerian cities became self-ruling, independent groups.

MY RESEARCH QUESTIONS

Supporting Question 1:

_____

_____

Supporting Question 2:

_____

_____

Supporting Question 3:

_____

_____

ESSENTIAL QUESTION

How does geography influence the way people live?

As you gather evidence to answer the Essential Question, think about:

- the location of the first settlements between the Tigris and the Euphrates rivers.

- the Fertile Crescent, which is an area of rich farmland between the Mediterranean Sea and the Persian Gulf.

My Notes

The Sumerians

DIRECTIONS: Search for evidence in Lesson 1 to help you answer the following questions.

1A IDENTIFYING CAUSE AND EFFECT How did Mesopotamia's geography attract settlements?

_____

_____

_____

_____

1B ANALYZING What water supply challenges were faced by people who settled near rivers in Mesopotamia?

_____

_____

_____

_____

2 GEOGRAPHY How did the geography of Mesopotamia contribute to Sumerian cities becoming independent city-states?

_____

_____

_____

_____

3 IDENTIFYING CAUSE AND EFFECT Fill in the chart below to describe how the seasons affected the settlers' source of water. Describe how settlers responded to the changes.

Seasonal Changes in Water Supplies	People's Responses Over Time
SUMMER	
SPRING	

4 ECONOMICS Use the chart below to record the details of the effects of irrigation.

Some Results of Using Irrigation

An Early Chariot

ESSENTIAL QUESTION

How does geography influence the way people live?

DIRECTIONS: Examine the artifact below and answer the accompanying questions.

EXPLORE THE CONTEXT: The invention of the wheel changed the lives of Sumerians in important ways, such as transportation. This Sumerian artifact from around 2500 B.C.E. shows a wheeled chariot. Chariots were a form of transportation used by the Sumerians. A chariot driver stood above the axle and gripped his legs around a wooden centerpiece, which was often covered with fleece for comfort.

PRIMARY SOURCE: PHOTOGRAPH

1 **DESCRIBING** Describe the mode of transportation shown and how it provided something more than a cart did. How do you think the drivers directed the donkeys or horses? What main advantage would chariot drivers have over cart users?

_____

_____

_____

_____

_____

2 **ANALYZING** Who do you think would be the most likely users of chariots in Mesopotamia? Explain why you think so.

_____

_____

_____

_____

_____

3 **COMPARING** Does your analysis agree with the text description of the chariot's development and usage?

_____

_____

_____

_____

4 **HISTORY** How do you believe the invention of the chariot affected the culture at that time?

_____

_____

_____

_____

Sumerian Tools

ESSENTIAL QUESTION

How does geography influence the way people live?

DIRECTIONS: Study the following image and answer the accompanying questions.

EXPLORE THE CONTEXT: This image shows early Sumerian tools from around 2000 B.C.E. The Sumerians were the first people to put copper and tin together to make a beautiful and strong metal called bronze. Before they discovered bronze, some tools were made of clay.

PRIMARY SOURCE: PHOTOGRAPH

1 **DESCRIBING** Do you recognize the tools in the images? How do you think these tools were used?

_____

_____

_____

_____

_____

2 HISTORY In what ways do you think life changed for the Sumerians after these tools were created?

_____

_____

_____

_____

_____

_____

3 **ANALYZING TEXT EVIDENCE** After referring to the text, describe what you know about the technology of toolmaking in Mesopotamia. What led to an improvement in tool making?

_____

_____

_____

_____

_____

_____

4 **DRAWING CONCLUSIONS** How do you think geography influenced the development of these tools?

_____

_____

_____

_____

_____

_____

ESSENTIAL QUESTION

How does geography influence the way people live?

As you gather evidence to answer the Essential Question, think about:

- why the rulers desired more land.
- how empires developed through conquest.

My Notes

_____

_____

_____

_____

_____

_____

_____

Mesopotamian Empires

DIRECTIONS: Search for evidence in Lesson 2 to help you answer the following questions.

1 HISTORY   Use the chart to identify some results of the spread of empires in Mesopotamia.

Results of Empire Building

2 **INTERPRETING** Consider how the government of the Assyrian Empire was able to rule such a large area of land. What allowed for such an expansion of power?

_____

_____

3 **CITING TEXT EVIDENCE** Use the graphic organizer to cite reasons for the fall of the Assyrian Empire.

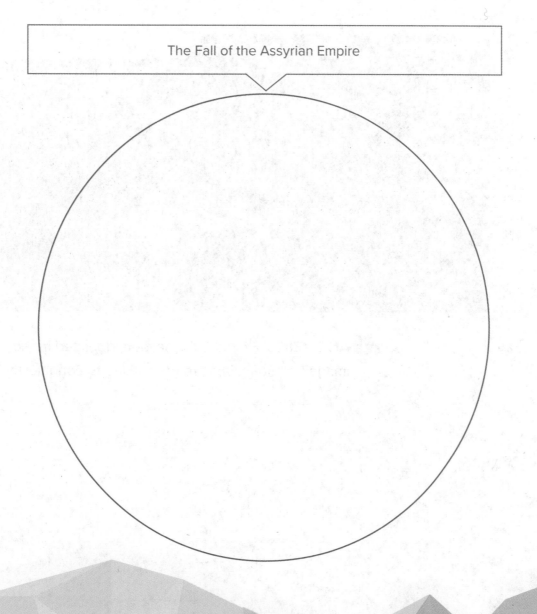

The Fall of the Assyrian Empire

Assyrians at War

ESSENTIAL QUESTION

How does geography influence the way people live?

DIRECTIONS: Examine the following image and answer the accompanying questions.

EXPLORE THE CONTEXT: A relief is a carving on a wall. The relief below is from Assyria's Central Palace, built around 728 B.C.E. This relief sculpture illustrates some early techniques and weapons that the Assyrians used to capture a city.

PRIMARY SOURCE: PHOTOGRAPH

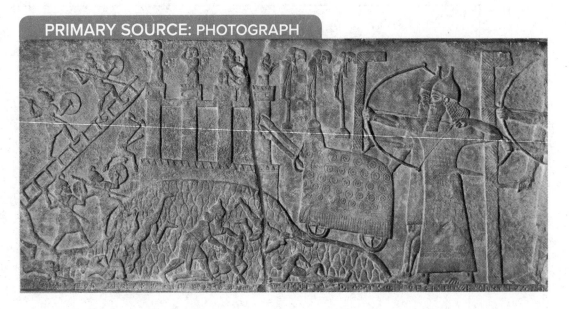

1 **ANALYZING** How are the soldiers depicted in the image? What actions are they taking to conquer the city?

_____

_____

_____

_____

_____

_____

_____

_____

_____

2 **DRAWING CONCLUSIONS** Why do you think cities were surrounded by tall walls with watchtowers? How would enemy soldiers get into the cities to conquer them?

_____

_____

_____

_____

_____

_____

3 **COMPARING AND CONTRASTING** Compare and contrast the text information describing the Assyrian army's weapons and actions with the image. How are the two alike and different?

_____

_____

_____

_____

_____

_____

4 **HISTORY** How did the attacks of the city-states change the lives of the conquered citizens? What were some of the effects after a new ruler was in charge?

_____

_____

_____

_____

_____

_____

Herodotus on Babylon

ESSENTIAL QUESTION

How does geography influence the way people live?

DIRECTIONS: Read the following excerpt and answer the accompanying questions.

EXPLORE THE CONTEXT: Herodotus was an early Greek historian who traveled and described the actions and sights he witnessed. This excerpt gives us a view of the defense system of the great city of Babylon.

PRIMARY SOURCE: EXCERPT FROM HERODOTUS 1:181: GREEK REPORTS OF BABLYLONIA, CHALDEA, AND ASSYRIA

" I.181: The outer wall is the main defense of the city. There is, however, a second inner wall, of less thickness than the first, but very little inferior to it in strength. The center of each division of the town was occupied by a fortress. In the one stood the palace of the kings, surrounded by a wall of great strength and size; in the other was the sacred precinct of Jupiter Belus [Bel], a square enclosure two furlongs each way, with gates of solid brass; which was also remaining in my time. In the middle of the precinct there was a tower of solid masonry, a furlong in length and breadth, upon which was raised a second tower, and on that a third, and so on up to eight. The ascent to the top is on the outside, by a path which winds round all the towers. When one is about halfway up, one finds a resting place and seats, where persons are wont to sit some time on their way to the summit. On the topmost tower there is a spacious temple, and inside the temple stands a couch of unusual size, richly adorned [decorated], with a golden table by its side. There is no statue of any kind set up in the place, nor is the chamber occupied of nights by any one but a single native woman, who, as the Chaldaeans, the priests of this god, affirm, is chosen for himself by the deity out of all the women of the land. "

— Herodotus, Histories, c. 430 B.C.E.

VOCABULARY

precinct: a district or area

Jupiter Belus: a reference to the Akkadian God Bel

enclosure: an area shut in by walls or fences

furlong: a distance of approximately one-eighth of a mile, or 220 yards

masonry: something built with bricks or stones

breadth: width

wont: a habit or something a person is used to doing

chamber: a private room

1 **CITING TEXT EVIDENCE** According to Herodotus, which areas inside the city's walls received the most protection?

_____

_____

2 **DETERMINING MEANING** Examine the location of the temple room as described by Herodotus. Why would the location of the temple be important for Herodotus to describe in such detail?

_____

_____

_____

3 **CITING TEXT EVIDENCE** Which words did Herodotus use to describe how the city was protected against intruders? Underline the words he used.

_____

_____

_____

_____

4 **HISTORY** Whose point of view does Herodotus use to explain the presence of the lady in the temple room?

_____

_____

_____

_____

① Think About It

ESSENTIAL QUESTION

How does geography influence the way people live?

Review the Supporting Questions that you developed at the beginning of the chapter. Review the evidence that you gathered in this chapter. Were you able to answer each Supporting Question?

If there was not enough evidence to answer your Supporting Questions, what additional evidence do you think you need?

_____

_____

_____

_____

② Organize Your Evidence

Use the graphic organizer below to organize the evidence you will use to support your position statement.

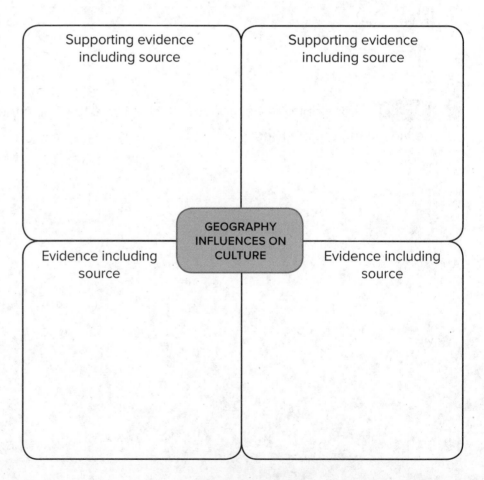

Supporting evidence including source	Supporting evidence including source

GEOGRAPHY INFLUENCES ON CULTURE

Evidence including source	Evidence including source

③ Write About It

A position statement related to the Essential Question should reflect your conclusion about the evidence. Write a position statement for the ESSENTIAL QUESTION: *How does geography influence the way people live?*

_____

_____

_____

_____

_____

_____

_____

_____

_____

④ Connect to the Essential Question

On a separate piece of paper, create at least five good interview questions as if you were interviewing a person who lived in the Mesopotamian valley in one of the early Sumerian city-states. Think about asking why he or she settled where they did, what the advantages and disadvantages were, how they needed to adapt to the environment, etc.

After deciding what questions to ask, and using the Essential Question about geography's influence as your central idea, write how an early Sumerian might have answered your questions.

_____

_____

_____

TAKING ACTION

MAKE CONNECTIONS Think about how the geography of your region affects your home, family, and community. What are the natural resources in your area that affect the way you live?

DIRECTIONS: If geography and its natural resources are important in shaping the lives of people, how can you become involved in the care of it? If you need to, contact an organization you believe is helping care for your geographical resources. Ask if you can participate in some way. Then promote this need to other students using Twitter or other social media. (If you do not have a Twitter account, create a statement using only 280 characters to sell your idea to your friends.)

Ancient Egypt and Kush

ESSENTIAL QUESTION

Why do civilizations rise and fall?

Think about how this question might relate to civilization in the Nile River valley.

TALK ABOUT IT

Discuss with a partner what type of information you would need to know to answer this question. For example, one question might be: How did the geography of the area encourage development along the Nile River in northeastern Africa?

DIRECTIONS: Now write down three additional questions that would help you explain why the Nile River valley became a desirable region for empire building.

MY RESEARCH QUESTIONS

Supporting Question 1:

_____

_____

Supporting Question 2:

_____

_____

Supporting Question 3:

_____

ESSENTIAL QUESTION

Why do civilizations rise and fall?

As you gather evidence to answer the Essential Question, think about:

- the location of the first settlements near the Nile River.
- whether the river valley contributed to population growth.

My Notes

_____

_____

_____

_____

_____

_____

_____

_____

The Nile River

DIRECTIONS: Search for evidence in Lesson 1 to help you complete the following items.

1 **DESCRIBING** Use the graphic organizer below to show ways the Nile River valley influenced the life of its early settlers.

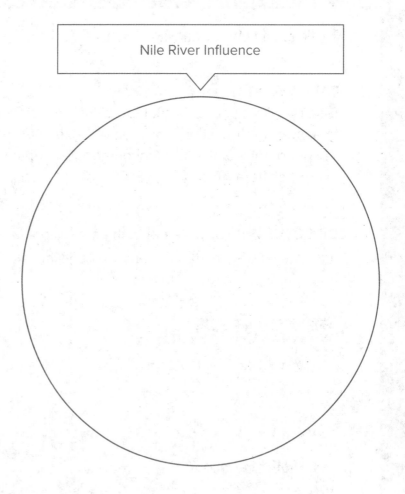

Nile River Influence

2 **IDENTIFYING CAUSE AND EFFECT** What factors allowed the Egyptian civilization to develop peacefully?

_____

_____

_____

_____

_____

3 ECONOMICS   How was the economy of Egypt influenced by the geography of the Nile River region?

_____

_____

_____

_____

_____

4 HISTORY   How did the Nile's predictable flooding help the people become resourceful and inventive? Use the graphic organizer below to organize the information.

_____

_____

_____

_____

_____

_____

_____

_____

_____

```
┌──────────────┐         ┌──────────────────────────────┐
│              │  ──────▶│                              │
│ Nile Flooding│  ──────▶│                              │
│              │         └──────────────────────────────┘
│              │         ┌──────────────────────────────┐
│              │  ──────▶│                              │
└──────────────┘         └──────────────────────────────┘
                         ┌──────────────────────────────┐
                         │                              │
                         └──────────────────────────────┘
```

A Shadoof

DIRECTIONS: Examine the image below and answer the questions.

EXPLORE THE CONTEXT: This image of a modern day shadoof shows a way that Egyptian farmers were able to fill the water basins used for irrigation of their fields. Irrigation revolutionized farming by helping the farmers control their water supply.

PRIMARY SOURCE: PHOTOGRAPH

1 **DESCRIBING** Describe the scene shown in the image.

_____

_____

_____

_____

_____

_____

_____

2 **ANALYZING CAUSE AND EFFECT** How did climate affect the need for the creation of irrigation tools?

_____

_____

_____

_____

_____

_____

3 **IDENTIFYING EFFECTS** How did people in the Nile River valley take advantage of annual flooding? How was the Nile easier to control than the Tigris and Euphrates Rivers?

_____

_____

_____

_____

_____

_____

4 **EXPLAINING EFFECTS** What was the effect of irrigation in the Nile River valley?

_____

_____

_____

_____

_____

_____

The Nile River

ESSENTIAL QUESTION

Why do civilizations rise and fall?

DIRECTIONS: Read the following excerpt and answer the questions.

EXPLORE THE CONTEXT: This excerpt from *The Nile Tributaries of Abyssinia and the Sword Hunters of the Hamran Arabs,* by Sir Samuel W. Baker, gives insight into the formation of the Nile River and its effect on the land that formed the delta region in Egypt.

VOCABULARY

affluents: streams of water flowing freely into larger streams or bodies of water
unnavigable: a stream not deep or wide enough for ships
Abyssinia: a region now known as Ethiopia, Africa

arteries: waterways
Blue Nile, Atbara: rivers in northeast Africa, both which flow into the Nile
inundates: to flood
inundation: a flooded condition
fertility: readiness to produce crops

1 DETERMINING MEANING Baker states that the two important rivers, the Blue Nile and the Atbara, change significantly due to rainfall. What causes this change, and why is this important?

_____

_____

_____

_____

_____

SECONDARY SOURCE: BOOK

❝ The two grand affluents of Abyssinia are, the Blue Nile and the Atbara, which join the main stream respectively in N. lat. 15 degrees 30 minutes and 17 degrees 37 minutes. These rivers, although streams of extreme grandeur during the period of the Abyssinian rains, from the middle of June until September, are reduced during the dry months to utter insignificance; the Blue Nile becoming so shallow as to be unnavigable, and the Atbara perfectly dry. At that time the water supply of Abyssinia having ceased, Egypt depends solely upon the equatorial lakes and the affluents of the White Nile, until the rainy season shall again have flooded the two great Abyssinian arteries. That flood occurs suddenly about the 20th of June, and the grand rush of water pouring down the Blue Nile and the Atbara into the parent channel, inundates Lower Egypt, and is the cause of its extreme fertility.

NOT only is the inundation the effect of the Abyssinian rains, but the deposit of mud that has formed the Delta, and which is annually precipitated by the rising waters, is also due to the Abyssinian streams, more especially to the river Atbara, which, known as the Bahr el Aswat (Black River), carries a larger proportion of soil than any other tributary of the Nile; therefore, to the Atbara, above all other rivers, must the wealth and fertility of Egypt be attributed.

It may thus be stated: The equatorial lakes FEED Egypt; but the Abyssinian rivers CAUSE THE INUNDATION. **"**

— Sir Samuel W. Baker, *The Nile Tributaries of Abyssinia and the Sword Hunters of the Hamran Arabs,* 1867 C.E.

2 ANALYZING From this description, why did people choose to live near a changing water supply?

_____

_____

_____

3 EXPLAINING CAUSES Reread Baker's description, and explain what caused the fertility of the delta.

_____

_____

_____

_____

4 ECONOMICS Describe how the Abyssinian streams affected the economic growth of the Nile River valley civilization.

_____

_____

_____

_____

_____

ESSENTIAL QUESTION

Why do civilizations rise and fall?

As you gather evidence to answer the Essential Question, think about:

- the power and authority of the Egyptian pharaohs.

- the role of religion in the life of the early Egyptians.

- the social groups in ancient Egypt and how they lived.

My Notes

Life in Ancient Egypt

DIRECTIONS: Search for evidence in Lesson 2 to help you answer the following question.

1 CITING EVIDENCE Use the graphic organizer below to identify ways the pharaoh influenced the Egyptian culture.

Pharaoh
_____
_____
_____
_____
_____

2 EXPLAINING CAUSE AND EFFECT How did religion influence the culture of ancient Egypt?

3 DRAWING CONCLUSIONS Analyze the roles of Egyptians and their lifestyles. Is there a connection among jobs, social ranking, and lifestyle? Use the table to organize your answers.

JOB	SOCIAL RANK	LIFESTYLE
King/pharaoh	highest	

CONCLUSIONS:

The Gateway of the Temple of Edfu

DIRECTIONS: Study the following image and answer the accompanying questions.

EXPLORE THE CONTEXT: The Temple of Edfu, built between 237 and 57 B.C.E., gives insight about the lifestyle and the impact of religion on the culture of ancient Egyptians.

PRIMARY SOURCE: RELIEF SCULPTURE

1 **COMPARING AND CONTRASTING** Compare the picture of the Temple of Edfu with the images of the pyramids in Lesson 2. Describe any similarities and differences you notice.

_____

_____

_____

_____

_____

_____

2 **DRAWING CONCLUSIONS** Why would the Egyptians build enormous and elaborate temples and tombs? Cite text from Lesson 2 to support your conclusions.

_____

_____

_____

_____

_____

_____

3 **EVALUATING EVIDENCE** Evaluate the images in the lesson and the text describing the roles of ancient Egyptians. Why were pharaohs and priests the most powerful and wealthy people in ancient Egypt?

_____

_____

_____

_____

_____

_____

4 **DRAWING CONCLUSIONS** What does the ability to devote resources to building great monuments and temples suggest about the wealth and strength of an empire? Cite details from Lesson 2 to support your conclusions.

_____

_____

_____

_____

_____

_____

Education in Ancient Egypt

ESSENTIAL QUESTION

Why do civilizations rise and fall?

DIRECTIONS: Study the following excerpt and answer the accompanying questions.

EXPLORE THE CONTEXT: In this excerpt, James Baikie describes a privileged Egyptian child who was being tutored, unlike most children of the early Egyptian times.

SECONDARY SOURCE: BOOK

66 When Tahuti grew a little older, and had fairly mastered the rudiments of writing, his teacher set him to write out copies of different passages from the best known Egyptian books, partly to keep up his hand-writing, and partly to teach him to know good Egyptian and to use correct language. Sometimes it was a piece of a religious book that he was set to copy, sometimes a poem, sometimes a fairy-tale. For the Egyptians were very fond of fairy-tales, and later on, perhaps, we may hear some of their stories, the oldest fairy-stories in the world. But generally the piece that was chosen was one which would not only exercise the boy's hand, and teach him a good style, but would also help to teach him good manners, and fill his mind with right ideas. Very often Tahuti's teacher would dictate to him a passage from the wise advice which a great King of long ago left to his son, the Crown Prince, or from some other book of the same kind. And sometimes the exercises would be in the form of letters which the master and his pupils wrote as though they had been friends far away from one another. Tahuti's letters, you may be sure, were full of wisdom and of good resolutions, and I dare say he was just about as fond of writing them as you are of writing the letters that your teacher sometimes sets as a task for you. 99

—James Baikie, *Peeps at Many Lahds: Ancient Egypt,* 1916 C.E.

VOCABULARY

rudiments: basics

hand: refers to handwriting

dictate: to read aloud something for another person to transcribe, or write down

resolutions: deciding to take a certain action

1 CITING TEXT EVIDENCE Which sentences from this excerpt explain why early Egyptian students were required to copy text from books?

_____

_____

_____

2 DRAWING CONCLUSIONS What character qualities might a student gain from this type of educational experience?

_____

3 DETERMINING CONTEXT How do you think education may have contributed to a rise in Egypt's civilization?

_____

_____

_____

4 ANALYZING POINT OF VIEW Discuss with a partner what you think the author wants you to know about Tahuti's attitude. What is the author suggesting about you and Tahuti as students then and now? Use evidence from the excerpt to support your answer.

_____

_____

_____

_____

5 MAKING CONNECTIONS If your teacher asked you to write letters to him or her about something you have read, what do you think the purpose would be?

_____

_____

Egypt's Empire

DIRECTIONS: Search for evidence in Lesson 3 to help you complete the following items.

ESSENTIAL QUESTION

Why do civilizations rise and fall?

As you gather evidence to answer the Essential Question, think about:

- the number of kingdoms that flourished but yet declined.
- the growth and prosperity that resulted during established kingdoms.

1 IDENTIFYING STEPS Use the text and the graphic organizer below to identify what events led to the rise and fall of these kingdoms.

DATE	KINGDOM	EVENTS CAUSING RISE	EVENTS CAUSING FALL
2055 B.C.E.	MIDDLE KINGDOM		
1600s B.C.E.	HYKSOS		
1550 B.C.E.	THE NEW KINGDOM		

My Notes

_____

_____

_____

_____

_____

_____

_____

2 **ANALYZING EVENTS** Describe any patterns in the chart you made in the first question that might explain how a once flourishing kingdom could collapse.

_____

_____

_____

_____

3 ECONOMICS Using text evidence, how was the Egyptian economy affected by the change of kingdoms? Use the organizer below.

KINGDOM	ECONOMY
MIDDLE KINGDOM	
HYKSOS	
THE NEW KINGDOM	

Egyptian Pottery

DIRECTIONS: Study the following image and answer the accompanying questions.

EXPLORE THE CONTEXT: This image of two dishes, a bracelet, and a small box shows pottery from the New Kingdom period of ancient Egypt. The New Kingdom lasted from 1550 B.C.E. to 1070 B.C.E. Pottery from this period was made from a ground quartz and covered with a fired glaze that was most commonly blue or green in color. Vases, small animal and human figures, and decorative wall tiles were frequently made using this difficult technique.

PRIMARY SOURCE: ARTIFACT

1 **CITING TEXT EVIDENCE** Is there a connection between this period of empire building and Egypt's development in the arts? Cite the text reference from Lesson 3 and explain.

_____

_____

_____

_____

2 **DESCRIBING** Examine the details on the dishes and bracelet, and describe them. What do the designs reveal about Egyptian life? Explain.

_____

_____

_____

_____

_____

3 **INFERRING** How might religious beliefs be reflected in pottery?

_____

_____

_____

_____

_____

4 ECONOMICS How did the economy impact the development of pottery?

_____

_____

_____

_____

_____

Egyptian Tomb Complex

DIRECTIONS: Study the following image and answer the accompanying questions.

EXPLORE THE CONTEXT: The Middle Kingdom, which lasted from about 2055 B.C.E. to 1650 B.C.E., was a time of growth and prosperity for Egypt. During this time, the arts and literature flourished. This era also brought forth historic and massive building projects, which included burial tombs. Pyramids were still built. Other types of monuments, however, such as this one seen in this modern day photo, were being built for the dead.

PRIMARY SOURCE: PHOTOGRAPH

1 **SUMMARIZING** List three facts you learned in this chapter about pyramids.

_____

_____

_____

_____

_____

2 **DESCRIBING** Describe the image of the tomb and its entrance.

_____

_____

_____

_____

3 **COMPARING AND CONTRASTING** Using what you learned about pyramids, how does the landscape around this tomb compare to the landscape around the pyramid? How are the pyramids and the Middle Kingdom tombs alike? How would the challenges of building tombs into the cliffs differ from the challenges of building a pyramid?

_____

_____

_____

_____

_____

4 GEOGRAPHY How did Egyptians make use of the different physical landscapes for their benefit?

_____

_____

_____

ESSENTIAL QUESTION

Why do civilizations rise and fall?

As you gather evidence to answer the Essential Question, think about:

- how Egypt influenced the kingdoms they conquered.
- why the Nubians grew wealthy and powerful.

My Notes

The Kingdom of Kush

DIRECTIONS: Search for evidence in Lesson 4 to help you answer the following questions.

1 **EXPLAINING CAUSE AND EFFECT** How did Nubia grow wealthy?

2 GEOGRAPHY How did the Egyptian culture influence the Nubian and Kush cultures?

3 ANALYZING INFORMATION What did Nubia and Kush adopt from Egyptian culture? Use the chart to answer this question with details.

	Adopted From Egyptian Culture
Nubians	
Kushites	Adopted From Egyptian Culture

Nubia and Kush

ESSENTIAL QUESTION

Why do civilizations rise and fall?

DIRECTIONS: Study the following excerpt and answer the accompanying questions.

EXPLORE THE CONTEXT: Nubia and Kush were thriving civilizations in Africa, located just south of Egypt. As empires spread, it was logical that these kingdoms near the Nile would be targets for conquest. Kush and Nubia were prosperous, with fertile land and gold to be mined. The following excerpt is from the story of a sailor, written about 2200 B.C.E., who claimed to have been shipwrecked on an island in or near Punt, which was located along the coast of modern-day Ethiopia and Djibouti. The story may be fiction, but the resources noted were items Egyptians received from trade with Nubians and the land of Punt.

PRIMARY SOURCE: BOOK

> ❝ Let thy heart be satisfied, O my lord, for that we have come back to the country...Moreover, we have come back in good health, and not a man is lacking; although we have been to the ends of Wawat [Nubia], and gone through the land of Senmut [Kush], we have returned in peace, and our land—behold, we have come back to it. ...
>
> They had said that the wind would not be contrary, or that there would be none. But as we approached the land, the wind arose, and threw up waves eight cubits high. As for me, I seized a piece of wood; but those who were in the vessel perished, without one remaining. A wave threw me on an island, after that I had been three days alone, without a companion beside my own heart. I laid me in a thicket, and the shadow covered me. Then stretched I my limbs to try to find something for my mouth. I found there figs and grain, melons of all kinds, fishes, and birds. Nothing was lacking.
>
> And I satisfied myself; and left on the ground that which was over, of what my arms had been filled withal. I dug a pit, I lighted a fire, and I made a burnt offering unto the gods...
>
> Then I bowed myself before [a serpent calling himself the Prince of Punt], and held my arms low before him, and he, he gave me gifts

VOCABULARY

contrary: hostile, causing problems

cubits: a cubit was the length of the forearm, 17–21 inches

thicket: underbrush, bushes

withal: with it all

burnt offering: a ritual to honor the Gods

. . . continued

of precious perfumes, of cassia, of sweet woods, of kohl, of cypress, an abundance of incense, of ivory tusks, of baboons, of apes, and all kinds of precious things. **"**

—from *The World's Story: A History of the World in Story, Song And Art,* 1914 C.E.

1 **DETERMINING POINT OF VIEW** Discuss with a partner the tone of the traveler who is discussing his journey. Does he suggest he is angry about the experience, amazed at his findings, relieved that it is over, or some other emotion? Use evidence from the text to support your answers.

_____

_____

_____

2 **DRAWING CONCLUSIONS** What does the writer suggest about Egypt's relationship with Kush and Nubia?

_____

_____

3 **MAKING CONNECTIONS** If you had been shipwrecked and later wrote about your experience, what do you think would be the most important detail to describe?

_____

_____

4 **INFERRING** Consider how the traveler refers to Nubia and Kush. What can you infer from the way he talks about these empires?

_____

_____

_____

_____

Herodotus on Ethiopia

DIRECTIONS: Study the following excerpt and answer the questions.

EXPLORE THE CONTEXT: Herodotus was an ancient Greek historian who traveled the ancient world, observing the lives of people and recording his reflections in narrative, or story form. He writes about the region south of Egypt in eastern Africa known as Ethiopia in these excerpts.

PRIMARY SOURCE: BOOK

❝Where the south declines towards the setting sun lies the country called Ethiopia, the last inhabited land in that direction. There gold is obtained in great plenty, huge elephants abound, with wild trees of all sorts, and ebony; and the men are taller, handsomer, and longer lived than anywhere else.❞

–from *Herodotus: The Histories, Book III,* c. 430 B.C.E.

❝The Ethiopians were clothed in the skins of leopards and lions, and had long bows made of the stem of the palm-leaf, not less than four cubits in length. On these they laid short arrows made of reed, and armed at the tip, not with iron, but with a piece of stone, sharpened to a point, of the kind used in engraving seals. They carried likewise spears, the head of which was the sharpened horn of an antelope; and in addition they had knotted clubs. When they went into battle they painted their bodies, half with chalk, and half with vermilion. . . .❞

–from *The History of Herodotus, Vol. IV,* c. 430 B.C.E.

VOCABULARY

Ethiopia: once called Abyssinia, an ancient region in northeastern Africa that borders Egypt and the Red Sea

ebony: a heavy, black wood

cubits: a measurement taken with the forearm, about 17–21 inches long

reed: the straight stalk of a plant

vermilion: a bright red or orange-red color

1 **CITING TEXT EVIDENCE** Which sentences provide the best description of the Ethiopian people?

_____

_____

_____

2 **COMPARING AND CONTRASTING** How do the descriptions of Ethiopia by Herodotus compare or contrast with the details about Nubia found in Lesson 4?

_____

_____

_____

3 **DRAWING CONCLUSIONS** What do these excerpts suggest about the potential for this Ethiopian civilization?

_____

_____

_____

_____

4 **DETERMINING CENTRAL IDEAS** Herodotus describes Ethiopia as the last inhabited land in the direction of the setting sun. What do you think was the overall impression of Herodotus concerning this land? Write your understanding of the main idea below. Underline details that support your main idea.

_____

_____

_____

_____

_____

_____

① Think About It

Review the supporting questions you developed at the opening of the chapter. Review the evidence you found in this chapter. Were you able to answer each of your Supporting Questions?

If you didn't find enough evidence to answer your Supporting Questions, what do you think you need to consider?

_____

_____

_____

② Organize Your Evidence

Use a chart like the one below to organize the evidence you will use to support your position statement. Then, create a position statement for the ESSENTIAL QUESTION: *Why do civilizations rise and fall?*

Sources of Information	Evidence from Sources to Cite	How the Evidence Supports Your Position Statement

3 Talk About It

Discuss your position statement and the evidence you have gathered with a small group or partner. Check your group's understanding and answer any questions members may have. Consider any additional advice or input they may have.

4 Connect to the Essential Question

On a separate piece of paper, write an autobiographical journal entry from the viewpoint of a child living in Kush during the Middle Kingdom. As the son or daughter of a farmer, how did the rise of the Assyrian kingdom affect the way you and your family lived? Your journal page should include answers to the **ESSENTIAL QUESTION:** *Why do civilizations rise and fall?*

_____

_____

_____

_____

CITIZENSHIP
TAKING ACTION

MAKE CONNECTIONS Many civilizations have risen and fallen during recorded history. These include Mesopotamia, Egypt, Rome, and the British Empire. Empires do not exist today in the same way they once did, although individual countries can have great influence over other countries, sometimes through economic policies, sometimes through military intervention. Syria is a country in Western Asia that formed as a modern nation after the end of World War II. In 2011 C.E., civil war broke out, with armed rebels seeking to remove the president. One of the country's largest cities, Aleppo, has been at the center of this conflict. Once a thriving metropolis, it has been largely destroyed. Many of the people who once lived there fled to other parts of the country or to other countries.

DIRECTIONS: Consider nations in the world that are in conflict today. Choose one conflict and research its causes and current status. Write a letter to your representative(s) to Congress outlining your position on the conflict. Suggest an action you would like that representative to take as a member of Congress.

_____

_____

_____

_____

_____

_____

The Israelites, 1800 B.C.E. to 70 C.E.

ESSENTIAL QUESTION

How does religion shape society?

Think about how this question might connect the history of Israelite society and Judaism with the history and development of other religions.

TALK ABOUT IT COLLABORATE

Discuss with a partner what type of information you would need to know to answer this question. For example, one question might be: How does understanding religious practices and daily life in Israelite societies relate to modern religious practices and their effect on societies?

DIRECTIONS: Now write down three additional questions that you need to answer to be able to explain how the development of Judaism shaped daily life for the Israelites and led to practices in modern Judaism.

MY RESEARCH QUESTIONS

Supporting Question 1:

_____

_____

Supporting Question 2:

_____

_____

Supporting Question 3:

_____

ESSENTIAL QUESTION

How does religion shape society?

As you gather evidence to answer the Essential Question, think about:

- the stories of Abraham's interactions with God and of Abraham's descendants.
- the reactions of the Israelites to the new Pharaoh and to Moses.

My Notes

Beginnings

DIRECTIONS: Search for evidence in Lesson 1 to help you answer the following questions.

1 **RELATING EVENTS** Which leaders led the Israelites first to Canaan, then to Egypt, and then out of Egypt and back to Canaan?

_____

_____

_____

_____

_____

2 **EXPLAINING CAUSE AND EFFECT** How did the leaders of the Israelites know where to bring their people?

_____

_____

_____

_____

_____

_____

_____

3 GEOGRAPHY In the graphic organizer below, write the name of the leader in each listed account from the Hebrew Bible. Then describe the influence the individual had on the way the Israelites lived.

Account in the Hebrew Bible	Influence on Israelites' Society
Journey to Canaan:	
Journey to Egypt:	
Journey Out of Egypt:	
Journey to Retake Canaan:	

4 ANALYZING EVENTS What religious belief inspired the Israelites under Joshua to fight to establish Canaan as their new homeland?

5 **SUMMARIZING AND DESCRIBING** In the graphic organizer below, use your own words to provide the meaning of each of the commandments listed in the first column.

Commandment	Meaning
First Commandment	
Third Commandment	
Fifth Commandment	
Seventh Commandment	
Eighth Commandment	
Ninth Commandment	

The Birth of Isaac

ESSENTIAL QUESTION

How does religion shape society?

DIRECTIONS: Read the following excerpt and answer the accompanying questions.

EXPLORE THE CONTEXT: Abraham is considered to be the father of Judaism and Sarah its mother. According to the Hebrew Bible, Abraham and Sarah wanted children. This is the account of the beginning of their family and of the Israelites' family tree.

PRIMARY SOURCE: BOOK

"21:1 And HaShem [God] remembered Sarah as He had said, and HaShem did unto Sarah as He had spoken.

21:2 And Sarah conceived, and bore Abraham a son in his old age, at the set time of which G-d had spoken to him.

21:3 And Abraham called the name of his son that was born unto him, whom Sarah bore to him, Isaac. . . .

21:5 And Abraham was a hundred years old, when his son Isaac was born unto him.

21:6 And Sarah said: 'G-d hath made laughter for me; every one that heareth will laugh on account of me.'

21:7 And she said: 'Who would have said unto Abraham, that Sarah should give [have] children? . . . for I have borne him a son in his old age.'"

—from the Hebrew Bible, Genesis 21:1–7

VOCABULARY

conceived: became pregnant
bore: gave birth

1 **DETERMINING MEANING** What is happening in this account from the Hebrew Bible?

_____

_____

_____

2 **INFERRING** This account in Genesis says that God "did unto Sarah as He had spoken." Then Sarah became pregnant. What can you infer from this account about what God did for Sarah and why Sarah needed God's help?

_____

_____

3 **CITING TEXT EVIDENCE** What evidence in the text can you find for how Sarah feels about giving birth to Isaac? How does she feel about becoming a mother? Why is this birth unusual?

_____

_____

_____

_____

_____

_____

4 **ANALYZING TEXT** After Abraham died, his son Isaac and later his grandson Jacob headed the family. How does this account of Isaac's birth show that God of the Hebrew Bible was involved in what happened to the ancestors of the ancient Israelites?

_____

_____

_____

_____

God's Message to Joshua and the Israelites

ESSENTIAL QUESTION
How does religion shape society?

DIRECTIONS: Read the following excerpt and answer the accompanying questions.

EXPLORE THE CONTEXT: In the Hebrew Bible, the book of Joshua describes all of the ways in which God helped the Israelites through crises and provided for them. Joshua is said to have received this information from God, after which he related it to his people.

VOCABULARY

dwelt: lived in
plagued: set troubles upon

wilderness: unsettled area
labor: work

SECONDARY SOURCE: BOOK

❝ 24:2 And Joshua said unto all the people, Thus saith the LORD God of Israel, Your fathers dwelt on the other side of the flood in old time, even Terah, the father of Abraham, and the father of Nachor: and they served other gods.

24:3 And I took your father Abraham from the other side of the flood, and led him throughout all the land of Canaan, and multiplied his seed, and gave him Isaac.

24:4 And I gave unto Isaac Jacob and Esau: and I gave unto Esau Mount Seir, to possess it; but Jacob and his children went down into Egypt.

24:5 I sent Moses also and Aaron, and I plagued Egypt, according to that which I did among them: and afterward I brought you out.

24:6 And I brought your fathers out of Egypt: and ye came unto the sea; and the Egyptians pursued after your fathers with chariots and horsemen unto the Red sea.

24:7 And when they cried unto the LORD, he put darkness between you and the Egyptians, and brought the sea upon them, and covered them; and your eyes have seen what I have done in Egypt: and ye dwelt in the wilderness a long season. . . .

24:11 And you went over Jordan, and came unto Jericho: and the men of Jericho fought against you, the Amorites, and the Perizzites, and the Canaanites, and the Hittites, and the Girgashites, the Hivites, and the Jebusites; and I delivered them into your hand.

24:13 And I have given you a land for which ye did not labor, and cities which ye built not, and ye dwell in them; of the vineyards and oliveyards which ye planted not do ye eat.

24:14 Now therefore fear the LORD, and serve him in sincerity and in truth: and put away the gods which your fathers served on the other side of the flood, and in Egypt; and serve ye the LORD. . .

24:24 And the people said unto Joshua, The LORD our God will we serve, and his voice will we obey. **99**

—from the Hebrew Bible, Joshua 24:3–7, 11, 13–14, 24

1 **DETERMING MEANING** In the biblical account, what does God mean by "plagued Egypt" and why would he do such a thing?

_____

_____

_____

_____

_____

_____

2 **CITING TEXT EVIDENCE** What evidence can you find in the text of the miracle that Moses is said to have performed in order to rescue the Israelites? What did Moses do, and what happened to the Egyptians?

_____

_____

_____

_____

_____

_____

_____

_____

_____

3 ANALYZING EVENTS Why does God tell the Israelites about all of the things he has done for their people? What goal is he trying to reach by sharing this information with them?

_____

_____

_____

_____

_____

_____

_____

_____

4 ANALYZING IDEAS How were the Israelites' ideas of worship similar to those of their ancestors two generations before?

_____

_____

_____

_____

_____

_____

_____

ESSENTIAL QUESTION

How does religion shape society?

As you gather evidence to answer the Essential Question, think about:

- how King David and King Solomon were both able to keep the peace.

- how inability to overcome divisions led to the downfall of Israel, Judah, and the destruction of the First Temple.

My Notes

The Israelite Kingdom

DIRECTIONS: Search for evidence in Lesson 2 to help you answer the following questions.

1 **ANALYZING INDIVIDUALS** How did King David and King Solomon include Judaism as a part of their rule?

_____

_____

_____

_____

_____

_____

_____

_____

2 **ANALYZING EVENTS** How did the split between Israel and Judah lead to the downfall of both kingdoms?

_____

_____

_____

_____

_____

_____

_____

3 DESCRIBING What role did the prophets play in the downfall of Judah?

_____

_____

_____

_____

_____

_____

_____

_____

4 CIVICS In the graphic organizer below, in your own words, write the teachings of two of the Israelite Prophets as discussed in the text. Find examples in the text that show how people in Israelite communities were influenced by each prophet's teachings.

Prophet and Teaching	Example in Israelite Daily Life

King David and the Prophet Nathan

ESSENTIAL QUESTION
How does religion shape society?

DIRECTIONS: Read the following excerpt and answer the accompanying questions.

EXPLORE THE CONTEXT: King David took the attractive wife of one of his soldiers, a man named Uriah. He, then, assigned Uriah to a very dangerous military action. David knew this would result in Uriah's death. When he was killed, the prophet Nathan confronted David.

VOCABULARY

ewe: female sheep
reared: raised

bosom: chest
dress: prepare for cooking

PRIMARY SOURCE: BOOK

❝1 And HaShem [God] sent Nathan unto David. And he came unto him, and said unto him: 'There were two men in one city: the one rich, and the other poor.

2 The rich man had exceeding many flocks and herds;

3 but the poor man had nothing save one little ewe lamb, which he had bought and reared; and it grew up together with him, and with his children; it did eat of his own morsel, and drank of his own cup, and lay in his bosom, and was unto him as a daughter.

4 And there came a traveller unto the rich man, and he spared to take of his own flock and of his own herd, to dress for the wayfaring man that was come unto him, but took the poor man's lamb, and dressed it for the man that was come to him.'

5 And David's anger was greatly kindled against the man; and he said to Nathan: 'As HaShem liveth, the man that hath done this deserveth to die;

6 and he shall restore the lamb fourfold, because he did this thing, and because he had no pity.'

7 And Nathan said to David: 'Thou art the man. Thus saith HaShem, the G-d of Israel: I anointed thee king over Israel, and I delivered thee out of the hand of Saul;

8 and I gave thee thy master's house, and thy master's wives into thy bosom, and gave thee the house of Israel and of Judah; and if that were too little, then would I add unto thee so much more.

9 Wherefore hast thou despised the word of HaShem, to do that which is evil in My sight? Uriah the Hittite thou hast smitten with the sword, and his wife thou hast taken to be thy wife, and him thou hast slain with the sword of the children of Ammon.

10 Now therefore, the sword shall never depart from thy house; because thou hast despised Me, and hast taken the wife of Uriah the Hittite to be thy wife. . . .

13 And David said unto Nathan: 'I have sinned against HaShem.' And Nathan said unto David: 'The HaShem also hath put away thy sin; thou shalt not die. 99

—from the Hebrew Bible, II Samuel 12:1–10, 13

1 IDENTIFYING Which of the Ten Commandments did David break by taking Uriah's wife and putting Uriah in a situation in which David knew Uriah would be killed? How did his actions go against these commandments?

_____

_____

_____

_____

_____

_____

2 DESCRIBING How does the excerpt help you to understand David as a ruler of the Israelites?

_____

_____

_____

_____

_____

_____

_____

3 **CITING TEXT EVIDENCE** What evidence in the text can you find for David's recognition of wrong action?

_____

_____

_____

_____

_____

_____

_____

4 **ANALYZING INDIVIDUALS** Why did David recognize the sin of another but not his own?

_____

_____

_____

_____

_____

_____

_____

_____

Isaiah's Message to the Israelites to Help the Hungry and the Poor

How does religion shape society?

DIRECTIONS: Read the following excerpt and answer the accompanying questions.

EXPLORE THE CONTEXT: This chapter of Isaiah is read in the synagogue on Yom Kippur (the Day of Atonement), the one day per year when people admit that they have sinned and seek God's forgiveness. They spend the day in prayer, trying to focus on being the good people that God wants them to be.

VOCABULARY

transgression: wrongdoing
forsook: turned away from, left
ordinance: law
wherefore: why
fast: to not eat

strife: trouble
smite: hit
afflicted: diseased or burdened
sabbath: day of the week set aside for rest and worship

PRIMARY SOURCE: BOOK

" 58:1 Cry aloud, spare not, lift up thy voice like a trumpet, and show my people their transgression, and the house of Jacob their sins.

58:2 Yet they seek me daily, and delight to know my ways, as a nation that did righteousness, and forsook not the ordinance of their God: they ask of me the ordinances of justice; they take delight in approaching to God.

58:3 Wherefore have we fasted, say they, and thou seest not? wherefore have we afflicted our soul, and thou takest no knowledge? Behold, in the day of your fast ye find pleasure, and exact all your labours.

58:4 Behold, ye fast for strife and debate, and to smite with the fist of wickedness: ye shall not fast as ye do this day, to make your voice to be heard on high.

58:5 Is it such a fast that I have chosen? a day for a man to afflict his soul? is it to bow down his head as a bulrush, and to spread sackcloth and ashes under him? wilt thou call this a fast, and an acceptable day to the LORD?

58:6 Is not this the fast that I have chosen? to loose the bands of wickedness, to undo the heavy burdens, and to let the oppressed go free, and that ye break every yoke?

58:7 Is it not to deal thy bread to the hungry, and that thou bring the poor that are cast out to thy house? when thou seest the naked, that thou cover him; and that thou hide not thyself from thine own flesh?

58:8 Then shall thy light break forth as the morning, and thine health shall spring forth speedily: and thy righteousness shall go before thee; the glory of the LORD shall be thy reward.

58:9 Then shalt thou call, and the LORD shall answer; thou shalt cry, and he shall say, Here I am. If thou take away from the midst of thee the yoke, the putting forth of the finger, and speaking vanity;

58:10 And if thou draw out thy soul to the hungry, and satisfy the afflicted soul; then shall thy light rise in obscurity, and thy darkness be as the noon day:

58:11 And the LORD shall guide thee continually, and satisfy thy soul in drought, and make fat thy bones: and thou shalt be like a watered garden, and like a spring of water, whose waters fail not.

58:12 And they that shall be of thee shall build the old waste places: thou shalt raise up the foundations of many generations; and thou shalt be called, The repairer of the breach, The restorer of paths to dwell in.

58:13 If thou turn away thy foot from the sabbath, from doing thy pleasure on my holy day; and call the sabbath a delight, the holy of the LORD, honourable; and shalt honour him, not doing thine own ways, nor finding thine own pleasure, nor speaking thine own words:

58:14 Then shalt thou delight thyself in the LORD; and I will cause thee to ride upon the high places of the earth, and feed thee with the heritage of Jacob thy father: for the mouth of the LORD hath spoken it. **"**

—from the Hebrew Bible, Isaiah 58:1-14

1 **DETERMINING MEANING** How does this text explain the purpose of a fast?

_____

_____

_____

_____

_____

_____

2 **DETERMINING MEANING** What similes does the author of this document use to describe the changes in people after a fast? What do each of the similes mean?

_____

_____

_____

_____

_____

_____

_____

_____

_____

_____

_____

_____

3 DETERMINING CENTRAL IDEAS What is the main idea of this passage?

_____

_____

_____

_____

_____

_____

_____

4 COMPARING AND CONTRASTING How is the main idea of this text similar to the main ideas expressed in the Ten Commandments?

_____

_____

_____

_____

_____

_____

_____

_____

ESSENTIAL QUESTION

How does religion shape society?

As you gather evidence to answer the Essential Question, think about:

- how the Israelites went from being led by kings to being led by temple priests and scribes.

- why the Torah serves as the center of a worship service.

My Notes

The Development of Judaism

DIRECTIONS: Search for evidence in Lesson 3 to help you answer the following questions.

1 **ANALYZING IDEAS** How is the Hebrew Bible a multipurpose document for the Jewish people?

2 **INFERRING** How does the account of the prophet Daniel demonstrate to Jews that God will rescue them from harm and that good will triumph over evil?

3 **COMPARING AND CONTRASTING** How is the biblical account of Daniel similar to other accounts of Israelites in crisis in the Hebrew Bible?

4 ANALYZING INDIVIDUALS In the graphic organizer below, write the roles of each member of a Jewish family in the time of the ancient Israelites. Then describe how a person described in the Hebrew Bible is used to reinforce those roles in the family.

Roles of Ancient Israelite Family Members	Examples of Roles in the Hebrew Bible
Father	
Daughter	
Son	

5 ANALYZING TEXT In the graphic organizer below, choose two laws of Judaism described in the text that are still observed today. Then describe how they were observed by ancient Israelites.

Jewish Law Observed Today	How the Law Was Observed By Ancient Israelites

Moses Maimonides on Jewish Dietary Laws

ESSENTIAL QUESTION
How does religion shape society?

DIRECTIONS: Read the following excerpt and answer the accompanying questions.

EXPLORE THE CONTEXT: The dietary laws of the Jewish people are called kashrut. Moses Maimonides (my•MON•ih•deez), a twelfth-century scholar who was born in what is now Spain and completed his career in Egypt, wrote works of philosophy and Jewish law. In this excerpt, he interprets the laws regarding animals.

PRIMARY SOURCE: BOOK

❝It is prohibited to cut off a limb of a living animal and eat it, because such [an] act would produce cruelty, and develop it: besides, the heathen kings used to do it: it was also a kind of idolatrous worship to cut off a certain limb of a living animal and to eat it. . . . Since, therefore, the desire of procuring good food necessitates the slaying of animals, the Law enjoins that the death of the animal should be the easiest. It is not allowed to torment the animal by cutting the throat in a clumsy manner, by poleaxing, or by cutting off a limb whilst the animal is alive. . . . It is also prohibited to kill an animal with its young on the same day, in order that people should be restrained and prevented from killing the two together in such a manner that the young is slain in the sight of the mother; for the pain of the animals under such circumstances is very great. There is no difference in this case between the pain of man and the pain of other living beings. ❞

—from *Guide for the Perplexed* (1190)

VOCABULARY

kashrut: Jewish religious laws concerning food and diet
poleaxing: slaughtering with a battle-ax
prohibited: not allowed
slain: killed
circumstances: conditions; situation

1 **DETERMINING MEANING** What does Maimonides mean by "torment," and what activities in the document fall into that category of behavior?

_____

_____

_____

_____

_____

2 **CITING TEXT EVIDENCE** What evidence in the text can you find for why it is not allowed in Jewish dietary laws to use meat from an animal that has had a limb cut off while it was still alive? How do each of these reasons help you understand the laws of kashrut?

_____

_____

_____

_____

3 **INFERRING** Based on this excerpt about Jewish dietary laws, what can you infer about how animals should be treated when they are being killed for food?

_____

_____

_____

_____

4 **ANALYZING PERSPECTIVES** How does this text reveal the Jewish perspective on similarities between animals and humans?

_____

_____

_____

_____

ESSENTIAL QUESTION
How does religion shape society?

Nehemiah and the Rebuilding of the Walls of Jerusalem

DIRECTIONS: Read the following excerpt and answer the accompanying questions.

EXPLORE THE CONTEXT: Nehemiah was authorized by the Persian king to rebuild the walls of Jerusalem. There was, however, strong opposition from the neighboring people, spearheaded by their leader Sanballat.

PRIMARY SOURCE: BOOK

" 33: But it came to pass that, when Sanballat heard that we built the wall, he was full of wrath, and took great indignation, and mocked the Jews.

34: And he spoke before his brethren and the army of Samaria, and said: 'What do these feeble Jews? will they restore at will? will they sacrifice? will they make an end this day? will they revive the stones out of the heaps of rubbish, seeing they are burned?'

35: Now Tobiah the Ammonite was by him, and he said: 'Even that which they build, if a fox go up, he shall break down their stone wall.'

36: Hear, O our G-d; for we are despised; and turn back their reproach upon their own head, and give them up to spoiling in a land of captivity;

37: and cover not their iniquity, and let not their sin be blotted out from before Thee; for they have vexed Thee before the builders.

38: So we built the wall; and all the wall was joined together unto half the height thereof; for the people had a mind to work. "

—from the Hebrew Bible, Nehemiah 3: 33-38

VOCABULARY

wrath: anger
indignation: offense
feeble: weak
reproach: disapproval

iniquity: morally wrong behavior
vexed: upset

1 **DETERMINING MEANING** What does Tobiah mean by referring to the fox climbing the wall?

_____

_____

_____

_____

_____

2 **CITING TEXT EVIDENCE** What evidence can you find in the text that Jerusalem was extremely important to the Jews?

_____

_____

_____

_____

3 **ANALYZING INDIVIDUALS** How did the Jews react to being mocked?

_____

_____

_____

4 **MAKING CONNECTIONS** How does this text reflect principles of Judaism found in the text about the Yom Kippur fast?

_____

_____

_____

_____

_____

ESSENTIAL QUESTION

How does religion shape society?

As you gather evidence to answer the Essential Question, think about:

- the different reasons for translating the Hebrew Bible into Greek.
- the importance of the Dead Sea Scrolls to our understanding of the practice of Judaism.

My Notes

The Jews in The Mediterranean World

DIRECTIONS: Search for evidence in Lesson 4 to help you answer the following questions.

1 IDENTIFYING CAUSE AND EFFECT How did the Jewish-Roman wars lead to the diaspora?

_____

_____

_____

_____

_____

_____

_____

2 ANALYZING IDEAS What role do rabbis and synagogues play in the preservation of the Jewish religion?

_____

_____

_____

_____

_____

_____

3 DESCRIBING In the graphic organizer below, describe the different groups of Jews under Roman rule. Then describe the ways that each group practiced their religion.

Jewish Communities Under Roman Rule	Jewish Religious Practices
Sadducees	
Pharisees	
Essenes	
Zealots	

Mattathias and the King

ESSENTIAL QUESTION

How does religion shape society?

DIRECTIONS: Read the following excerpt and answer the accompanying questions.

EXPLORE THE CONTEXT: Mattathias (mah•tah•TYE•uhs) was an Israelite leader whose story is known as an example of the persistence of the Israelites' religious faith.

VOCABULARY

renegade: traitors
Gentiles: non-Jewish people
covenant: agreement

profane: distasteful and wrong, against religious law
ordinances: laws

PRIMARY SOURCE: BOOK

❝11 In those days [the reign of Antiochus Epiphanes] certain renegades came out from Israel and misled many, saying, "Let us go and make a covenant with the Gentiles around us, for since we separated from them many disasters have come upon us." 12 This proposal pleased them, 13 and some of the people eagerly went to the king, who authorized them to observe the ordinances of the Gentiles. 14 So they built a gymnasium in Jerusalem, according to Gentile custom, 15 and removed the marks of circumcision, and abandoned the holy covenant. . . .

41 Then the king wrote to his whole kingdom that all should be one people, 42 and that all should give up their particular customs. 43 All the Gentiles accepted the command of the king. Many even from Israel gladly adopted his religion; they sacrificed to idols and profaned the sabbath. 44 And the king sent letters by messengers to Jerusalem and the towns of Judah; he directed them to follow customs strange to the land, 45 to forbid burnt offerings and sacrifices and drink offerings in the sanctuary, to profane sabbaths and festivals, 46 to defile the sanctuary and the priests, 47 to build altars and sacred precincts and shrines for idols, to sacrifice swine and other unclean animals, 48 and to leave their sons uncircumcised. They were to make themselves abominable by everything unclean

and profane, 49 so that they would forget the law and change all the ordinances. 50 He added,[e] "And whoever does not obey the command of the king shall die.". . .

62 But many in Israel stood firm and were resolved in their hearts not to eat unclean food. 63 They chose to die rather than to be defiled by food or to profane the holy covenant; and they did die. 64 Very great wrath came upon Israel. . . .

19 But Mattathias answered and said in a loud voice: "Even if all the nations that live under the rule of the king obey him, and have chosen to obey his commandments, every one of them abandoning the religion of their ancestors, 20 I and my sons and my brothers will continue to live by the covenant of our ancestors. 21 Far be it from us to desert the law and the ordinances. 22 We will not obey the king's words by turning aside from our religion to the right hand or to the left. 🙾

—from the Hebrew Bible, I Maccabees 1: 11-15, 41-50, 62-64; 2: 19-22

1 DETERMINING MEANING Based on your reading of the text, what do you think the writer of this document means by the "holy covenant"?

_____

_____

_____

_____

_____

2 DESCRIBING How does this document describe the notion of "unclean"?

_____

_____

_____

_____

_____

_____

_____

_____

_____

_____

_____

_____

③ CITING TEXT EVIDENCE What evidence in the text can you find for how Mattathias feels about the laws of his religion and the role they play in his life?

_____

_____

_____

_____

_____

_____

_____

_____

④ ANALYZING How do Mattathias's actions reflect the historical precident of keeping the faith? Who in past stories of the Israelites has a similar reaction to this type of challenge?

_____

_____

_____

_____

_____

_____

_____

_____

Capital Cases

ESSENTIAL QUESTION

How does religion shape society?

DIRECTIONS: Read the following excerpt and answer the accompanying questions.

EXPLORE THE CONTEXT: The following excerpt is a discussion of Jewish law.

PRIMARY SOURCE: BOOK

❝How were witnesses admonished in capital cases? They were brought in, and admonished to the effect that 'what you say may be merely your own opinion, or hearsay, or secondhand, or derived from a trustworthy person. Perhaps you do not know that we intend to question you by examination and inquiry. Know, moreover, that capital cases are not like non-capital cases: in non-capital cases a man may pay money and so make expiation; but in capital cases the blood of the accused and of his posterity may cling to him (the witness) to the end of the world. For so we find it in the case of Cain, who slew his brother, as it is written: THE VOICE OF THE BLOODS OF THY BROTHER CRIES TO ME FROM THE GROUND; —not the blood of thy brother, but the bloods of thy brother—his blood and that of his posterity.'

For this reason man was created one and alone in the world: to teach that whosoever destroys a single soul is regarded as though he destroyed a complete world, and whosoever saves a single soul is regarded as though he saved a complete world; and for the sake of peace among created beings that one man should not say to another, "My father was greater than thine," and that heretics should not say, "There are many ruling powers in heaven "; also to proclaim the greatness of the King of kings of kings, blessed be He! for mankind stamps a hundred coins with one seal, and they are all alike, but the King of kings of kings, blessed be He! has stamped every man with the seal of the first Adam, and not one of them is like his fellow. 1 So every single person is forced to say, The world was created for my sake. ❞

—from Mishnah Sanhedrin 4:5, c. 200s C.E.

VOCABULARY

admonished: warned

hearsay: evidence that has no concrete proof, heard from someone else

expiation: the act of repaying for wrongdoing

posterity: future generations

Danby, Herbert, trans. 1919. Tractate Sanhedrin, Mishnah and Tosetta:The Judicial Procedure of the Jews as Codified Towards the End of the Second Century A.D. London: Society for Promoting Christian Knowledge. New York: The Macmillan Company.

1 **DETERMINING MEANING** What does the writer mean by "the blood of the accused and of his posterity may cling to him. . . ."? What does the writer mean by "his posterity"?

_____

_____

2 **INFERRING** The writer makes a distinction between capital and non-capital cases. What is the difference between the two kinds of cases?

_____

_____

3 **ANALYZING** Why does the murder of one person, from this writer's perspective, equal the murder of an entire world?

_____

_____

_____

_____

_____

_____

_____

4 **MAKING CONNECTIONS** How are this document and the document on Jewish dietary laws similar regarding the views of Judaism on the taking of a life? How do these similarities help you understand the Jewish perspective on the power of human beings to take lives or refrain from taking them?

_____

_____

_____

_____

_____

ESSENTIAL QUESTION

How does religion shape society?

1 Think About It

Review the supporting questions that you developed at the beginning of the chapter. Review the evidence that you gathered in this chapter. Were you able to answer each Supporting Question?

If there was not enough evidence to answer your Supporting Questions, what additional evidence do you think you need to consider?

2 Organize Your Evidence

Use a chart like the one below to organize the evidence you will use to support your position statement.

Source of Information	Specific evidence from the source to cite From the Source	How does the evidence support my position statement?	How does this evidence connect to modern life?

3 Write About It

A position statement related to the Essential Question should reflect your conclusion about the evidence. Write a position statement for the ESSENTIAL QUESTION: *How does religion shape society?*

_____

_____

_____

_____

_____

_____

_____

_____

4 Talk About It

Work in a small group to present your position statement and evidence. Gather feedback from your classmates before you write your final conclusion. You may choose to refine your position statement after you have discussed it with your classmates. Group members should listen to one another's arguments, ask questions, and offer constructive advice to help each other create clear position statements.

_____

_____

_____

5 Connect to the Essential Question

On a separate piece of paper, develop an interview with an ancient Israelite person who is your age to answer the ESSENTIAL QUESTION: *How does religion shape society?*

CITIZENSHIP
TAKING ACTION

MAKE CONNECTIONS Jews throughout history have faced discrimination and persecution. Hostility or prejudice against Jews is called anti-Semitism. Hostility towards Jewish people reached its height in Europe before and during World War II, when Jews were murdered by the Nazis in the Holocaust. The Nazis were defeated, but anti-Semitism continues, even in the United States. Hate groups sometimes target Jews and Jewish organizations with violent acts. American Jews can face discrimination in employment and other parts of society.

DIRECTIONS: The Anti-Defamation League (ADL) was founded in the United States to fight anti-Semitism. Use the Internet to find the nearest office of the ADL in your state or region. Find out what steps the ADL recommends for schools and communities to take action against anti-Semitism. Then discuss as a class what actions would be effective in responding to anti-Semitic incidents among students and in the wider society.

The Ancient Greeks

ESSENTIAL QUESTION

Why does conflict develop?

Think about how this question might relate to the Ancient Greek civilization.

TALK ABOUT IT  COLLABORATE

Discuss with a partner what information you would need in order to answer this question. For example, one question might be: Did the geography of Greece affect the development of conflict within its civilization?

DIRECTIONS: Write down three more questions that might help you explain the influence of conflict as the Greeks developed as a civilization.

MY RESEARCH QUESTIONS

Supporting Question 1:

_____

_____

Supporting Question 2:

_____

_____

Supporting Question 3:

_____

_____

Rise of Greek Civilization

DIRECTIONS: Search for evidence in Lesson 1 to help you answer the following questions.

1 **ANALYZING** What problems or benefits did the people of ancient Greece experience as a result of being surrounded by seas and mountains?

_____

_____

_____

_____

_____

2 **COMPARING AND CONTRASTING** In what ways were the Mycenaeans and Minoans alike and different?

ESSENTIAL QUESTION

Why does conflict develop?

As you gather evidence to answer the Essential Question, think about:

- the distance between the communities in Greece.
- reasons for the Dark Age and the later recovery of Greece.

My Notes

_____

_____

_____

_____

_____

_____

_____

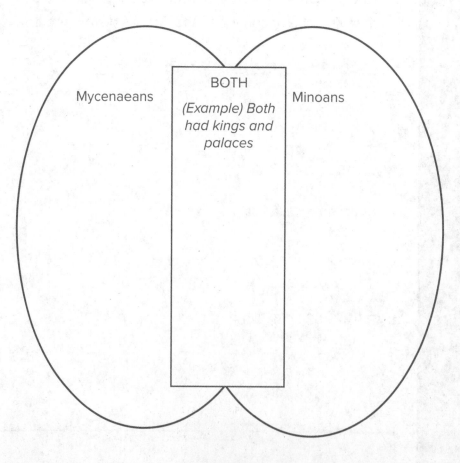

Mycenaeans

BOTH
(Example) Both had kings and palaces

Minoans

3 **IDENTIFYING CAUSE AND EFFECT** Fill in the chart below to show the relationship between the fall of the Mycenaeans and its effects during the Dark Age. Use details to fill in what the effects were for each event listed.

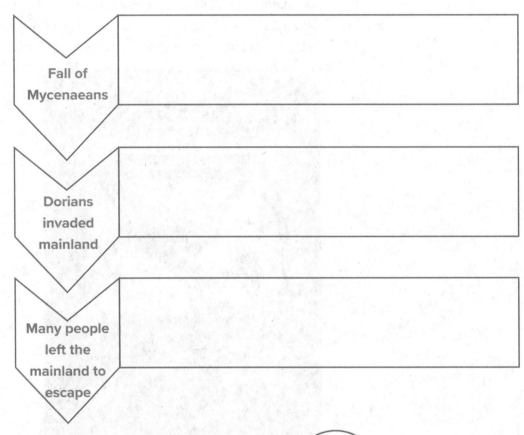

Fall of Mycenaeans

Dorians invaded mainland

Many people left the mainland to escape

4 **HISTORY** What were the historic developments in the restoration of Greece? Fill in the web with details of Greek accomplishments after the Dark Age.

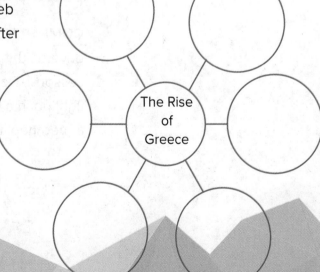

The Rise of Greece

Chariot Race

DIRECTIONS: Study the following image and answer the accompanying questions.

EXPLORE THE CONTEXT: This photo of a vase created around 500 B.C.E. to 480 B.C.E. includes an image of a chariot. Chariots had a great impact on ancient Greek Civilization.

PRIMARY SOURCE: IMAGE

1A **COMPARING** Compare the image of the chariot and its driver with the picture of the Greek city-state hoplites in Lesson 1. Describe any advantages or disadvantages of fighting in a chariot as compared with being a heavily armed hoplite.

_____

_____

_____

_____

_____

1B **ANALYZING** How did the use of chariots contribute to the development of conflict?

_____

_____

_____

_____

_____

2 HISTORY Why would chariot racing have become a sporting event when the chariots were designed for war?

_____

_____

_____

3 **DRAWING CONCLUSIONS** By examining the image, can you determine how the nobles controlled their horses? Why would control be important? Support your opinion with reasons.

_____

_____

_____

_____

_____

4 **ANALYZING POINT OF VIEW** Whose point of view, the hoplites or the nobles, is illustrated in the image? Why do you think this image would have been painted onto vases and walls of palaces? What evidence can you supply from Lesson 1 to support your answer?

_____

_____

_____

_____

_____

_____

Hesiod on Conflict

ESSENTIAL QUESTION

Why does conflict develop?

DIRECTIONS: Read the following excerpt and answer the accompanying questions.

EXPLORE THE CONTEXT: The excerpt from *The Ancient Olympics*, by Nigel Spivey, provides insight from poetry written by Hesiod, an early Greek writer.

SECONDARY SOURCE: BOOK

66 It was one of the earliest surviving Greek poets, Hesiod, composing his verses probably around 700 BC, who not only made 'Strife' (Eris) a supernatural force to be reckoned with, but also divided this force into one Strife that was useful and productive (Eris agathos) and another that caused nothing but grief for humankind. This malevolent Strife, 'exulting in bad things' (kakochartos), was the bringer of war and dissent to the world. Good Strife . . . encouraged mortals to make the most of their brief time on earth; Bad Strife sets up lusts for battle and bloodshed. Good Strife nurtured desires for wealth and fame; Bad Strife was a destroyer of lives and property. Good Strife urged creative industry, stirring the energies of emulation. So craftsmen competed amongst themselves, so farmers toiled to get the best from their land, so even beggars vied in their begging, and poets challenged other poets. 99

— Nigel Spivey, *The Ancient Olympics: A History,* 2004 C.E.

VOCABULARY

strife: quarrel, conflict
supernatural: something related to a God or Deity
reckoned with: dealt with
malevolent: having an evil influence

exulting: rejoicing, feeling joy or happiness
mortals: humans
emulation: imitation of something admired
vied: competed for superiority

1 **DETERMINING MEANING** Spivey explains the importance of *Strife*, according to Hesiod. Examine the meaning of the word *strife* as it is usually defined today. How does that compare with Hesiod's point of view concerning *Strife*? Explain.

_____

_____

_____

_____

2 CITING TEXT EVIDENCE Which phrases or lines from Hesiod would relate to the Olympics, both then and now?

_____

_____

_____

_____

_____

3 EXPLAINING EFFECTS Review Lesson 1 to see how Greek citizens viewed their individual city-states. Describe the effects of "good strife" in the individual polis and the effects of "bad strife" among the city-states of Greece.

_____

_____

_____

_____

_____

4 DRAWING CONCLUSIONS What character qualities would a person choosing Hesiod's "good strife" exhibit? Explain.

_____

_____

_____

5 RELATING EVENTS If you faced a competition at school and felt you were not ready, what ideas could you apply from Hesiod's poetry theme?

_____

_____

_____

_____

ESSENTIAL QUESTION

Why does conflict develop?

As you gather evidence to answer the Essential Question, think about:

- the resentment people had toward the control of the wealthy nobles.

- the reign of controlling tyrants before the rise of oligarchies and democracies.

My Notes

Sparta and Athens: City-State Rivals

DIRECTIONS: Search for evidence in Lesson 2 to help you answer the following questions.

1 **DETERMINING SUPPORTING DETAILS** Complete the chart to define and compare the differences in the following types of government.

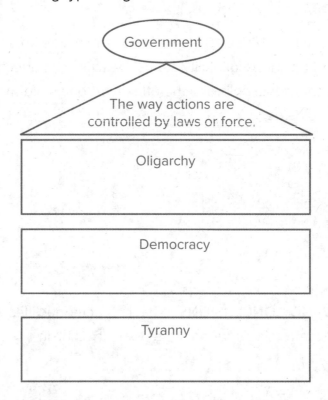

2 ECONOMICS How might Sparta's culture affect its relationships with other city-states?

_____

_____

_____

3 INFERRING In the graphic organizer below, list ways Spartan men and women were raised and the roles each played in Sparta. Then make an inference about what kind of city-state Sparta was.

Spartan Men	Spartan Women
1.	1.
2.	2.
3.	3.

4 EXPLAINING CAUSE AND EFFECT How did debt and slavery cause reform in the city-state of Athens? List a chain of effects that resulted from this reform.

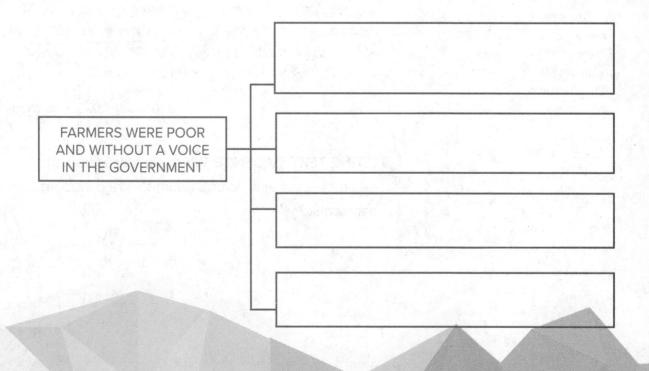

FARMERS WERE POOR AND WITHOUT A VOICE IN THE GOVERNMENT

Democratic Reforms

ESSENTIAL QUESTION

Why does conflict develop?

VOCABULARY

magistracies: control of territory

appraisement: a statement of the value of something

measures: a standard unit used to measure quantity

administration: the people who manage the government

disputes: an argument or difference of opinion

deprived: lacking something considered necessary

DIRECTIONS: Study the following excerpt and answer the accompanying questions.

EXPLORE THE CONTEXT: Plutarch was a Greek biographer and essayist whose excerpt describes reforms put in place by Solon.

> **PRIMARY SOURCE: BOOK**
>
> ❝[W]ishing to leave all the magistracies in the hands of the well-to-do, as they were, but to give the common people a share in the rest of the government, of which they had hitherto [so far] been deprived, Solon made an appraisement of the property of the citizens. Those who enjoyed a yearly increase of five hundred measures (wet and dry), he placed in the first class, and called them Pentakosiomedimnoi; the second class was composed of those who were able to keep a horse, or had a yearly increase of three hundred measures, and they were called Hippada Telountes, since they paid a Knight's tax; the members of the third class, whose yearly increase amounted to two hundred measures (wet and dry together), were called Zeugitai. All the rest were called Thetes; they were not allowed to hold any office, but took part in the administration only as members of the assembly and as jurors. This last privilege seemed at first of no moment [importance], but afterwards proved to be of the very highest importance, since most disputes finally came into the hands of these jurors.❞
>
> —from *Plutarch's Lives,* c. 96-98 C.E.

1 CITING TEXT EVIDENCE Which sentences from the excerpt explain why Solon's reforms were considered democratic?

_____

_____

_____

_____

_____

_____

2 **COMPARING AND CONTRASTING** Compare and contrast Plutarch's description of democratic reforms with the text in Lesson 2.

_____

_____

_____

_____

_____

_____

3 **DETERMINING POINT OF VIEW** Discuss with a partner what you think Plutarch believes about Solon's ideas of governing. What does Plutarch suggest by the word choices in this sentence: "to give the common people a share in the rest of the government, of which they had hitherto [so far] been deprived." Why might he have chosen the word *deprived*?

_____

_____

_____

_____

_____

_____

_____

4 **DRAWING CONCLUSIONS** From reading the excerpt, how do you think the people responded to Solon's reforms? Compare your conclusion with the explanation in Lesson 2.

_____

_____

_____

_____

Spartan Sayings

ESSENTIAL QUESTION

Why does conflict develop?

DIRECTIONS: Study the following excerpt and answer the accompanying questions.

EXPLORE THE CONTEXT: Plutarch, the Greek writer, also collected quotations from the people of Sparta. These quotes will help explain the ideas and attitudes of the citizens of ancient Sparta.

PRIMARY SOURCE: BOOK

66 **ANAXANDRIDAS**

When another person asked why the Spartans, in their wars, ventured boldly into danger, he said, 'Because we train ourselves to have regard for life and not, like others, to be timid about it.'

ANDROCLEIDAS

Androcleidas the Spartan, who had a crippled leg, enrolled himself among the fighting-men. And when some persons were insistent that he be not accepted because he was crippled, he said, 'But I do not have to run away, but to stay where I am when I fight the opposing foe.'

ARISTON

1 When someone inquired how many Spartans there were in all, he said, 'Enough to keep away our enemies.'

2 When one of the Athenians read a memorial oration in praise of those who fell at the hands of the Spartans, he said, 'What kind of men, then, do you think ours must be who vanquished these?'

ZEUXIDAMUS

3 When someone inquired why they kept the laws in regard to bravery unwritten, and did not have them written down and thus give them to the young men to read, Zeuxidamus said, 'Because the young ought to accustom themselves to deeds of manly valour, a better thing than to apply their mind to writings.' **99**

— Plutarch, *Apophthegmata Laconica,* c. 96-98 C.E.

VOCABULARY

ventured: took a risk to go out and do something

valour: courage, bravery

memorial: a time or event set aside to remember

oration: speech

vanquished: conquered

1 **INFERRING** What character traits were most valued by the Spartans and how did these traits affect their culture? Use evidence from the excerpts to support your ideas.

_____

_____

_____

_____

_____

_____

_____

_____

_____

_____

2 CITING TEXT EVIDENCE Discuss with a partner the tough mindset that was characteristic of the Spartans. Use evidence from the quotations to support your answer.

_____

_____

_____

_____

_____

_____

3 CONTRASTING How do the Spartan values stated in the quotations contrast with the values of Athenians described in Lesson 2?

_____

_____

_____

4 DRAWING CONCLUSIONS What do the quotations suggest about the military strength of ancient Sparta? Support your answer with details.

_____

_____

_____

5 CIVICS Imagine that our nation passed laws that schools would no longer teach reading but, instead, focus solely on building physical strength. How do you think our society would change? Explain.

_____

_____

_____

ESSENTIAL QUESTION

Why does conflict develop?

As you gather evidence to answer the Essential Question, think about:

- how Persia's great King Cyrus built a growing empire.

- the clash between Greece and Persia as the Persians tried to move into Europe.

My Notes

Greece and Persia

DIRECTIONS: Search for evidence in Lesson 3 to help you answer the following questions.

1 **CITING TEXT EVIDENCE** How is Persia's king, Cyrus, described? Fill in the chart below with factual evidence from the text.

Who is This King Cyrus?

Text evidence #1:

Text evidence #2:

Text evidence #3:

2 **SEQUENCING** Identify the events in the expansion of the Persian Empire after Cyrus. Write the events in the organizer according to the historical sequence.

Sequence of Events in the Expansion of the Persian Empire
1
2
3
4
5
6

3 IDENTIFYING CAUSE AND EFFECT In the graphic organizer below, describe how the Greeks responded to each advance by the Persians.

Persians landed at Marathon ready for battle	
Xerxes invaded Greece with 200,000 troops and many warships.	
The Persian fleet entered the strait of Salamis near Athens.	
The Persian soldiers marched into Athens.	
The Persians had 100,000 troops at Plataea, in 479 B.C.E.	

King Darius

DIRECTIONS: Study the following image of King Darius I of Persia and answer the accompanying questions.

EXPLORE THE CONTEXT: This photo shows a relief wall from King Darius's palace in Persepolis, the ancient capital of Persia. Construction of the capital's buildings began around 518 B.C.E.

PRIMARY SOURCE: RELIEF SCULPTURE

1 **DETERMINING POINT OF VIEW** Using the image as a resource, whose viewpoint is best shown, the citizens of Persia or King Darius I? What emotions do you think this image was meant to point out to all who viewed it? Use evidence from Lesson 2 to support your answer.

_____

_____

_____

_____

_____

_____

2 **DRAWING CONCLUSIONS** What role does Zoroastrianism play in how King Darius I is depicted in the image? Reread the description in your text and decide if it corresponds with the image shown. Explain.

_____

_____

_____

_____

_____

_____

3 **COMPARING AND CONTRASTING** What does the image suggest about the authority of kings of Persia? How did the rule of Persian kings contrast with the Greek form of government? How are both systems similar?

_____

_____

_____

_____

_____

4 **DRAWING CONCLUSIONS** What does King Darius I's image suggest to you about the reason for conflict between Persia and Greece?

_____

_____

_____

_____

_____

_____

ESSENTIAL QUESTION

Why does conflict develop?

The Defeat of Xerxes at the Battle of Salamis

DIRECTIONS: Study the following excerpt and answer the accompanying questions.

EXPLORE THE CONTEXT: Artemisia was a courageous Greek woman who had married King Halicarnassus in 500 B.C.E. After he died, she accepted her role as Queen. She became loyal to Persia and made herself famous by becoming a naval commander.

SECONDARY SOURCE: BOOK

❝He said that he would consult some of the other commanders upon the subject. He did so, and then, before coming to a final decision, he determined to confer with Artemisia. He remembered that she had counseled him not to attack the Greeks at Salamis, and, as the result had proved that counsel to be eminently wise, he felt the greater confidence in asking her judgment again. He accordingly sent for Artemisia, and, directing all the officers, as well as his own attendants, to retire, he held a private consultation with her in respect to his plans.

'Mardonius proposes,' said he, 'that the expedition should on no account be abandoned in consequence of this disaster, for he says that the fleet is a very unimportant part of our force, and that the army still remains unharmed. He proposes that, if I should decide myself to return to Persia, I should leave three hundred thousand men with him, and he undertakes, if I will do so, to complete, with them, the subjugation of Greece. Tell me what you think of this plan. You evinced so much sagacity in foreseeing the result of this engagement at Salamis, that I particularly wish to know your opinion.'**❞**

— Jacob Abbott, *Makers of History: Xerxes*, 1878 C.E.

VOCABULARY:

confer: to seek someone else's opinion

eminently: exceptionally

consultation: a meeting to gather another's ideas

expedition: a journey or trip

undertakes: begins

subjugation: defeat

evinced: demonstrated

sagacity: wisdom

1 ANALYZING Which words describing Artemisia show how much Xerxes admired her?

_____

_____

2 DRAWING CONCLUSIONS Using information about Salamis in Lesson 3, why do you think Artemisia counseled Xerxes not to attack there?

_____

_____

_____

_____

3 HISTORY Discuss with a partner what you can infer about the role of females in this time period. What is the author suggesting about Artemisia in this passage when Xerxes calls her for a consultation?

_____

_____

_____

4 INFERRING Why do you think Xerxes wanted a private consultation with Artemisia about the possibility of a future battle with the Greeks?

_____

_____

_____

_____

5 IDENTIFYING CONNECTIONS If you had an important decision to make, who would you consult? Would you go to a trusted friend or to someone you knew had experience in the area of concern?

_____

_____

_____

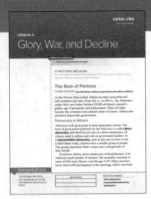

Glory, War, and Decline

DIRECTIONS: Search for evidence in Lesson 4 to help you answer the following questions.

ESSENTIAL QUESTION

Why does conflict develop?

As you gather evidence to answer the Essential Question, think about

- how the economic and political strength of Athens gave them more influence.

- how Sparta became the head of an alliance of city-states to rival Athens.

1 IDENTIFYING CAUSES Use the chart to record important details that resulted from the leadership of Pericles in Athens.

Athens Under the Leadership of Pericles

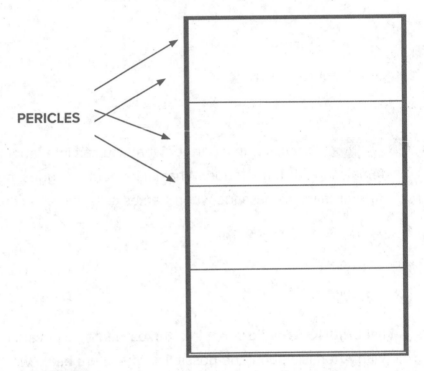

PERICLES

My Notes

_____

_____

_____

_____

_____

_____

_____

2 HISTORY If Athens prospered under the leadership of Pericles, what went wrong? What was the trigger, or initial cause, of conflict?

_____

_____

_____

_____

_____

_____

_____

3 **ANALYZING** What were the democratic principles encouraged in the famous speech, now known as Pericles's Funeral Oration?

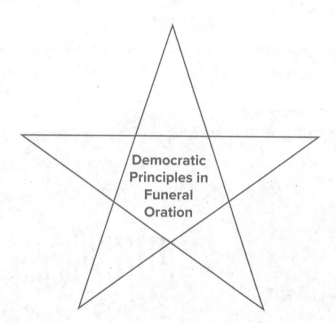

Democratic
Principles in
Funeral
Oration

4 **IDENTIFYING CAUSES** Use the chart below to record events that caused Athens to finally lose the Peloponnesian War.

Causes of the Surrender Of Athens

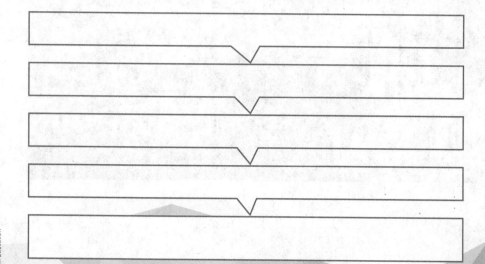

The Acropolis

ESSENTIAL QUESTION
Why does conflict develop?

DIRECTIONS: Study the following image and answer the accompanying questions.

EXPLORE THE CONTEXT: This image depicts a famous example of the center point of most ancient Greek city-states, an acropolis. This modern-day photo shows the acropolis that was built in ancient Athens, where the temple to the Goddess Athena was eventually added.

PRIMARY SOURCE: IMAGE

1A **DESCRIBING** Describe the famous Acropolis as seen in this image.

_____

_____

1B **IDENTIFYING CONNECTIONS** Describe the features of the Acropolis that have been used in more modern architecture. Describe any important buildings you may know of in America using those ancient Greek features.

_____

_____

_____

_____

2 **ANALYZING** How was the Acropolis protected?

_____

_____

3 **DRAWING CONCLUSIONS** Does this image of the Athenian Acropolis correspond to the description of Greek acropolis structures in Lesson 1? Explain.

_____

_____

_____

4 **CITING TEXT EVIDENCE** In Lesson 4, reread about the days after the Persian Wars and Pericles. Why did the Athenian victory and leadership of Pericles contribute to the building of additional monuments at the Acropolis?

_____

_____

_____

_____

_____

The Plague in Athens

ESSENTIAL QUESTION

Why does conflict develop?

DIRECTIONS: Study the following excerpt and answer the accompanying questions.

EXPLORE THE CONTEXT: Thucydides, another well-known historian from Ancient Greece, wrote about the war between Athens and Sparta. The war was called the Peloponnesian War because of Sparta's location in the Peloponnesus, a peninsula in southern Greece. In addition to the problems of war, Athens was struck by an epidemic, killing many Athenians, including the leader Pericles. Attica is the region around and including Athens.

VOCABULARY

thence: from there
thither: onward in a new direction
lazar-house: a place where people with leprosy were confined
epidemic: a rapid spread of disease

scourge: suffering, calamity
copious: plentiful, a large amount
draughts: cups
oblivion: forgetting or not knowing

PRIMARY SOURCE: BOOK

❝At the beginning of the next summer the Peloponnesians again entered Attica, and resumed their work of devastation, destroying the young crops, and wrecking whatever had been spared in the previous year. Before they had been many days in Attica, a new and far more terrible visitation came upon the Athenians, threatening them with total extinction as a people. We have seen how the whole upper city, with the space between the Long Walls, and the harbour-town of Peiraeus, was packed with a vast multitude of human beings, penned together, like sheep in a fold. Into these huddled masses now crept a subtle and unseen foe, striking down his victims by hundreds and by thousands. That foe was the Plague, which beginning in Southern Africa, and descending thence to Egypt, reached the southern shores of the Mediterranean, and passed on to Peiraeus, having been carried thither by seamen who trafficked between northern Africa and Greece. . . .

From the description of the symptoms we may conclude that this epidemic was similar to that dreadful scourge of mankind which has been almost conquered by modern science, the small-pox. The patient who had taken the

infection was first attacked in the head, with inflammation of the eyes, and violent headache. By degrees the poison worked its way into the whole system, . . . One of the most distressing features of the disease was a raging thirst, which could not be appeased by the most copious draughts of water; and the internal heat, which produced this effect, caused also a frightful irritability of the skin, so that the sufferer could not bear the touch of the lightest and most airy fabrics, . . . Of those who recovered, many bore the marks of the sickness to their graves, by the loss of a hand, a foot, or an eye; while others were affected in their minds, remaining in blank oblivion, without power to recognise themselves or their friends. **99**

— from *Stories from Thucydides*, c. 400s B.C.E.

1 **ANALYZING SOURCES** In the first two sentences, what emotions do you think the author wanted the reader to feel? What evidence can you provide to support your answer?

_____

_____

_____

_____

_____

_____

_____

_____

2 **COMPARING AND CONTRASTING** In Lesson 4, the city-state of Athens is described at its height after the Persian Wars. What words would best describe Athens then? Compare and contrast this condition to that of Athens at the time of the writing by Thucydides.

_____

_____

_____

_____

_____

_____

_____

3 SUMMARIZING Describe the impact of the plague on the people of Athens and why it would have affected the outcome of the war with Sparta.

_____

_____

_____

_____

_____

_____

_____

4 CITING TEXT EVIDENCE How does the author Thucydides elaborate the main idea that Athens was destroyed during the Peloponnesian War? Use evidence from the excerpt to support your ideas.

_____

_____

_____

_____

_____

_____

_____

_____

_____

ESSENTIAL QUESTION

Why does conflict develop?

1 Think About It

Review the supporting questions that you developed at opening of the chapter. Review the evidence you found in the chapter. Were you able to answer each of your Supporting Questions?

If you didn't find enough evidence to answer your Supporting Questions, what do you think you need to consider?

_____

_____

_____

_____

_____

2 Organize Your Evidence

Use a chart like the one below to organize the evidence you will need to support your position statement.

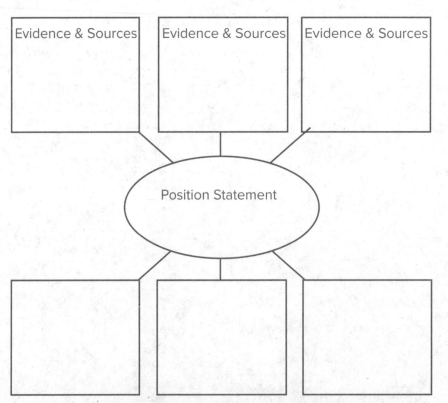

③ Talk About It

In a small group or with a partner, discuss your position statement and the evidence you have gathered. Check your group's understanding of your evidence and respond to questions your members may have while considering their input.

⑤ Connect to the Essential Question

On a separate piece of paper, write a decree, or instruction, to your citizens as if you were an important leader in ancient Athens. What wisdom would you pass onto the people in a young democracy? Be sure to address the answers to the ESSENTIAL QUESTION: *Why does conflict develop?* What advice could you give your followers that would help them live peacefully, using what you've learned about conflict?

CITIZENSHIP
TAKING ACTION

MAKE CONNECTIONS: Many kings and city-state leaders fought to gain land and power in the days of ancient Greece. Though we have not experienced a foreign power attempting to gain territory *within* America today, some world leaders still seek dominion over other countries. One place that was recently overtaken by Russia was the Crimea region of Ukraine. Many members of the international community of nations placed sanctions (penalties, often with trade agreements) on Russia for their invasion. However, Russia continues to occupy the region militarily.

DIRECTIONS: Research the causes of this specific conflict. Determine if the events that caused Russia to act aggressively are similar to reasons you discovered for conflicts among Greeks and Persians.

Write a speech that you could present to the United Nations to promote an international agreement to turn around Russia's invasion in Ukraine.

_____

_____

_____

_____

_____

_____

_____

_____

_____

_____

Greek Civilization

ESSENTIAL QUESTION

What makes a culture unique?

Think about how this question might relate to the culture of ancient Greece.

COLLABORATE

TALK ABOUT IT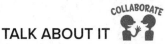

Discuss with a partner what type of information you would need to know to answer this question. For example, one question might be: What kind of cultural advancements happened in ancient Greece?

DIRECTIONS: Now write down three additional questions that would help you explain the parts of society that makes a culture unique.

MY RESEARCH QUESTIONS

Supporting Question 1:

_____

_____

Supporting Question 2:

_____

_____

Supporting Question 3:

_____

_____

ESSENTIAL QUESTION

What makes a culture unique?

As you gather evidence to answer the Essential Question, think about:

- the religion adopted by people in ancient Greece.
- how theater and literature influenced the thought of ancient Greek communities.

My Notes

_____

_____

_____

_____

_____

_____

_____

Greek Culture

DIRECTIONS: Search for evidence in Lesson 1 to help you answer the following questions.

1 SUMMARIZING Use the chart below to make notes about the religious beliefs and practices of ancient Greece.

Religious Beliefs	Religious Practices

2 SUMMARIZING Ancient Greek drama and literature remain parts of western culture today. As you reread the chapter, fill out the KWL chart below to record what you know, what you learned, and what you would like to learn about ancient Greek literature and drama.

Know	Want to Learn	Learned

3 **ANALYZING** Reread the section of the chapter about ancient Greek comedies and tragedies. Now think about the movies, plays, and stories you know of today. Write the name of one tragedy and one comedy that you have seen on television, in a theater, or read in literature.

_____

_____

_____

_____

_____

_____

_____

_____

4 **HISTORY** Look at the drawing of the Parthenon. What does the architecture tell you about the people who used it?

_____

_____

_____

_____

_____

_____

_____

_____

Greek Papyrus

DIRECTIONS: Examine the image below and answer the accompanying questions.

EXPLORE THE CONTEXT: This artifact from around the 300s B.C.E., which describes the battle of Salamis, is made of a plant material called papyrus. Papyrus grows best in wet areas of warm climates, like along the Nile River or in Mediterranean locations like Greece. This material was used as paper by early cultures. The ancient Greek people used papyrus to record their laws, poetry, and stories. Some papyrus artifacts have been recovered from graves. Others have been found wrapped and placed alongside mummies. Today, papyrus artifacts are preserved carefully in museums. They help modern historians understand what life was like many years ago.

PRIMARY SOURCE: ARTIFACT

1 GEOGRAPHY What can you tell about the climate and environment of ancient Greece from the artifact?

_____

_____

_____

_____

2 **INTEGRATING VISUAL INFORMATION** What type of document is pictured in this image? How does this help you understand ancient Greek culture?

_____

_____

_____

_____

3 **INFERRING** The writing on the papyrus tells the story of an important battle in which a Greek fleet overpowered Persian naval forces that were much greater in number. What inference can you make about how documents such as this were shared among people in ancient Greece?

_____

_____

_____

_____

4 **DRAWING CONCLUSIONS** What conclusion can you draw about the artifact from knowing that it has been preserved from ancient times?

_____

_____

_____

_____

The Temple of Apollo at Delphi

DIRECTIONS: Look at the image and answer the accompanying questions.

EXPLORE THE CONTEXT: The image shows the ruins of the Temple of Apollo at Delphi. The temple was built around the 700s B.C.E. Temples were often dedicated to specific Gods and Goddesses, especially Apollo, the God of the sun. The grand temple was home to the Oracle of Delphi and would have been considered a sacred site. Today it draws thousands of visitors who want to understand the culture of people who lived long ago.

PRIMARY SOURCE: ARCHITECTURE

1 **DETERMINING CONTEXT** What was the purpose of the temple? Why was it built?

_____

_____

_____

_____

2 **ANALYZING** What can you tell about the number of people who likely visited the temple when it was built? What type of people likely visited the temple? What evidence can you gather from the image that helps you answer that question?

_____

_____

_____

_____

_____

_____

_____

3 GEOGRAPHY What features of the setting of the temple of Apollo at Delphi help you understand its meaning and importance?

_____

_____

_____

_____

4 ECONOMICS What could you learn about the culture of ancient Greece from visiting the ruins of the temple of Apollo at Delphi?

_____

_____

_____

ESSENTIAL QUESTION

What makes a culture unique?

As you gather evidence to answer the Essential Question, think about:

- the thinkers that shaped ancient Greek philosophy.

- how people use facts and beliefs to build ideas about science.

- how our own ideas about science and medicine are built on the culture of ancient Greece.

My Notes

_____

_____

_____

_____

_____

_____

_____

_____

_____

The Greek Mind

DIRECTIONS: Search for evidence in Lesson 2 to help you answer the following question.

1 SUMMARIZING Take notes using the Cornell Note Taking organizer below on the ideas of the ancient Greek philosophers. Summarize the sections and the images from your textbook to take notes.

Philosophers	Notes
Sophists	
Socrates	
Plato	
Aristotle	

2 HISTORY The Greek word *philosophy* means "love of wisdom." How does that help you understand ancient Greek culture?

_____

_____

_____

_____

_____

3 **ANALYZING** Which Greek philosopher's work laid the groundwork for the study of science? Provide some examples of his studies.

_____

_____

_____

4 **COMPARING AND CONTRASTING** How were the historians Herodotus and Thucydides alike in their thinking, and how were they different?

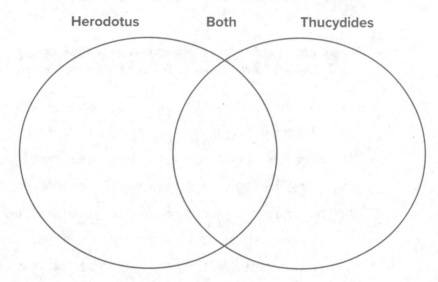

Herodotus   Both   Thucydides

5 **DETERMINING CENTRAL IDEAS** Important ancient Greek scientists are listed in the first column of the chart below. In the second column, write details explaining what each scientist is famous for.

Scientist	Major Contribution
Thales	
Pythagoras	
Hippocrates	

Athenian Constitution

ESSENTIAL QUESTION

What makes a culture unique?

DIRECTIONS: Study the following excerpt and answer the accompanying questions.

EXPLORE THE CONTEXT: Aristotle wrote many works on government. He was interested in how people interacted with their rulers. Each city in ancient Greece had its own system of government. In the passage below, Aristotle explains the political system of the ancient Greek city of Athens.

PRIMARY SOURCE: POLITICAL TREATISE

66 There should be a Council of Four Hundred, as in the ancient constitution, forty from each tribe, chosen out of candidates of more than thirty years of age, selected by the members of the tribes. This Council should appoint the magistrates and draw up the form of oath which they were to take; and in all that concerned the laws, in the examination of official accounts, and in other matters generally, they might act according to their discretion. They must, however, observe the laws that might be enacted with reference to the constitution of the state, and had no power to alter them nor to pass others. 99

— Aristotle, *The Athenian Constitution,* 350 B.C.E.

VOCABULARY

magistrate: judge

1   HISTORY   What type of document is this? How does this information help you understand the document?

_____

_____

_____

_____

_____

_____

② **EXPLAINING** How were the members of the council chosen?

_____

_____

_____

_____

_____

_____

_____

③ **ANALYZING SOURCES** What details from the source give information about the rules council members were required to follow?

_____

_____

_____

_____

_____

_____

④ CIVICS What can you tell about the government of ancient Athens from the document?

_____

_____

_____

_____

_____

_____

_____

Hippocrates

ESSENTIAL QUESTION
What makes a culture unique?

DIRECTIONS: Study the following excerpt and answer the accompanying questions.

EXPLORE THE CONTEXT: Hippocrates lived from around 460 to 370 B.C.E. He wrote many essays on medical issues. Some of his works include *On Injuries of the Head, On the Heart, On the Glands, On the Veins,* and *On the Diseases of Women*. He wrote so many essays on health and anatomy that he is sometimes called the "father of modern medicine." This excerpt is from his work called *Regimen in Acute Diseases*.

PRIMARY SOURCE: BOOK

❝The course I recommend is to pay attention to the whole of the medical art. Indeed all acts that are good and correct should be in all cases well or correctly performed; if they ought to be done quickly, they should be done quickly, if neatly, neatly, if painlessly, they should be managed with a minimum of pain; and all such acts ought to be performed excellently, in a manner better than that of one's own fellows.❞

— Hippocrates, *Regimen in Acute Diseases*, 400 B.C.E.

---

1 **HISTORY** What type of document is this? What does it help you understand?

_____

_____

_____

_____

_____

Copyright © McGraw-Hill Education   Translated 1923 by W. H. S. Jones. Hippocrates, Vol II. London: William Heinemann Ltd; Cambridge, Massachusetts: Harvard University Press.

2 **ASKING QUESTIONS** Does Hippocrates want something specific to happen by writing this document? What is his motive for writing?

_____

_____

_____

_____

_____

_____

3 **DRAWING CONCLUSIONS** When was the document written? How does that help you understand it?

_____

_____

_____

_____

_____

_____

_____

4 **EVALUATING EVIDENCE** What inference can you make about Hippocrates from the details in the document? What evidence do you use to make your inference?

_____

_____

_____

_____

_____

_____

ESSENTIAL QUESTION

What makes a culture unique?

As you gather evidence to answer the Essential Question, think about:

- how Phillip II of Macedonia changed the culture of ancient Greece.
- the role of Alexander the Great in ancient Greek culture.
- the culture of the Hellenistic Era.

My Notes

_____

_____

_____

_____

_____

_____

_____

_____

Alexander's Empire

DIRECTIONS: Search for evidence in Lesson 3 to help you answer the following questions.

1 **SEQUENCING** Use information from the text and the sequence of events organizer below to list events, beginning with the Macedonian conquest of ancient Greece to the period of the Hellenistic kings.

2 **EXPLAINING CAUSE AND EFFECT** Use the cause-and-effect organizer below to explain what caused Alexander the Great to come to power and the effect of his leadership.

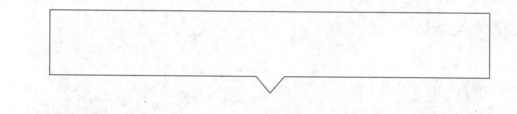

3 CIVICS How did Alexander the Great and the later Hellenistic rulers spread ancient Greek culture?

_____

_____

_____

_____

_____

_____

_____

ESSENTIAL QUESTION

What makes a culture unique?

Map of Alexander the Great's Territory

DIRECTIONS: Study the following image and answer the accompanying questions.

EXPLORE THE CONTEXT: Alexander the Great had a vision of uniting Macedonia, Greece, Egypt, and Asia Minor into one empire. The map in this image, created in 1862 C.E., marks the area that he ruled when he was at his greatest power.

SECONDARY SOURCE: MAP

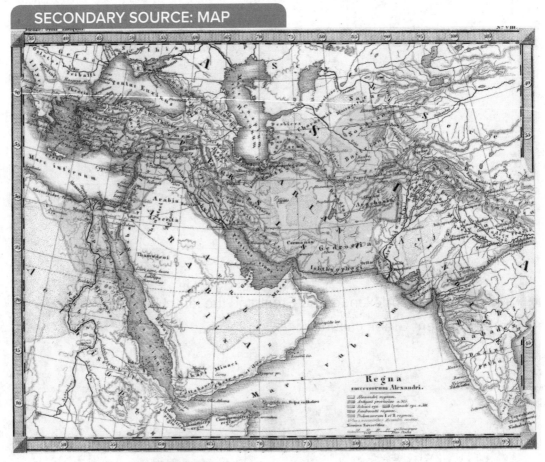

1   GEOGRAPHY   What are the beneficial natural features that Alexander has access to in his vast territory?

_____

_____

_____

_____

2 GEOGRAPHY How does the geography of Greece, the homeland of Hellenistic rule, present challenges for Alexander the Great's rule?

_____

_____

_____

_____

_____

3 CIVICS How does the vast territory with its challenging geographic features place limits on the government that Alexander the Great imagined?

_____

_____

_____

_____

4 DESCRIBING Alexander the Great's empire stretched from the shores of the Mediterranean Sea and across southern Asia to the Indian subcontinent. Which modern-day countries within the boundaries of that ancient empire have been in the news lately? Name at least two countries and explain what has happened there.

_____

_____

_____

_____

_____

On Alexander from the Works of Christina Queen of Sweden

DIRECTIONS: Study the following passage and answer the accompanying questions.

EXPLORE THE CONTEXT: Christina, Queen of Sweden, lived from 1626 to 1689 C.E. She became queen at age 6 when her warrior king father died. Christina was educated as a prince and cared deeply about reading and the arts. She loved exciting stories and admired Alexander the Great for his adventure and bravery.

SECONDARY SOURCE: BOOK EXCERPT

" But this great, this invincible Alexander, who so well discharged the duties of his rank, however engrossed by ambition, however employed in great and important affairs, read almost as much as if he had been retired. Greece at that time, learned as it was, could not furnish him with books enough. Homer and his sword lay always by his side. He loved letters little less than glory. He favored every fine genius; he was liberal to profusion in encouraging arts and sciences, as appeared in many shining instances. . . . Philosophers, orators, poets, sculptors, and every able man in his age partook of his liberality and shared in his fortune. "

—from *The Works of Christina Queen of Sweden*, 1753 C.E.

VOCABULARY

Homer: a Greek poet and his written works
profusion: large amount
orators: public speakers
partook: took part in
liberality: open-mindedness

1. **DETERMINING CONTEXT** Who wrote the passage? What was her occupation and background? How does this information help you understand the document?

_____

_____

_____

_____

2. **ANALYZING POINTS OF VIEW** How does the author describe Alexander the Great? What does she call out as his best qualities?

_____

_____

_____

_____

3. **ANALYZING SOURCES** When was the passage written? Where was it written? How does this information help you understand the credibility of the information in this document?

_____

_____

_____

_____

4. **DRAWING CONCLUSIONS** What was the author's purpose in writing about Alexander the Great's passion for cultural activities?

_____

_____

_____

ESSENTIAL QUESTION

What makes a culture unique?

As you gather evidence to answer the Essential Question, think about:

- how poets and playwrights illustrate the culture of a society.

- the connection between happiness and reason.

- how mathematics and science reveal information about a culture.

My Notes

_____

_____

_____

_____

_____

_____

_____

_____

Hellenistic Culture

DIRECTIONS: Search for evidence in Lesson 4 to help you answer the following questions.

1 EXPLAINING CAUSE AND EFFECT For each effect listed in the graphic organizer below, write the cause of that effect.

Cause	Effect
	Alexandria became the Greek capital of Egypt.
	Hellenistic kings built public building projects.
	Hellenistic rulers supported talented writers.

2 COMPARING AND CONTRASTING Use the diagram below to compare and contrast Epicureanism and Stoicism. How are they alike, and how are they different?

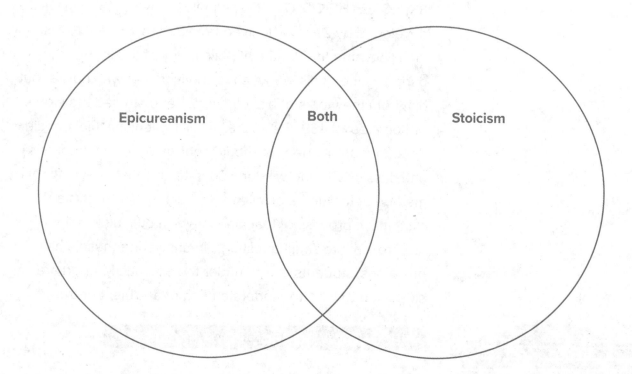

Epicureanism   Both   Stoicism

3 SUMMARIZING The Greek scientists and mathematicians made important discoveries in ancient Greece. Summarize what you learned about each figure on the lines that follow.

_____

_____

_____

_____

_____

_____

Stoicism

DIRECTIONS: Study the following excerpt, and answer the accompanying questions.

EXPLORE THE CONTEXT: The philosophy of Stoicism was developed by Zeno, who lived from 334 to 262 B.C.E. His ideas became the dominant philosophy of the Hellenistic period. None of his works have survived, but we know about him from the works of his followers. Zeno studied the works of Socrates (c. 469–399 B.C.E.) as all Hellenistic thinkers did. Zeno taught that people should control their own emotions and passions to find wisdom. Socrates is most known for his method of tackling a problem. His Socratic Method is a systematic process of teaching in which difficult problems are broken into small questions. In answering these small questions, students taught under the Socratic Method are slowly led to a better understanding of a subject or truth.

SECONDARY SOURCE: BOOK EXCERPT

❝The study of Stoicism cannot be properly begun without some attempt to trace its germs in earlier speculation, and to note what was the state of Greek society in which it first took root before it was transferred to other and perhaps to kindlier soils. Like all the famous systems which divided the earnest thinkers of the old Greek world, its real starting-point is to be found in the life and thought of Socrates, whose original and striking figure fills so marked a place in the pictures of the social life at Athens towards the close of the fifth century before our era. Not that Greek philosophy began with him. There had been no lack before of serious efforts to solve some of the many problems which had forced themselves upon men's thoughts when they looked out upon the universe around them, or tried to think about their own relations to the world unseen, and to the infinities that lay before and after.❞

— Rev. W.W. Capes, *Stoicism*, 1880 C.E.

Copyright © McGraw-Hill Education   Capes, Rev. W. W. 1880. Stoicism. London: Society for Promoting Christian Knowledge: New York: Pott, Young, & Co.

VOCABULARY

germ: beginning
speculation: thought, theories

striking: impressive
infinities: endless unknowns

1 DETERMINING CONTEXT What type of document is this? How does knowing this help you understand the passage?

_____

_____

_____

_____

2 CITING TEXT EVIDENCE What point is the author making in his comparison of Stoicism to the ideas of Socrates? What evidence from the passage suggests that the author considers this point controversial?

_____

_____

_____

_____

3 HISTORY Why was the passage written? How does the purpose for writing help you understand it?

_____

_____

_____

_____

4 DISTINGUISHING FACT FROM OPINION The author includes some of his own opinions in the passage. In his argument about the roots of Stoicism, the author mixes his opinions with established facts. Identify the opinions and the facts in the author's argument.

_____

_____

_____

_____

_____

Winged Victory of Samothrace

DIRECTIONS: Study the following image and answer the accompanying questions.

EXPLORE THE CONTEXT: The statue pictured here is called the Winged Victory of Samothrace. It is a statue of the Goddess Nike from the Hellenistic period, probably created around 200 B.C.E. to honor a naval battle at the Greek island of Samothrace. Nike is the ancient Greek Goddess of victory. The statue now stands in a famous museum in Paris, France, called the Louvre. Although historians have preserved Roman copies of Hellenistic statues, this Winged Victory of Samothrace is one of the few original sculptures from that period.

PRIMARY SOURCE: STATUE

1 `HISTORY` Describe the statue pictured in this image. What does its appearance help you understand about the work of art and the culture it came from?

_____

_____

_____

_____

_____

2 **INFERRING** We know that the statue honors the Goddess of victory on the occasion of a battle triumph. What does this fact help you understand about the values of the ancient Greeks?

_____

_____

_____

_____

3 `HISTORY` What was happening in the region during the 200s B.C.E. that influenced the creation of this statue?

_____

_____

_____

_____

4 `CIVICS` The Winged Victory of Samothrace is held in a famous museum and considered one of the world's treasures. What does this fact say about western culture today?

_____

_____

_____

_____

ESSENTIAL QUESTION

What makes a culture unique?

1 Think About It

Review the supporting questions you developed at the opening of the chapter. Review the evidence you found in the chapter. Were you able to answer each of your Supporting Questions?

If you didn't find enough evidence to answer your Supporting Questions, what do you think you need to consider?

_____

_____

_____

_____

_____

_____

2 Organize Your Evidence

Use a web like the one below to organize the evidence you will use to support your position statement.

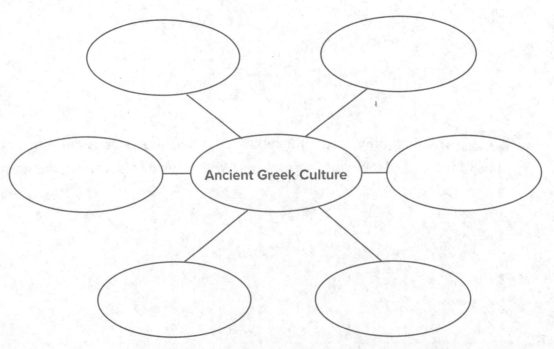

Ancient Greek Culture

3 Talk About It

Discuss the evidence you have gathered with a small group or partner. Check your group's understanding of the qualities that make a culture unique, and answer any questions members may have. Consider any additional advice or input they may have.

4 Connect to the Essential Question

On a separate piece of paper, write a scene for a play in the style of a Greek tragedy or comedy. Include information about the culture of ancient Greece and details that reveal how it made ancient Greek culture unique. Your scene should answer the ESSENTIAL QUESTION: *What makes a culture unique?*

CITIZENSHIP
TAKING ACTION

MAKE CONNECTIONS In ancient Greece, culture thrived, and poets and playwrights became important, famous people. Today, ancient Greek poetry and drama remain part of Western culture. We are able to understand the day-to-day lives of the ancient Greeks, the issues they cared deeply about, and their values through their literature. Yet the window into a culture through literature is not unique to ancient Greece. That window exists for most cultures that have a well-developed literary tradition. This includes the United States today. Although you may not read poetry every day, there are countless modern American poets who capture the feeling, frustrations, and triumphs of modern culture through verse and drama.

DIRECTIONS: Use what you have learned about what makes a culture unique to participate in a modern poetry reading. Research modern American poets and select a poem or short work of literature that captures an idea about the culture you experience today. Then take turns among your classmates to read your selection aloud. Discuss as a class how the details of the poem you chose reveal information about the culture today.

_____

_____

_____

_____

_____

_____

_____

Ancient India

ESSENTIAL QUESTION

What makes a culture unique?

Think about how this question might relate to ancient India.

TALK ABOUT IT

Discuss with a partner what type of information you would need to know to answer this question. For example, one question might be: What factors contributed to the development of ancient Indian culture that set it apart from other cultures?

DIRECTIONS: Now write three additional questions that would help you explain what made ancient Indian culture unique.

MY RESEARCH QUESTIONS

Supporting Question 1:

_____

_____

Supporting Question 2:

_____

_____

Supporting Question 3:

_____

_____

Early Civilizations

DIRECTIONS: Search for evidence in Lesson 1 to help you answer the following questions.

1 **EXPLAINING CAUSE AND EFFECT** How did geography and climate influence ancient cultures in India?

_____

_____

_____

_____

_____

_____

_____

2 **HISTORY** Describe the elements responsible for progress in the Indus civilization. Use the text's discussion of these elements and the chart below to help you organize the facts.

The Indus Cultural Development

Farming

Building

Trading

ESSENTIAL QUESTION

What makes a culture unique?

As you gather evidence to answer the Essential Question, think about:

- the landforms and climate of India's subcontinent.
- development of ancient cultures along the Indus and the later impact of the Aryans.

My Notes

_____

_____

_____

_____

_____

_____

3 **RELATING EVENTS** How did the Aryans influence the culture of India? Use the organizing web to show the various ways Aryans influenced India.

4 `CIVICS` How did the varnas affect ancient Indians and their civic choices?

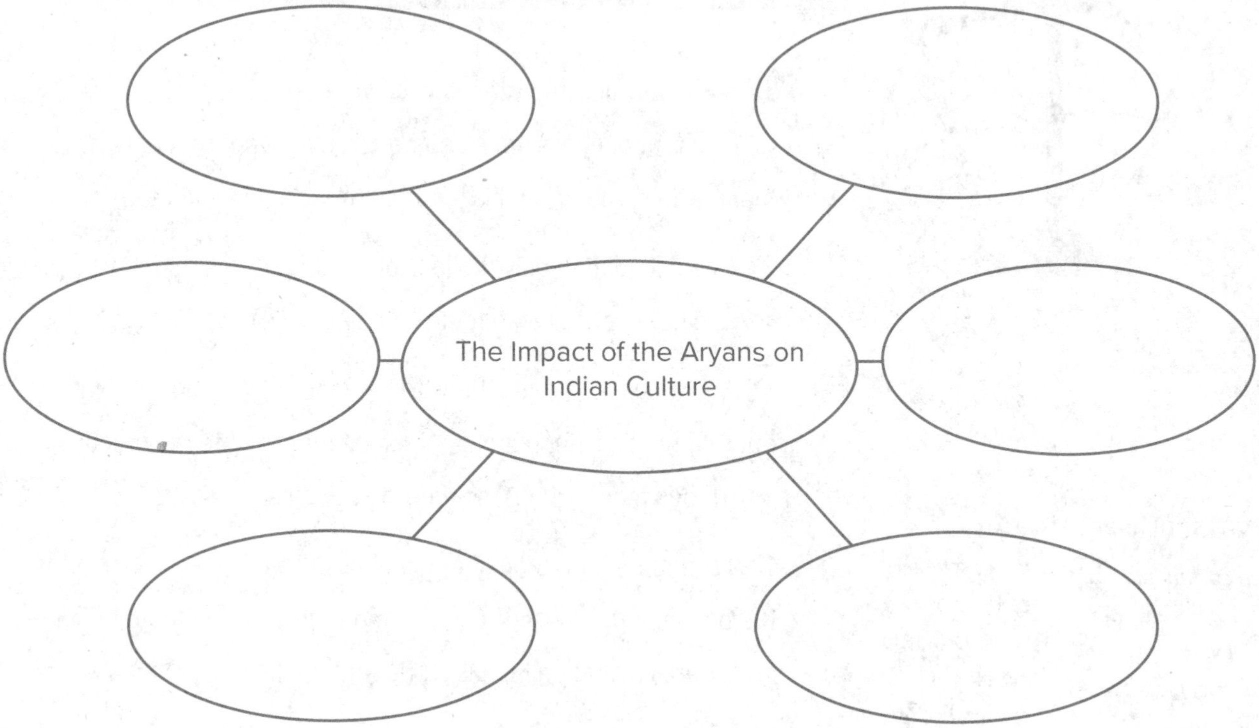

_____

_____

_____

_____

The Impact of the Aryans on
Indian Culture

The Laws of Manu

DIRECTIONS: Study the excerpt below and answer the accompanying questions.

EXPLORE THE CONTEXT: The Laws of Manu are believed to have been written around 200 C.E. They contain one of Asia's first written codes of law, both moral and religious. The laws were specific and detailed about how class or varna relationships were to be conducted in India.

PRIMARY SOURCE: LEGAL CODE

❝ But in order to protect this universe He, the most resplendent one, assigned separate (duties and) occupations to those who sprang from his mouth, arms, thighs, and feet.

91. One occupation only the lord prescribed to the Sudra, to serve meekly even these (other) three castes. . . .

127. (Sudras) who are desirous to gain merit, and know (their) duty, commit no sin, but gain praise, if they imitate the practice of virtuous men without reciting sacred texts.

128. The more a (Sudra), keeping himself free from envy, imitates the behaviour of the virtuous, the more he gains, without being censured, (exaltation in) this world and the next.

129. No collection of wealth must be made by a Sudra, even though he be able (to do it); for a Sudra who has acquired wealth, gives pain to Brahmanas. ❞

—from *The Laws of Manu* (Sacred Books of the East, Volume 25)

VOCABULARY

resplendent: magnificent, with glowing light
prescribed: assigned
caste: assigned position or social status

merit: spiritual credit
virtuous: principled, moral
censured: criticized
exaltation: honor, praise
Brahmanas: sacred writings about the Vedas

Buhler, Georg. Translated 1886. The Laws of Manu - With Extracts From Seven Commentaries. Oxford: Clarendon Press.

Copyright © McGraw-Hill Education

1 **DETERMINING POINT OF VIEW** Discuss this excerpt with a partner. Whose point of view is being proclaimed? Does this suggest that there are other points of view to be considered? Use evidence from the text to support your answers.

COLLABORATE

_____

_____

_____

_____

2 **ECONOMICS** How did the Laws of Manu impact the economy of the Sudra? Would the greater economy of India also have been impacted? Support your answer with details using the text and the excerpt.

_____

_____

_____

_____

_____

3 **ANALYZING TEXT** How does the first sentence of instruction (91) contribute to the development of these rules for the Sudra? Explain, citing references in the text.

_____

_____

_____

_____

4 **DETERMINING MEANING** Based on the excerpt, what is the only hope of the Sudra who follows the Laws of Manu? Use details to support your answer.

_____

_____

_____

Life in Harappa and Mohenjo-Daro

DIRECTIONS: Study the excerpt below and answer the accompanying questions.

EXPLORE THE CONTEXT: This excerpt is from a study on the ancient cities of Harappa and Mohenjo-Daro. It takes a look at the archaeological evidence and provides insights into what life might have been like when the cities thrived.

SECONDARY SOURCE: BOOK EXCERPT

"The ruins of Harappa and Mohenjo-Daro reveal that they were the products of the first city planning in history. Wide, straight streets divide residential areas into square city blocks. Archaeologists have excavated houses, granaries, public halls, and shops. Both cities had extensive sewer systems. Walled fortresses with towers provided protection. To create such well-planned cities, the people needed a knowledge of surveying and geometry. Furthermore, only a strong central government in each city could have supervised the planning and construction. Scholars are not sure who ruled the Indus Valley cities, but they think that a priest-king probably headed the government of each city. The rulers must have had considerable power because the governments exercised strict control. For example, they controlled construction of new buildings and established standards of weight and measures. Because of the tight control, writing, building styles, street plans, and even the size of bricks remained unchanged for nearly 1,000 years. . . . Evidence from the diggings shows that the Indus Valley civilization began to decline many years before it finally ended about 1500 B.C. Builders abandoned the uniform standards of earlier times, and quality of work declined. The arts showed less creativity, and trade with Mesopotamia dwindled."

—from *World History: Patterns of Civilization* by Burton Beers, 1990 C.E.

VOCABULARY

archaeologists: people who study earlier cultures by examining their artifacts and writings

excavated: dug holes in the earth to find remains of cultures

granaries: storage buildings for harvested grain

extensive: wide and broad in size

surveying: figuring the exact size and form of something using mathematics, geometry, and trigonometry

decline: weaken

uniform: all the same; consistent

dwindled: decreased

1 **EVALUATING ARGUMENTS** What evidence does the author use to suggest the cities had strong, powerful governments?

_____

_____

_____

2 **COMPARING AND CONTRASTING TEXTS** How is this excerpt similar to the text description of Mahenjo-Daro and Harappa? How are the two sources different?

_____

_____

_____

_____

_____

_____

3 GEOGRAPHY **AND** HISTORY Considering the geography and history of these great cities, what might have led to their ruin? List evidence from your text and the excerpt that supports your ideas.

_____

_____

_____

_____

_____

_____

4 **MAKING CONNECTIONS** The excerpt notes that the quality of work declined in these ancient cities once uniform standards were abandoned. Give examples of how uniform standards help ensure quality in the United States today.

_____

_____

ESSENTIAL QUESTION

What makes a culture unique?

As you gather evidence to answer the Essential Question, think about:

- how religions and philosophies are established.
- how beliefs and philosophies influence the way people live.

My Notes

Religions of Ancient India

DIRECTIONS: Search for evidence in Lesson 2 to help you answer the following questions.

1 EXPLAINING CAUSE AND EFFECT How did the Hindu belief in reincarnation contribute to people's acceptance of the *jati* system?

_____

_____

_____

_____

_____

_____

_____

2 COMPARING AND CONTRASTING How does Hinduism compare or contrast with Buddhism in the belief about how to live life successfully? Use the chart below to organize your answer.

BELIEFS ABOUT HOW TO LIVE SUCCESSFULLY	
Hinduism	
Buddhism	

3 ECONOMICS Complete the following chart to analyze the relationship between religion and economics in ancient India. Use details from the text to complete the chart.

Religions	What were the core beliefs of each religion, and how did they influence India's economy?
Hinduism	
Buddhism	
Jainism	

4 ANALYZING IDEAS What is a similar belief in both Hinduism and Jainism that shaped the way Hindus and Jains live? Cite details from the text to support your ideas.

_____

_____

_____

Jain Ethics

DIRECTIONS: Study the excerpt below and answer the accompanying questions.

EXPLORE THE CONTEXT: There were five challenging vows the monks had to follow in order to be spiritual leaders of the Jain teachings. The monks had to be free from relationships with their families and with everything of the world. For those followers of the faith who remained in their families, there were twelve specific, but easier, vows to follow.

VOCABULARY

ethics: principles of morality

layperson: a follower as opposed to leader

intentionally: on purpose

motive: the reason behind an action

negligence: ignoring a problem; carelessness

institute: a place where work is carried on

occupational: relating to a person's employment

SECONDARY SOURCE: BOOK EXCERPT

Non-violence Anuvrat (small vow)

❝ In this vow, a person must not intentionally hurt any living being (plants, animals, humans etc.) or their feeling either by thought, word or deed, himself, or through others, or by approving such an act committed by somebody else. Intention in this case applies selfish motive, sheer pleasure and even avoidable negligence. He may use force, if necessary, in the defense of his country, society, family, life, property, religious institute.

His agricultural, industrial, occupational living activities do also involve injury to life, but it should be as minimum as possible, through carefulness and due precaution. ❞

— Ahimsa Anuvrata, c. 500s B.C.E. quoted in *Twelve Vows of Layperson*, compiled by Pavin K. Shah, 1993 C.E.

1 **ANALYZING TEXT** What does the word *intentionally* mean? What does the use of this word mean for those taking this vow? Explain your answer using details from the excerpt.

_____

_____

_____

_____

_____

2 **EXPLAINING POINTS OF VIEW** What does the Jain vow have in common with the Buddhist Eightfold Path and the Hindu belief in reincarnation and karma? Support your answer with evidence from Lesson 2.

_____

_____

_____

_____

_____

_____

_____

_____

3 CIVICS Which part of the vow makes it possible for Jains to serve in the military?

_____

_____

4 **MAKING CONNECTIONS** How would a commitment to be kinder to one another change the environment of your school?

_____

_____

_____

Copyright © McGraw-Hill Education   Pâli. Translated 1881 by Davids, T. W. Rhys and Oldenberg, Hermann. Vinaya Texts - Part I The Pâtimokkha. Oxford: Clarendon Press.

Nidāna: The Words of Disburdenment

DIRECTIONS: Study the excerpt below and answer the accompanying questions.

EXPLORE THE CONTEXT: *The Twelve Nidānas* are Buddhist writings that show cause-and-effect relationships between each of their twelve doctrines. In Sanskrit, the term *nidāna* means "motivation" or "link between things." The writings of Theravada Buddhism are written in Pâli, a language that developed in northern India between the fifth and second centuries B.C.E.

SECONDARY SOURCE: BOOK EXCERPT

Reverence to the Blessed One, the Holy One, the Fully Enlightened One: *Nidana: The Words of Disburdenment*

❝ Now, venerable Sirs, it is by your silence, that I shall know whether you are pure. As to each one question put there must be an answer, so, in such a meeting as this, each question is put as many as three times. Then if any Bhikkhu, when it has been three times put, knowingly omit to declare a fault incurred, he is guilty of uttering a conscious lie. Venerable Sirs, the uttering of a deliberate lie has been declared by the Blessed One to be a condition hurtful (to spiritual progress). Therefore a fault, if there be one, should be declared by that Bhikkhu who remembers it, and desires to be cleansed therefrom. For a fault, when declared, shall be light to him.

Venerable Sirs, the Introduction is now recited.

Thus do I question you, venerable Sirs, 'Are you pure in this matter?'

A second time do I question you, 'Are you pure in this matter?'

A third time do I question you, 'Are you pure in this matter?'

The venerable ones are pure herein. Therefore do they keep silence. Thus I understand. ❞

— Siddhartha Gautama, c. 500 B.C.E., as recorded in *The Pâtimokkha, Vol. XIII of The Sacred Books of the East,* translated from Pâli by T.W. Rhys Davids and Hermann Oldenberg

ESSENTIAL QUESTION

What makes a culture unique?

VOCABULARY

reverence: deep respect or awe

enlightened: having achieved knowledge through spiritual practice

disburdenment: the removal of a burden or a problem

venerable: worthy of respect because of age or spiritual status

bhikkhu: a male Buddhist monk, or spiritual teacher

incurred: brought upon oneself

uttering: speaking

1 ANALYZING IDEAS Analyze how the writer introduced the topic. Describe the central idea. Where did you locate it? How did the writer make the central idea clear through examples or supporting details?

ESSENTIAL QUESTION

What makes a culture unique?

2 **COMPARING AND CONTRASTING TEXTS** Examine the description of Buddhist beliefs in Lesson 2. Does this excerpt match what you read? Explain whether the ideas in the two sources are in agreement or not, and support with text evidence.

_____

_____

_____

_____

_____

_____

_____

_____

_____

_____

3 CIVICS How might this Buddhist principle apply to government and citizenship? Explain your ideas.

_____

_____

_____

_____

_____

_____

_____

_____

_____

_____

4 DETERMINING MEANING What purpose do you believe was served by the repetition of the questions at the end? Explain your ideas.

_____

_____

_____

_____

_____

_____

_____

_____

_____

_____

The Mauryan Empire

DIRECTIONS: Search for evidence in Lesson 3 to help you answer the following questions.

1 IDENTIFYING CAUSE AND EFFECT What events set Chandragupta Maurya in place as ruler of the Mauryan dynasty?

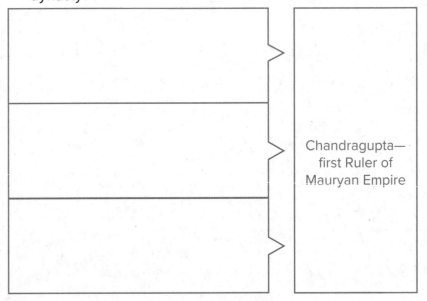

2 ANALYZING IDEAS Analyze the methods the Mauryan king Ashoka used to govern his kingdom and how his ideas affected Indian culture. Use the chart below to organize your information, citing references from Lesson 3.

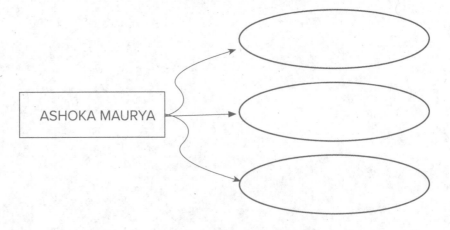

ESSENTIAL QUESTION

What makes a culture unique?

As you gather evidence to answer the Essential Question, think about:

- the development of the Mauryan and Gupta dynasties in ancient India.
- the contributions of the Mauryan and Gupta Empires to the Indian culture.

My Notes

3 HISTORY How did the Mauryan rulers who followed Ashoka govern India? What were the consequences of their rule for the Mauryan Empire? Explain.

_____

_____

_____

_____

4 **DETERMINING CENTRAL IDEAS** What influence did the Mauryan and Gupta Empires have on Indian culture? Collect details from your text. Use the chart below to organize your information, and then write a central idea statement.

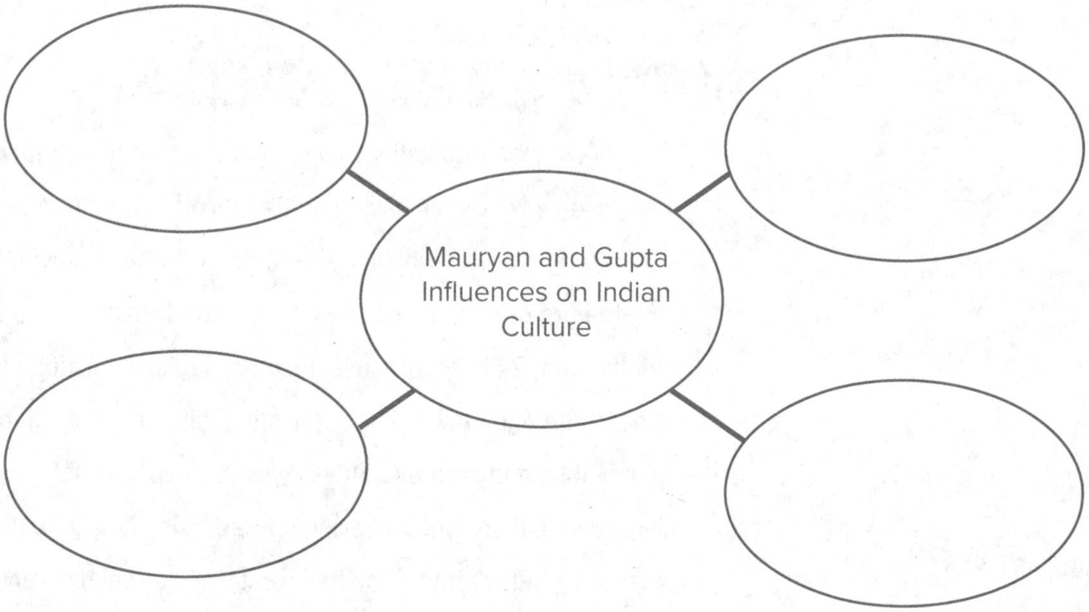

Mauryan and Gupta Influences on Indian Culture

_____

_____

The Bhagavad Gita

Copyright © McGraw-Hill Education   1899. The Bhagavad Gita: With An English Translation, Explanatory Notes, And An Examination Of Its Doctrines. Compiled From Various Writers. 2nd Edition. London: Christian Literature Society.

ESSENTIAL QUESTION

What makes a culture unique?

DIRECTIONS: Study the excerpt below and answer the accompanying questions.

EXPLORE THE CONTEXT: *The Bhagavad Gita* is a 700-verse Hindu scripture composed in Sanskrit, often referred to as "the Divine Song." It is part of an epic poem that is considered the longest in the world. Sections are broken out into numbered lines, often called verses. Historians believe the *Bhagavad Gita* was recorded in writing between 400 B.C.E. and 200 C.E.

PRIMARY SOURCE: BOOK EXCERPT

" 22 As a man throweth away old garments, and putteth on new, even so the soul, having quitted its old mortal frames, entereth into others which are new. 23 The weapon divideth it not, the fire burneth it not, the water corrupteth it not, the wind drieth it not; 24 It is indivisible, inconsumable, incorruptible, and is not to be dried away: it is everlasting, all-pervading, stable, immovable, and eternal; 25 it is invisible, inconceivable, and unalterable; therefore, believing it to be thus, thou shouldst not grieve. 26 But whether thou believest it of eternal birth and duration, or that it dieth with the body, still thou hast no cause to lament it. 27 Death is certain to one that is born, and to one that dieth birth is certain. Wherefore it doth not behove thee to grieve about that which is inevitable. 28 The former state of beings is unknown; the middle state is evident, and their future state is not to be discovered. Why then shouldst thou trouble thyself about such things as these? 29 Some regard the soul as a wonder, whilst some speak and others hear of it with astonishment; but no one knoweth it, although he may have heard it described. "

— from *The Bhagavad Gita*

VOCABULARY

quitted: released or let go

mortal frames: human bodies

indivisible: incapable of being divided or separated

inconsumable: cannot be used up

incorruptible: unable to be spoiled or corrupted

all-pervading: spread throughout

inconceivable: unable to be understood

unalterable: unchanging

lament: grieve or regret

behove: fit or suit a person

inevitable: sure to happen

1 **DETERMINING MEANING** How does the writer support his idea that when the human frame (the body) is finished, the soul (the spiritual or emotional part) is not?

_____

_____

_____

2 **ANALYZING POINT OF VIEW** What lines in the excerpt explain the writer's beliefs about rebirth, or reincarnation?

_____

_____

_____

_____

_____

_____

3 **ANALYZING TEXT** Why does the writer believe it is foolish to worry about death?

_____

_____

_____

_____

4 **HISTORY** What historic developments contributed to the writing of the *Bhagavad Gita*, and how might this excerpt have fit into the story? Cite evidence from Lesson 3 to support your answer.

_____

_____

_____

_____

_____

_____

The Iron Pillar near Delhi, India

ESSENTIAL QUESTION

What makes a culture unique?

DIRECTIONS: Examine the image below and answer the accompanying questions.

EXPLORE THE CONTEXT: The large iron pillar from the Gupta period is remarkable not only because of its size (about 23 feet, or 7 meters, tall), but because its metal is resistant to rust. The ancient writing on it remains well-preserved, and readable. The pillar was created around 400 C.E.

PRIMARY SOURCE: PHOTOGRAPH

1 **INTEGRATING VISUAL INFORMATION** Based on information from Lesson 3 and the photograph of the Iron Pillar, why do you think this pillar may have been built?

_____

_____

_____

2 **HISTORY** How does the pillar compare to other iron works from its era in size, structure, and resistance to rust? Use information in Lesson 3 to help you explain why this pillar is considered noteworthy.

_____

_____

_____

_____

_____

_____

3 **DRAWING CONCLUSIONS** What does the pillar suggest about the culture of the Gupta era? Explain.

_____

_____

_____

_____

4 **MAKING CONNECTIONS** If you saw a similar monument in Washington, D.C., what would you think about the builder's purpose? What might be inscribed on it?

_____

_____

_____

ESSENTIAL QUESTION

What makes a culture unique?

① Think About It

Review the Supporting Questions that you developed at the beginning of the chapter. Review the evidence that you gathered in this chapter. Were you able to answer each Supporting Question?

If there was not enough evidence to answer your Supporting Questions, what additional evidence do you think you need?

_____

_____

_____

② Organize Your Evidence

Use the chart to organize the evidence you will use to support your position statement.

WHAT MAKES A CULTURE UNIQUE?

❸ Talk About It

Work with a partner or small group to discuss your position statement and the evidence you have gathered. Before you write your final conclusion, gather ideas from your classmates. Group members should take turns sharing their ideas, asking questions, and offering insights. Use your lesson readings to guide you as you support your ideas.

❹ Write About It

Write your position statement for the ESSENTIAL QUESTION, using your gathered information: *What makes a culture unique?*

_____

_____

_____

_____

_____

_____

❺ Connect to the Essential Question

On a separate piece of paper, create a visual essay. Use the organizer from question 2 to prepare your case explaining how Indian culture is unique. Either draw pictures to represent the various influences that helped shape ancient Indian culture or find photographs to copy and insert into your essay.

MAKE CONNECTIONS Think about how the culture of your community impacts how you and your family live. What are the most important influences in your area that shape your personal culture?

DIRECTIONS: What is a belief you hold that is also important in your community's culture? How can you become involved in promoting this belief? Promote what you feel should be changed to make life better or to spread your belief. Promote your belief by choosing one of these ideas: organize a rally, write and perform a song about it, or create a promotional advertisement.

_____

_____

_____

_____

_____

_____

_____

_____

_____

_____

_____

_____

Early China

ESSENTIAL QUESTION

What makes a culture unique?

Think about how this question might relate to the culture of ancient China.

TALK ABOUT IT COLLABORATE

Discuss with a partner what type of information you would need to know to answer this question. For example, one question might be: What factors made the culture of early China different from the culture of its neighbors?

DIRECTIONS: Now write three additional questions that would help you explain the distinctive characteristics of early Chinese culture.

MY RESEARCH QUESTIONS

Supporting Question 1:

_____

_____

Supporting Question 2:

_____

_____

Supporting Question 3:

_____

_____

ESSENTIAL QUESTION

What makes a culture unique?

As you gather evidence to answer the Essential Question, think about:

- the rivers, mountains, and deserts that separated ancient China from other civilizations.

- the power of the dynasty kings over those they ruled.

The Birth of Chinese Civilization

DIRECTIONS: Search for evidence in Lesson 1 to help you answer the following questions.

1 **EXPLAINING CAUSE AND EFFECT** How did the geography of China help determine its development?

_____

_____

_____

_____

_____

_____

_____

2 **CITING TEXT EVIDENCE** Record supporting details to explain the idea that religion and government were related during the Shang dynasty.

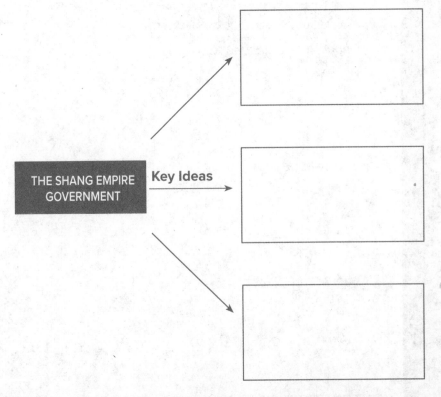

My Notes

_____

_____

_____

_____

_____

_____

_____

3 **ANALYZING EVENTS** What were the significant events that allowed the Zhou dynasty to rule China for more than 800 years? Use the organizer to record important ideas that shaped the culture under the Zhou reign.

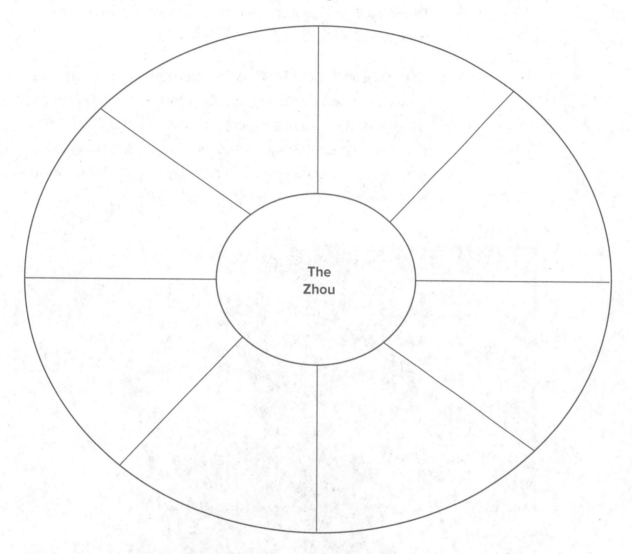

The
Zhou

4 **HISTORY** What were the effects of the Period of the Warring States?

_____

_____

_____

_____

_____

Bronze From Early Zhou Dynasty

DIRECTIONS: Examine the artifact below and answer the accompanying questions.

EXPLORE THE CONTEXT: When bronze-making techniques were developed during the Shang dynasty era, many objects were made. Bronze-making continued during the Zhou dynasty. Some were practical objects such as weapons, farming tools, urns, and cups. Others were meant as works of art, such as this bronze vessel created around 1027–771 B.C.E.

PRIMARY SOURCE: ARTIFACT

World History Archive/Alamy Stock Photo

Copyright © McGraw-Hill Education

1 **INTEGRATING VISUAL INFORMATION** Reread the text about bronze making and closely examine the object. Note the body of the vessel and the decorated elements, including the lid. What do you think this object may have been used for?

_____

_____

_____

2 **ECONOMY** What do you think such a piece of bronze tells about the development of the Zhou culture economically?

_____

_____

_____

3 **INTEGRATING VISUAL INFORMATION** Who would have been the most likely users of this kind of a bronze vessel during the Zhou dynasty?

_____

_____

_____

_____

4 **HISTORY** This bronze container was developed sometime during the lengthy 800-year Zhou reign. From the text, is there a period during which you think it is more or less likely that it would have been made?

_____

_____

_____

_____

Teachings of Confucius

ESSENTIAL QUESTION

What makes a culture unique?

VOCABULARY

standing: rank or position; how others regard you

disciple: follower, student, learner

inculcate: consistently teach

aye: a word that shows agreement

purport: meaning or sense

whole-heartedness: with full support

forbearance: complete self-control

DIRECTIONS: Read the following excerpt and answer the accompanying questions.

EXPLORE THE CONTEXT: This excerpt from an anonymous collection of quotations (compiled c. 475 B.C.E.—221 B.C.E.) provides insight into the mind of Confucius and his teachings.

PRIMARY SOURCE: BOOK EXCERPT

❝'One should not be greatly concerned at not being in office; but rather about the requirements in one's self for such a standing. Neither should one be so much concerned at being unknown; but rather with seeking to become worthy of being known.'

Addressing his disciple Tsang Sin, the Master said, 'Tsang Sin, the principles which I inculcate have one main idea upon which they all hang.' 'Aye, surely,' he replied.

When the Master was gone out the other disciples asked what was the purport of this remark. Tsang's answer was, 'The principles of our Master's teaching are these—whole-heartedness and kindly forbearance; these and nothing more.'❞

—from *Chinese Literature Comprising The Analects of Confucius, The Sayings of Mencius, The Shi-King, The Travels of Fâ-Hien, and The Sorrows of Han*

1 ANALYZING What does Confucius believe should be the highest concern of those who hold office, or wish they could?

_____

_____

_____

_____

2 **INFERRING** If Confucius had convinced the aristocrats, kings, and royal officials to live according to his philosophy, how would that have affected the dynasties?

_____

_____

_____

_____

_____

3 **DETERMINING MEANING** Use the text to help you explain what Confucius means by "seeking to become worthy of being known."

_____

_____

_____

_____

_____

4 **MAKING CONNECTIONS** If you heard a teacher today say something similar, what would you think about his or her purpose? Explain your answer.

_____

_____

_____

_____

5 **IDENTIFYING** Underline the phrases that refer to the central idea of Confucius's teaching.

_____

_____

_____

ESSENTIAL QUESTION

What makes a culture unique?

As you gather evidence to answer the Essential Question, think about:

- the impact that the philosophies of Confucius, Laozi, and Hanfeizi had on China.

- the effect class structure had on early China and the way people lived.

My Notes

_____

_____

_____

_____

_____

_____

_____

_____

_____

Society and Culture in Ancient China

DIRECTIONS: Search for evidence in Lesson 2 to help you answer the following questions.

1 **EXPLAINING CAUSE AND EFFECT** How did the different philosophies help shape the culture of early China?

CAUSE	EFFECT
Confucianism	
Daoism	
Legalism	

2 **CITING TEXT EVIDENCE** Analyze the four Chinese social classes using evidence from the text.

Aristocrats	Farmers	Artisans	Merchants

3 **COMPARING AND CONTRASTING** How were the roles of men and women similar and different in early China?

The Roles of Men and Women in Early China	
Similarities:	Differences:

4 ECONOMICS How did the practice of children inheriting land from their parents affect the income of the aristocratic families? What was the economic consequence to the land-owning families after several generations?

_____

_____

_____

The Tao and Its Characteristics

DIRECTIONS: Study the following excerpt and answer the accompanying questions.

EXPLORE THE CONTEXT: Laozi is believed to be the founder of the philosophy known as Daoism and is accepted as the author of the Dao, writings about these beliefs. This excerpt from his writings will reveal some core ideas that influenced the early Chinese culture.

PRIMARY SOURCE: BOOK EXCERPT

❝46. 1. When the Tao prevails in the world, they send back their swift horses to (draw) the dung-carts. When the Tao is disregarded in the world, the war-horses breed in the border lands.

2. There is no guilt greater than to sanction ambition; no calamity greater than to be discontented with one's lot; no fault greater than the wish to be getting. Therefore the sufficiency of contentment is an enduring and unchanging sufficiency.

49. 1. The sage has no invariable mind of his own; he makes the mind of the people his mind.

2. To those who are good (to me), I am good; and to those who are not good (to me), I am also good;—and thus (all) get to be good. To those who are sincere (with me), I am sincere; and to those who are not sincere (with me), I am also sincere;—and thus (all) get to be sincere.

3. The sage has in the world an appearance of indecision, and keeps his mind in a state of indifference to all. The people all keep their eyes and ears directed to him, and he deals with them all as his children. ❞

— Lao-Tse [Laozi], *The Tao Teh King, or The Tao and Its Characteristics*, Part II, c. 700s B.C.E.—200s B.C.E.

VOCABULARY

Tao: in Taoism, *Tao* refers to "the way," or right path of life (also spelled *Dao* and *Daoism*)

prevails: succeeds

dung-carts: carts used in farming to haul animal manure

sanction: approve

calamity: disaster

sufficiency: the state of having enough

enduring: lasting, constant

sage: wise person

invariable: unchanging

1 **CITING TEXT EVIDENCE** According to the Tao, what are positive effects of living the "right path"? Write only the key ideas.

_____

_____

_____

2 **COMPARING AND CONTRASTING** How does this short excerpt from the Tao compare and contrast with the ideas of Laozi found in Lesson 2?

_____

_____

_____

_____

_____

3 **ANALYZING POINTS OF VIEW** Discuss with a partner the point of view of Laozi in verse 49:2. What message do you believe the sage is sending?

_____

_____

_____

4 **MAKING CONNECTIONS** If you heard the philosophy of living peacefully with sincerity toward all people today, what would you think about the teacher's goal?

_____

_____

5 **DRAWING CONCLUSIONS** Why would the swift horses be used to pull dung-carts if people followed the teachings of Tao?

_____

_____

Instruction on Conduct for Chinese Women and Girls

DIRECTIONS: Study the following excerpt and answer the accompanying questions.

EXPLORE THE CONTEXT: The author of this instruction manual for women and girls in early China was a daughter of a high official living during the Han dynasty. She was well known for her literary achievements at the time. Here she offers advice to young women regarding the roles of women in China at this time.

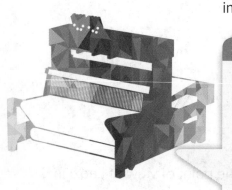

PRIMARY SOURCE: BOOK EXCERPT

Woman's Work.—Weaving Silk, etc.

❝All girls, everywhere, should learn woman's work. In weaving cloth, distinguish between the coarse and fine; When sitting at the loom, work carefully; when boiling the silk cocoons, collecting for them the mulberry and chia leaves, in all be very diligent. Protect the worms from wind and rain. If cold, warm them by the fire; keep them in a clean place. As the young ones grow, transfer them to baskets, but crowd them not; provide them leaves, not too many nor too few.

Making silk, be careful of the straight and cross threads, so you will make a perfect piece. When finished remove the gauze at once from the loom. Cotton cloth, fold and lay in boxes or baskets. Silk, cotton, and the two kinds of grass cloth, all learn perfectly to make, then you can sell to others, and yourself have clothing to wear. . . .

Do not imitate lazy women who from youth to womanhood have been stupid; not having exerted themselves in woman's work. They are prepared for neither cold nor warm weather. Their sewing is so miserable, people both laugh at and despise them. The idle girl, going forth to be married, injures the reputation of her husband's whole family. Her clothes are ragged and dirty. . . . She is a disgrace to her village. I thus exhort and warn the girls, let them hear and learn. ❞

—from *The Chinese Book of Etiquette and Conduct for Women and Girls*, c. 49 C.E.—120 C.E.

VOCABULARY

distinguish: recognize the differences
diligent: untiring, hardworking
cross threads: the crosswise or horizontal threads in weaving
gauze: lightweight woven fabric, usually of cotton or silk
idle: lacking in effort; lazy
exhort: caution; encourage to do something

1 **COMPARING AND CONTRASTING** How does the description of filial piety in Lesson 2 compare or contrast with the excerpt about the conduct of women and girls?

_____

_____

_____

2 **ANALYZING POINTS OF VIEW** According to the author, what character traits should girls and women conform to?

_____

_____

3 **MAKING CONNECTIONS** If you read instructions for today's girls that had the same tone as these, what would be your reaction? What parts might you agree with, and how might you disagree?

_____

_____

_____

4 **ECONOMICS** How would this set of instructions contribute to the economy of early China?

_____

_____

_____

5 **DRAWING CONCLUSIONS** From examining the central idea in this excerpt, what can you conclude was the primary role of girls and women in early China?

_____

_____

_____

The Qin and Han Dynasties

DIRECTIONS: Search for evidence in Lesson 3 to help you answer the following questions.

ESSENTIAL QUESTION

What makes a culture unique?

As you gather evidence to answer the Essential Question, think about:

- how the Qin emperor brought changes to the Chinese culture when he took control.

- the impact of the new government and time of peace during the Han Empire.

My Notes

_____

_____

_____

_____

_____

_____

_____

_____

_____

1 DESCRIBING Use the web organizer below to show the ways Qin changed the life of early Chinese.

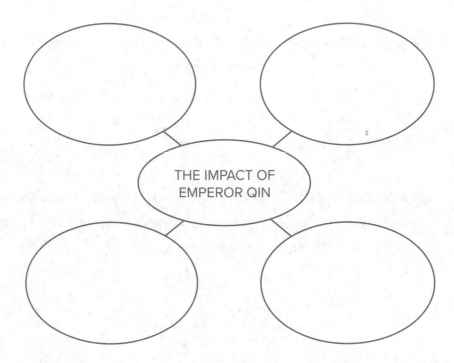

THE IMPACT OF EMPEROR QIN

2 IDENTIFYING CAUSE AND EFFECT What caused the end of the Qin dynasty?

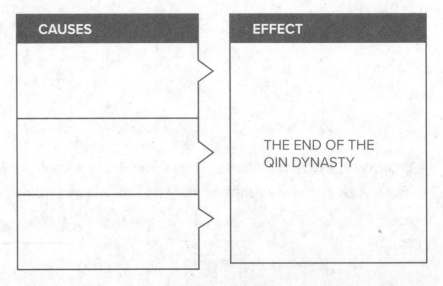

CAUSES

EFFECT

THE END OF THE QIN DYNASTY

3 HISTORY How did land ownership change because of the increase in population during the Han rule?

_____

_____

_____

_____

_____

_____

4 **ANALYZING EVENTS** Analyze the results of expanding trade and the development of the Silk Road during the Han dynasty. Use the organizer to support your analysis of the text.

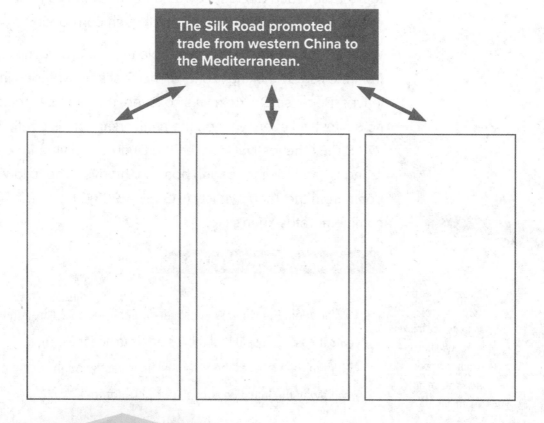

The Silk Road promoted trade from western China to the Mediterranean.

A Poem in Memory of a Chinese Poet and Prime Minister

DIRECTIONS: Read the following story and poem and answer the accompanying questions.

EXPLORE THE CONTEXT: Qu Yuan was a poet and prime minister in the Chu kingdom during the Warring States period. He loved his country and wanted to keep the Chu state free from the conquering Qin. Qu Yuan was vocal in his warnings and protests, but the Emperor rejected his opinions. Instead, he was punished by being sent to a remote area of the southern part of China. Traveling by boat to his exile, Yuan decided it would be far better to jump overboard and drown than live with such corruption.

While searching for Yuan, the people tried to protect his body from the fish by making "zong-zi," rice packets wrapped in leaves. Because Qu Yuan was so loved, the Chinese people hold a festival every year on the anniversary of his death, in 278 B.C.E. The festival is called the Duan Wu, a time for eating "zong-zi" and rowing dragon boats in the river. The following poem from the Tang dynasty (618 C.E.—907 C.E.) commemorates Yuan's life.

PRIMARY SOURCE: POEM

VOCABULARY

influence: the power to make other persons act a certain way

remote: distant

exile: force to leave home

corruption: dishonest behavior for personal gain

zong-zi: rice packets wrapped often in bamboo leaves

injustice: unfair treatment

❝ Whom did the Duan Wu Festival originally honor? Through the years it has been said that the festival is to honor Qu Yuan. Although the water of the River Mi Luo is vast enough, It cannot wash away the injustice a loyal official suffered. ❞

1 **DETERMINING POINT OF VIEW** Discuss with a partner the tone of this poem. Do you believe the writer wanted this poem to convey outrage, sympathy, sorrow, acceptance, or something else? Use evidence from the poem to support your answer.

_____

_____

_____

_____

2 **DRAWING CONCLUSIONS** What does this poem suggest about the ruling power, the Emperor of the Chu?

_____

_____

_____

_____

3 **HISTORY** What historic developments came after Qu Yuan's exile and death? Use Lesson 3 to help you support your ideas about what occurred after the Period of the Warring States when Qu Yuan lived in the Chu kingdom.

_____

_____

_____

_____

4 **CIVICS** How did the Emperor's decision to exile Qu Yuan impact the people he ruled? Explain your answer with supporting details.

_____

_____

_____

_____

ESSENTIAL QUESTION

What makes a culture unique?

A Gateway from Han Dynasty (202 B.C.E.–220 C.E.)

DIRECTIONS: Study the image and answer the accompanying questions.

EXPLORE THE CONTEXT: This newly-built gateway is located near the original gateway to China's first Buddhist temple, built around 68 C.E. Gateways were built for both memorial and decorative purposes. Some were made of stone or brick, while others were constructed of wood. Often, they were marked with moral principles, achievements of a certain family's ancestors, or descriptions of government achievements. They were usually placed in front of a temple, a tomb, a bridge, or at the entrance to a city or an area within a city.

PRIMARY SOURCE: ARCHITECTURE

Copyright © McGraw-Hill Education   China Images/Alamy Stock Photot

1 **DRAWING CONCLUSIONS** Why would the Chinese build such an elaborate and ornamental gateway? Cite text from Lesson 3.

_____

_____

_____

_____

2 **EVALUATING EVIDENCE** Evaluate what you observe in the image along with what you read in the text in Lesson 3 describing the growth of the Han Empire.

_____

_____

_____

_____

3 **COMPARING AND CONTRASTING** How does the gateway in the image compare with the Great Wall of China in appearance and purpose?

_____

_____

_____

_____

4 **INFERRING** Why might a government or group of people construct elaborate buildings?

_____

_____

_____

_____

1 Think About It

ESSENTIAL QUESTION

What makes a culture unique?

Review the supporting questions you developed at the opening of the chapter. Review the evidence you found in the chapter. Were you able to answer each of your Supporting Questions?

If you didn't find enough evidence to answer your Supporting Questions, what do you think you need to consider?

_____

_____

_____

_____

2 Organize Your Evidence

Use a chart like the one below to organize the evidence you will use to support your position statement.

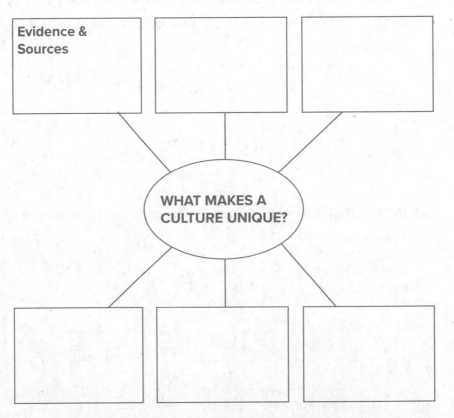

Evidence & Sources

WHAT MAKES A CULTURE UNIQUE?

③ Talk About It

Discuss your position statement and the evidence you have gathered with a small group or a partner. Check your group's understanding and answer any questions members may have. Consider any additional advice or input they may have.

④ Connect to the Essential Question

Create a slide-show presentation that shows various influences that can lead to the creation of unique cultures. Use this chapter's lessons and Inquiry Journal sources to help you identify geographies, people, governments, military forces, ideas, and philosophies that can change how a culture takes shape. Show the effect of such influences on culture development.

CITIZENSHIP
TAKING ACTION

MAKE CONNECTIONS Culture includes many things, such as the beliefs, art, and customs of a group. It can include the way people worship, the movies they watch, and the music they listen to. It also can include the way they interact, such as at home, in school or at work, or through social media.

Many forces create the culture in which people live. It was true in early China as well as today in modern China. It is true of the ever-changing culture of America. Examine some of the influences that make our culture the way it is, and consider an element you feel strongly about. Are there some aspects of American culture you believe should change? If so, think about what kind of informed action on your part might help change them.

DIRECTIONS: Consider some way of thought, government action, or philosophy of life you believe would be positive for your culture. Research the topic you feel you could campaign for, and take your knowledge into the real world. Write an example of how you would promote this idea to your classmates, hoping to benefit American culture starting in your very own school.

_____

_____

_____

_____

_____

_____

_____

_____

Rome: Republic to Empire

ESSENTIAL QUESTION

How do governments change?

Think about how this question might relate to Rome as it changed from a republic to an empire.

TALK ABOUT IT

Discuss with a partner what type of information you would need to know to answer this question. For example, one question might be: *How do individuals change the way a government is run?*

DIRECTIONS: Now write down three additional questions that would help you explain how the Roman government changed over time.

MY RESEARCH QUESTIONS

Supporting Question 1:

_____

_____

Supporting Question 2:

_____

_____

Supporting Question 3:

_____

_____

ESSENTIAL QUESTION

How do governments change?

As you gather evidence to answer the Essential Question, think about:

- legends about Rome's founding.
- the influence of the Etruscans.
- how Rome changed after overthrowing Etruscan rule.

My Notes

The Founding of Rome

DIRECTIONS: Search for evidence in Lesson 1 to help you answer the following questions.

1 HISTORY Fill in the chart below to describe two different legends about how Rome was founded.

Legends of Rome's Founding	
The Aeneid	
Romulus and Remus	

2 HISTORY Who were the Etruscans?

3 EXPLAINING EFFECTS How did the Etruscans influence Roman culture?

_____

_____

_____

_____

_____

_____

_____

4 CONTRASTING How did the new Roman Republic differ from Rome under Etruscan rule?

_____

_____

_____

_____

_____

_____

_____

_____

5 EXPLAINING Why were the Romans able to rule effectively?

_____

_____

_____

_____

_____

_____

Etruscan Artwork

DIRECTIONS: Examine the image below and answer the accompanying questions.

EXPLORE THE CONTEXT: Like some other ancient cultures, the Etruscans had skilled artists. Etruscan artists painted tomb walls with many types of colorful images, such as the scene in the painting below created in the 500s B.C.E.

PRIMARY SOURCE: PAINTING

1A **DESCRIBING** Describe the scene shown in the image.

_____

_____

_____

_____

_____

_____

_____

_____

_____

_____

_____

1B **ANALYZING** Why did the Etruscans most likely include these images?

_____

_____

_____

_____

_____

_____

2 HISTORY Why might the Etruscans have created paintings on the walls of tombs?

_____

_____

_____

_____

_____

_____

_____

Women in Etruscan Society

ESSENTIAL QUESTION

How do governments change?

DIRECTIONS: Read the following excerpt and answer the accompanying questions.

EXPLORE THE CONTEXT: Various cultures across time have had different opinions of women and their place in society. Many cultures in the past viewed women as second-class citizens. In the excerpt below, the author writes about the Etruscans' view of women.

SECONDARY SOURCE: BOOK

❝No one of these is more conspicuous than the position assigned to woman in Etruscan civilization. It was in astonishing contrast to her place among the polished Greeks. . . . With the Etruscans, evidently a strictly monogamous people, she was the equal and the companion of her husband. She sat by his side at the feasting board, she was cared for in the most attentive manner, her image was carved with his on their common tomb, and there are a thousand evidences that she was not merely the idol, but the honored helpmate of the man. It was from this Etruscan example that early Rome drew the principle of monogamy and of the substantial independence of woman. ❞

—from *The Ethnologic Affinities of the Ancient Etruscans,* 1889

VOCABULARY

conspicuous: obvious
evidently: clearly
monogamous: married to one person
attentive: thoughtfully helpful
helpmate: spouse, companion, helper, partner
substantial: sizeable, significant

1 EXPLAINING What were the Etruscans' views on marriage?

_____

_____

_____

_____

_____

2A **CONTRASTING** How did the Etruscans' views on women differ from those of many other cultures of the past?

_____

_____

_____

_____

_____

_____

2B **DESCRIBING** Describe how women were treated in Etruscan society.

_____

_____

_____

_____

_____

_____

_____

3 CIVICS How did the Etruscans' treatment of women affect Roman culture?

_____

_____

_____

_____

_____

_____

_____

ESSENTIAL QUESTION

How do governments change?

As you gather evidence to answer the Essential Question, think about:

- the social structure of Rome.
- how Rome's government changed.
- how the Punic Wars extended Rome's territory and rule.

My Notes

_____

_____

_____

_____

_____

_____

_____

_____

Rome as a Republic

DIRECTIONS: Search for evidence in Lesson 2 to help you answer the following questions.

1 **CIVICS** Use the chart to compare the lives of patricians and plebeians in Rome.

Patricians	Plebeians

2 **EXPLAINING** List the three branches of Roman government, and explain the function of each.

_____

_____

_____

_____

_____

_____

3 CIVICS How did the plebeians win their place in the Roman government?

_____

_____

_____

_____

4 HISTORY How did Rome gain control of Sicily?

_____

_____

_____

_____

_____

_____

_____

5 IDENTIFYING EFFECTS What was the effect on Rome of the Second Punic War?

_____

_____

_____

_____

_____

_____

6 RELATING EVENTS Why was the Third Punic War so significant?

_____

_____

_____

_____

Living Under Roman Laws

ESSENTIAL QUESTION

How do governments change?

DIRECTIONS: Read the following excerpt and answer the accompanying questions.

EXPLORE THE CONTEXT: The Roman justice system changed over time. One major change was posting the city's laws, known as the Twelve Tables, in the Forum for all to see. The Twelve Tables made up the first written code of law, drafted in 451 B.C.E. Below is an excerpt from Table VIII.

PRIMARY SOURCE: LEGAL CODE

❝Table VIII. Torts or Delicts

23. . . . Whoever is convicted of speaking false witness shall be flung from the Tarpeian Rock.

24a. If a weapon has sped accidentally from one's hand, rather than if one has aimed and hurled it, to atone for the deed a ram is substituted as a peace offering to prevent blood revenge.

24b. If anyone pastures on or cuts stealthily by night . . . another's crops . . . the penalty shall be capital punishment, and, after having been hung up, death as a sacrifice to Ceres, a punishment more severe than in homicide. ❞

—from *The Twelve Tables*, 451–450 B.C.E.

VOCABULARY

Torts: civil offenses or wrongdoings
Delicts: a civil crime requiring that money be paid
convicted: found guilty of a crime
atone: make amends

pastures on: to allow one's animals to graze upon
stealthily: in a sneaky manner
Ceres: the Roman Goddess of crops
homicide: murder

1 ANALYZING What does the punishment for "speaking false witness" tell you about the Romans?

_____

_____

_____

_____

_____

Copyright © McGraw-Hill Education   Johnson, Alan Chester, Paul Robinson Coleman-Norton, Frank Card Bourne, trans. 1961. Ancient Roman Statutes. Ed. Clyde Pharr. Clark, NJ: The Lawbook Exchange, LTD., 2003.

2A **CONTRASTING** Did the Romans make a distinction between causing accidental harm and causing deliberate harm to another person? How do you know this?

_____
_____
_____
_____
_____

2B **EXPLAINING** What does this distinction tell you about the Roman justice system?

_____
_____
_____
_____

3A CIVICS What is the punishment for stealing crops or allowing one's animals to graze on another person's crops?

_____
_____
_____
_____
_____

3B **ANALYZING** Why do you think this penalty was "more severe than in homicide"?

_____
_____
_____
_____
_____

Hannibal Wages War Against Rome

ESSENTIAL QUESTION
How do governments change?

DIRECTIONS: Read the following excerpt and answer the accompanying questions.

EXPLORE THE CONTEXT: Polybius was a Greek historian and statesman who lived in Rome. He wrote many books about Rome and its development into a powerful, important entity. In the excerpt below, he writes about the actions of Hannibal, Carthage's greatest general.

PRIMARY SOURCE: BOOK

❝Passing the winter in the Celtic territory, Hannibal kept his Roman prisoners in close confinement, supplying them very sparingly with food; while he treated their allies with great kindness from the first, and finally called them together and addressed them, 'alleging that he had not come to fight against them, but against Rome in their behalf; and that, therefore, if they were wise, they would attach themselves to him: because he had come to restore freedom to the Italians, and to assist them to recover their cities and territory which they had severally lost to Rome.' With these words he dismissed them without ransom to their own homes, wishing by this policy to attract the inhabitants of Italy to his cause, and to alienate their affections from Rome, and to awaken the resentment of all those who considered themselves to have suffered by the loss of harbors or cities under the Roman rule.❞

—from *Polybius, Book III, Chapter 77, Hannibal and the Punic Wars,* c. 200–118 B.C.E.

VOCABULARY

confinement: to be imprisoned

sparingly: in a poor or stingy way

alleging: claiming

severally: individually

alienate: to separate, to turn against

resentment: bitterness, anger, harsh feelings

1 **CONTRASTING** How did Hannibal's treatment of his prisoners differ?

_____

_____

_____

2 GEOGRAPHY Why might some Italians have resented Rome?

_____

_____

_____

_____

3 **EXPLAINING** What did Hannibal tell Rome's allies?

_____

_____

_____

_____

4 CIVICS Think about your responses to questions 2 and 3. Why did Hannibal behave this way?

_____

_____

_____

_____

5 **DRAWING CONCLUSIONS** Which part of the excerpt leads you to that conclusion?

_____

_____

_____

_____

_____

ESSENTIAL QUESTION

How do governments change?

As you gather evidence to answer the Essential Question, think about:

- how the poor were viewed by government officials.

- how powerful individuals changed the Roman government and people's lives.

My Notes

The End of the Republic

DIRECTIONS: Search for evidence in Lesson 3 to help you answer the following questions.

1 EXPLAINING Explain the policy of "bread and circuses."

_____
_____
_____
_____
_____
_____
_____

2A CONTRASTING How were Tiberius and Gaius Gracchus different from many other Roman government officials?

_____
_____
_____
_____
_____
_____

2B EXPLAINING EFFECTS What was the result of the brothers' actions?

_____
_____
_____
_____
_____
_____

3 CONTRASTING Complete the Venn diagram to show similarities and differences between the generals Marius and Sulla.

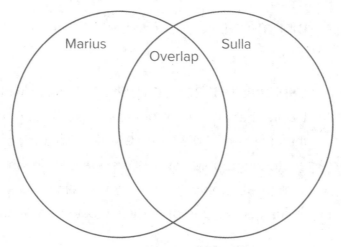

Marius   Overlap   Sulla

4 CIVICS How did Caesar's rise to power change Rome?

_____

_____

_____

5 HISTORY What was the relationship between Octavian and Antony? How did Antony's relationship with Cleopatra affect this relationship?

_____

_____

_____

_____

_____

6 CIVICS After Octavian assumed power, what was his opinion about Rome's republican form of government?

_____

_____

_____

ESSENTIAL QUESTION

How do governments change?

Plutarch on Julius Caesar's Rise to Power

DIRECTIONS: Read the following excerpt and answer the accompanying questions.

EXPLORE THE CONTEXT: Plutarch was a well-known biographer and writer of essays. His writing often focused on the culture of the ancient Greeks and ancient Romans. He wrote biographies of soldiers, statesmen, and other influential people. In the excerpt below, he writes about Julius Caesar, one of Rome's most famous leaders.

PRIMARY SOURCE: BIOGRAPHY

66 In his pleadings at Rome, his eloquence soon obtained him great credit and favor, and he won no less upon the affections of the people by the affability of his manners and address, in which he showed a tact and consideration beyond what could have been expected at his age; and the open house he kept, the entertainments he gave, and the general splendor of his manner of life contributed little by little to create and increase his political influence. His enemies slighted the growth of it at first, presuming it would soon fail when his money was gone; whilst in the meantime it was growing up and flourishing among the common people. . . . 99

—Plutarch, *Life of Caesar*, c. 96–98 C.E.

VOCABULARY

pleadings: public statements

eloquence: a persuasive and forceful way of speaking or writing

favor: approval, support

affability: friendliness, pleasantness

tact: a thoughtful or polite way of doing something

slighted: ignored

flourishing: thriving

1A **CIVICS** Which quality did Caesar possess that made him popular with his peers in Rome?

_____

_____

_____

1B IDENTIFYING Which quality did Caesar possess that made him popular with the common people of Rome?

_____

_____

_____

2 INFERRING Consider your answers to questions 1A and 1B. Why were these qualities most likely important?

_____

_____

_____

_____

_____

_____

_____

_____

3 ANALYZING What does Plutarch mean when he says that Caesar "showed a tact and consideration beyond what could have been expected at his age"?

_____

_____

_____

_____

4 EXPLAINING Why did Caesar's enemies think he would fail?

_____

_____

_____

_____

_____

Plutarch on Julius Caesar's Rival, Pompey

DIRECTIONS: Read the following excerpt and answer the accompanying questions.

EXPLORE THE CONTEXT: In this excerpt, Plutarch writes about the Roman senator Pompey. Julius Caesar, another senator named Crassus, and Pompey made up the First Triumvirate, equally sharing power in Rome. However, Pompey later became Caesar's main rival.

PRIMARY SOURCE: BIOGRAPHY

> **66** Never had any Roman the people's good-will and devotion more zealously throughout all the changes of fortune, more early in its first springing up, or more steadily rising with his prosperity, or more constant in his adversity than Pompey had. . . . In Pompey there were many [causes] that helped to make him the object of their love; his temperance, his skill and exercise in war, his eloquence of speech, integrity of mind, and affability in conversation and address; insomuch that no man ever asked a favor with less offence, or conferred one with a better grace. When he gave, it was without assumption; when he received, it was with dignity and honor. **99**

—Plutarch, *Life of Pompey*, 96–98 C.E.

VOCABULARY

zealously: eagerly, enthusiastically

prosperity: wealth

adversity: hardship, difficulty

affability: friendliness, pleasantness

temperance: restraint,

integrity: honesty, reliability

conferred: granted, presented

1 ANALYZING What does Plutarch mean when he says, "Never had any Roman the people's good-will and devotion more zealously throughout all the changes of fortune, more early in its first springing up, or more steadily rising with his prosperity, or more constant in his adversity than Pompey had?"

_____

_____

_____

Copyright © McGraw-Hill Education   Plutarch. 1904. "Pompey." In *A Source Book of Roman History*, ed. Dana Carleton Munro. Trans. Arthur Hugh Clough. Boston, USA: D.C. Heath & Co.

2 **EXPLAINING** What might be another way of saying "When he gave, it was without assumption; when he received, it was with dignity and honor?"

_____

_____

_____

_____

_____

_____

_____

3 **CIVICS** Why did the Roman people love Pompey?

_____

_____

_____

_____

_____

_____

4 **COMPARING** According to Plutarch, how were Pompey and Julius Caesar the same?

_____

_____

_____

_____

_____

_____

ESSENTIAL QUESTION

How do governments change?

As you gather evidence to answer the Essential Question, think about:

- the effects that various rulers had on Rome.
- how the borders of the Roman Empire expanded.
- how the Roman economy changed over time.

My Notes

_____

_____

_____

_____

_____

_____

_____

_____

_____

_____

Rome Builds an Empire

DIRECTIONS: Search for evidence in Lesson 4 to help you answer the following questions.

1 **CIVICS** Use the chart to describe reforms in Rome made by Caesar Augustus.

Caesar Augustus's Reforms	
Military	
Architecture	
Government	
Law	

2 **EXPLAINING CAUSES** Why did the Praetorian Guard execute Caligula?

_____

_____

_____

_____

3A **UNDERSTANDING CHRONOLOGY** Name the five "good emperors" in order of their reigns.

_____

_____

3B **CITING TEXT EVIDENCE** List at least one way that each of these emperors strengthened the Roman Empire.

_____

_____

_____

_____

_____

_____

_____

4 **IDENTIFYING** Where did the Roman Empire expand under Trajan's rule?

_____

_____

_____

_____

_____

_____

5 ECONOMICS How did the Roman navy aid Rome's economy?

_____

_____

_____

_____

_____

Polybius on the Army of the Roman Empire

DIRECTIONS: Read the following excerpt and answer the accompanying questions.

EXPLORE THE CONTEXT: Greek historian Polybius had a great deal to say about Rome, including its army. In this excerpt, he gives his opinion about the soldiers' readiness for battle.

PRIMARY SOURCE: BOOK

❝ The Roman order on the other hand is flexible; for every Roman, once armed and on the field, is equally well equipped for every place, time, or appearance of the enemy. He is, moreover, quite ready and needs to make no change, whether he is required to fight in the main body, or in a detachment, or in a single maniple, or even by himself. Therefore, as the individual members of the Roman force are so much more serviceable, their plans are also much more often attended by success than those of others. . . . ❞

— Polybius, *Book XVIII, Chapter 32, Flexibility of the Roman Order,* c. 200–118 B.C.E.

VOCABULARY

flexible: able to change easily

equipped: ready, armed with weapons

moreover: in addition

detachment: a military unit that is separate from the main body of troops

maniple: a military unit of 60 or 120 soldiers

serviceable: working, functioning

flourishing: thriving

1 ANALYZING What is Polybius's opinion of the Roman army?

_____

_____

_____

_____

_____

_____

2 **EXPLAINING** What does Polybius mean when he says that the soldiers need "to make no change, whether he is required to fight in the main body, or in a detachment, or in a single maniple, or even by himself?"

_____

_____

_____

_____

_____

_____

3 **CIVICS** Why does Polybius believe that Roman soldiers often defeat their enemies?

_____

_____

_____

_____

_____

_____

4 **INFERRING** Based on Polybius's statements, what quality are other armies lacking?

_____

_____

_____

_____

_____

_____

Tacitus on the Emperor Nero

ESSENTIAL QUESTION

How do governments change?

VOCABULARY

fancy: liking, desire

chariot: similar to a carriage

degrading: shameful

theatrical: dramatic, as if on the stage

sacred: blessed

prophetic: able to see into the future

deity: a God or Goddess

DIRECTIONS: Read the following excerpt and answer the accompanying questions.

EXPLORE THE CONTEXT: Tacitus was a public official in Rome. In his book *Annals,* he wrote about the Roman Empire during 14 C.E. to 68 C.E. In this excerpt, he wrote about Nero, an emperor famous for being cruel.

PRIMARY SOURCE: BOOK

❝He [Nero] had long had a fancy for driving a four-horse chariot, and a no less degrading taste for singing to the harp, in a theatrical fashion, when he was at dinner. This, he would remind people, was a royal custom, and had been the practice of ancient chiefs; it was celebrated, too, in the praises of poets, and was meant to show honor to the gods. Songs indeed, he said, were sacred to Apollo, and it was in the dress of a singer that that great and prophetic deity was seen in Roman temples as well as in Greek cities. ❞

— Tacitus, *Annals*, Book XIV, Chapter 14, Nero's Amusements, c. 105–109 C.E.

1 ANALYZING Based on this passage, what do you think was Tacitus's opinion of Nero and his behavior?

_____

_____

_____

_____

_____

2 **INFERRING** Tacitus thinks Nero's "fancy for driving a four-horse chariot" shows a degrading, or shameful, taste. What action of Nero's does Tacitus think shows "a no less degrading taste"?

_____

_____

_____

_____

_____

3 **IDENTIFYING CAUSES** Why did Nero sing at dinner?

_____

_____

_____

_____

_____

_____

_____

4 **HISTORY** How is the portrayal of Nero in this passage different from the description of Nero presented in your textbook?

_____

_____

_____

_____

_____

_____

_____

1 Think About It

ESSENTIAL QUESTION

How do governments change?

Review the Supporting Questions that you developed at the beginning of the chapter. Review the evidence that you gathered in this chapter. Were you able to answer each Supporting Question?

If there was not enough evidence to answer your Supporting Questions, what additional evidence do you think you need?

_____

_____

_____

_____

2 Organize Your Evidence

Use the chart below to organize the evidence you will use to support your position statement.

Source of information	Specific Evidence to Cite From the Source	How does the evidence support my position statement?	How does this evidence connect to modern life?

③ Write About It

A position statement related to the Essential Question should reflect your conclusion about the evidence. Write a position statement for the ESSENTIAL QUESTION: *How do governments change?*

_____

_____

_____

_____

_____

_____

_____

_____

④ Connect to the Essential Question

On a separate piece of paper, create at least five good interview questions as if you were interviewing a person who lived during the rise of the Roman Empire. Think about asking what his or her life was like, how life was different under the republic, or how life changed under different emperors, etc.

After deciding what questions to ask, and using the Essential Question about how governments change as your central idea, write about how a person during the rise of the Roman Empire might have answered your questions.

TAKING ACTION

MAKE CONNECTIONS Think about how leaders in your local government commit themselves to helping your community. Is there more that you think these local leaders could do to help your community?

DIRECTIONS: Go online to find the names of the government officials who serve your town or county. Learn about their activities to help the people in your community. Then, start a petition or write a letter to the editor of your local newspaper on an issue you believe is not being addressed.

Roman Civilization

ESSENTIAL QUESTION

Why do civilizations rise and fall?

Think about how this question might relate to the way culture and civilizations are connected today.

TALK ABOUT IT COLLABORATE

Discuss with a partner what type of information you would need to know to answer this question. For example, one question might be: *Where did Roman civilization come from?*

DIRECTIONS: Write three additional questions that would help you to explain why civilizations rise and fall.

MY RESEARCH QUESTIONS

Supporting Question 1:

_____

_____

Supporting Question 2:

_____

_____

Supporting Question 3:

_____

_____

ESSENTIAL QUESTION

Why do civilizations rise and fall?

As you gather evidence to answer the Essential Question, think about:

- the characteristics of Roman civilization.
- the influences that shaped Roman civilization.

My Notes

The Roman Way of Life

DIRECTIONS: Search for evidence in Lesson 1 to help you answer the following questions.

1 **GEOGRAPHY** How was Rome's location important for forming a new empire?

_____

_____

_____

_____

2A **DESCRIBING** What was the Forum in Rome, and what happened there?

_____

_____

_____

_____

_____

2B **CITING TEXT EVIDENCE** How does the text describe the powerful role a father had in the typical Roman family?

_____

_____

_____

2C **DESCRIBING** What factors contributed to the changing status and role of women in Rome at this time?

_____

_____

_____

_____

_____

3A EXPLAINING CAUSE AND EFFECT Discuss in pairs what changes occurred to the Roman people as its empire grew through its achievements in science and art. Fill in the graphic organizer to show specific examples of new ideas and advancements. Add more categories as you discuss the Romans' growing culture.

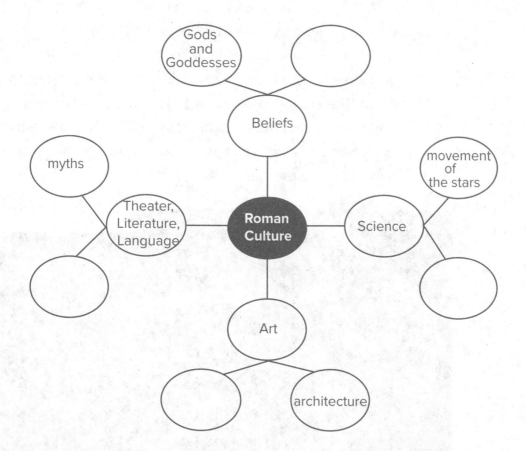

3B ANALYZING TEXT PRESENTATION The text states that the Romans "copied the Greeks in many ways but changed, or adapted, what they borrowed to match their own needs." Give two text examples showing ways the Romans borrowed from the Greeks and then changed it.

_____

_____

_____

_____

Gladiators

DIRECTIONS: Examine the image below and answer the accompanying questions.

EXPLORE THE CONTEXT: Gladiators became part of state-sponsored Roman entertainment called "bread and circuses." Romans enjoyed the spectacles of watching gladiators fight animals, and sometimes one another, to the death. The artwork below, created in 30 B.C.E., depicting the gladiators, shows how violent these entertainment events were. Some leaders, such as Seneca, warned against the corruption in these games.

PRIMARY SOURCE: RELIEF SCULPTURE

1 **INFERRING** Why might these games have been appealing to many Romans?

_____

_____

_____

_____

2 **IDENTIFYING CAUSES** Why do you think gladiators often came from the poor population of Rome?

_____

_____

_____

_____

_____

3 **MAKING CONNECTIONS** Why might the gladiator Spartacus have led a slave rebellion? Cite details in the image and text from Lesson 1 to support your answer.

_____

_____

_____

_____

_____

_____

4 **HISTORY** How does this artwork contribute to today's knowledge of the Romans?

_____

_____

_____

_____

_____

The Pantheon

DIRECTIONS: Study the following image and answer the accompanying questions.

EXPLORE THE CONTEXT: The building in this photograph is the Roman Pantheon, which was built as a temple to honor Roman Gods. Its construction was completed in about 125 C.E. by the Emperor Hadrian. The Pantheon is made mostly of concrete and consists of two main parts: a porch supported by columns and a large, circular room with a great dome as its ceiling. This was the largest dome ever built until modern times. The Pantheon remains in good shape today, and for more than 1,000 years it has been used as a Christian church.

PRIMARY SOURCE: IMAGE

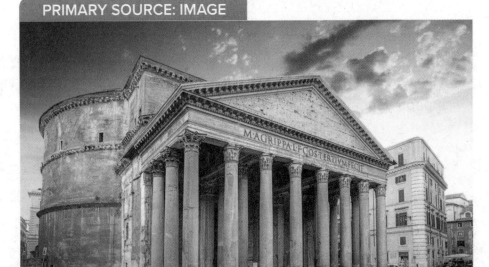

1 **DESCRIBING** What can you tell about the Pantheon from this photograph?

_____

_____

_____

2 DETERMINING CONTEXT In what ways does this building demonstrate the influence of Greek culture on ancient Rome?

_____
_____
_____
_____
_____
_____
_____

3 EXPLAINING Why is it significant that the Romans constructed this building using concrete?

_____
_____
_____
_____
_____
_____
_____

4 DRAWING CONCLUSIONS What conclusions can you draw about Roman architecture from this image of the Pantheon?

_____
_____
_____
_____
_____
_____
_____

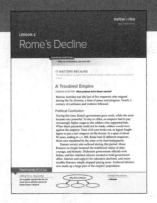

ESSENTIAL QUESTION

Why do civilizations rise and fall?

As you gather evidence to answer the Essential Question, think about:

- how the economic situation influenced the decline of Rome.
- what role emperors played in Rome's decline.

My Notes

Rome's Decline

DIRECTIONS: Search for evidence in Lesson 2 to help you complete the following questions.

1A **DETERMINING CENTRAL IDEAS** What are two major issues that caused Rome to decline in the period 100 C.E. to 500 C.E.?

_____

_____

_____

_____

_____

_____

_____

_____

1B **DESCRIBING** Were Diocletian's reforms helpful in slowing Rome's decline?

_____

_____

_____

2 **SUMMARIZING** How did the rule of Emperors Diocletian, Constantine, and Theodosius lead to the separation of the Roman Empire into two empires?

_____

_____

_____

_____

_____

3A IDENTIFYING EFFECTS The Romans let in the Visigoths and then treated them poorly. What effect did that treatment have on the Visigoths?

_____

_____

3B DESCRIBING How did attacks by the Vandals contribute to the weakening of Rome?

_____

_____

3C EXPLAINING CAUSE AND EFFECT What relationship did the later Roman Empire have with Germanic groups? How did this relationship help lead to the fall of Rome?

_____

_____

_____

_____

_____

4 SUMMARIZING Summarize in a few sentences which city led the Roman Empire when it was divided into two.

_____

_____

_____

_____

5 MAKING CONNECTIONS What are some examples of Rome's legacy to the modern world?

_____

_____

_____

Constantine

ESSENTIAL QUESTION

Why do civilizations rise and fall?

DIRECTIONS: Read the following excerpt and answer the accompanying questions.

EXPLORE THE CONTEXT: In 1776 C.E. English historian Edward Gibbon published the first volume of his most significant work, *The History of the Decline and Fall of the Roman Empire.* The six volumes of that work covered the empire's history from 98 C.E. to 1590 C.E. In this excerpt, Gibbon describes Constantine before he became Roman emperor.

SECONDARY SOURCE: BOOK

❝ Instead of following [his father] Constantius in the West, he [Constantine] remained in the service of [Emperor] Diocletian, signalized his valor in the wars of Egypt and Persia, and gradually rose to the honorable station of a tribune of the first order. The figure of Constantine was tall and majestic; he was dexterous in all his exercises, intrepid in war, affable in peace; in his whole conduct, the active spirit of youth was tempered by habitual prudence; and while his mind was engrossed by ambition, he appeared cold and insensible to the allurements of pleasure. The favor of the people and soldiers, who had named him as a worthy candidate for the rank of Caesar, served only to exasperate the jealousy of [the Roman Emperor] Galerius. . . . Every hour increased the danger of Constantine, and the anxiety of his father, who, by repeated letters, expressed the warmest desire of embracing his son. ❞

— Edward Gibbon, *The History of The Decline and Fall of the Roman Empire*

VOCABULARY

intrepid: consistently courageous

affable: easy to be around or approach

dexterous: able to think or act skillfully

allurements: objects attracting desire

exasperate: to increase anger or impatience

❶ IDENTIFYING Who did Constantine stay with when his father left for the West?

_____

2 IDENTIFYING CAUSES What was the cause of Constantine's rise to tribune?

_____

_____

_____

_____

3 INFERRING Why did people and soldiers think Constantine would make a good emperor, or Caesar?

_____

_____

_____

_____

4 MAKING CONNECTIONS Would Constantine, as described in this excerpt, be as respected as a leader today as he was then?

_____

_____

_____

_____

5 HISTORY What effect might jealousy among the emperors, such as Galerius's jealousy of Constantine, have had on the Roman Empire?

_____

_____

_____

_____

How Alaric Captured Rome

Procopius. 1916. History Of The Wars: The Vandalic War. Vol. 3 and 4 of History of the Wars. Trans. H.B. Dewing. London: William Heinemann Ltd.; Cambridge, Massachusetts: Harvard University Press.

ESSENTIAL QUESTION

Why do civilizations rise and fall?

DIRECTIONS: Read the following excerpt and answer the accompanying questions.

EXPLORE THE CONTEXT: Procopius, who lived and flourished during the years of about 490–560 C.E., wrote some of the most important sources on the Roman Empire and the Byzantine emperor Justinian. His work, *History of the Wars,* extended over eight books. This excerpt, taken from Books III and IV, describes the Vandalic War.

SECONDARY SOURCE: BOOK

❝[Alaric] chose out three hundred whom he knew to be of good birth and possessed of valour beyond their years, and told them secretly that he was about to make a present of them to certain of the patricians in Rome, pretending that they were slaves. And he instructed them that, as soon as they got inside the houses of those men, they should display much gentleness and moderation. . . . When all those who were to be their masters would most likely be already asleep after their meal, they should all come to the gate called Salarian and with a sudden rush kill the guards, who would have no previous knowledge of the plot, and open the gates as quickly as possible.

After making this declaration and sending the youths not long afterwards, he commanded the barbarians to make preparations for the departure, and he let this be known to the Romans. . . . And all the youths at the time of the day agreed upon came to this gate, and, assailing the guards suddenly, put them to death; then they opened the gates and received Alaric and the army into the city at their leisure. And they set fire to the houses which were next to the gate, among which was also the house of Sallust, who in ancient times wrote the history of the Romans, and the greater part of this house has stood

VOCABULARY

assailing: attacking
plundering: stealing
perished: died or disappeared

1 ANALYZING What tone does the author's first sentence convey in this excerpt?

_____

_____

_____

_____

_____

_____

_____

. . . continued

half-burned up to my time; and after plundering the whole city and destroying the most of the Romans, they moved on. At that time they say that the Emperor Honorius in Ravenna received the message from one of the eunuchs, evidently a keeper of the poultry, that Rome had perished. And he cried out and said, 'And yet it has just eaten from my hands!' . . . The eunuch comprehending his words said that it was the city of Rome which had perished at the hands of Alaric. . . . **"**

— Procopius, *The Vandalic War,* c. 550 C.E.

2 **CITING TEXT EVIDENCE** How does the author show that Alaric made use of the element of surprise in his attack on Roman leaders?

_____

_____

_____

_____

3 **INFERRING** Rome fell in 476 C.E. What detail in the excerpt suggests that Rome struggled to recover after Alaric's attack?

_____

_____

_____

_____

4 **ASSESSING CREDIBILITY** Is this source a reliable account of the fall of Rome? Why or why not?

_____

_____

_____

_____

ESSENTIAL QUESTION

Why do civilizations rise and fall?

As you gather evidence to answer the Essential Question, think about:

- how and why Constantinople became the "new Rome."
- how Byzantine civilization developed.

My Notes

_____

_____

_____

_____

_____

_____

_____

The Byzantine Empire

DIRECTIONS: Search for evidence in Lesson 3 to help you complete the following items.

1A **DRAWING CONCLUSIONS** How did Constantinople's location contribute to the initial success of the Byzantine Empire?

_____

_____

_____

_____

_____

1B **IDENTIFYING CAUSES** At first, Constantinople was known as "The New Rome," but over time it developed its own character. What caused this change?

_____

_____

_____

_____

2A **EXPLAINING** What responsibilities did Justinian have as ruler of the Byzantine Empire?

_____

_____

_____

_____

2B CITING TEXT EVIDENCE What aspects of civil society are evident in the way Justinian and Theodora cooperated in their government? Find an example in the text to support Justinian and Theodora's actions.

_____

_____

_____

_____

3 ANALYZING TEXT PRESENTATION What might the historian, Procopius, have meant when he reported Theodora's words of warning to Justinian?

_____

_____

_____

_____

4 HISTORY What events or actions were important to Justinian's legacy? Choose the three actions you think are most important and record them in the graphic organizer.

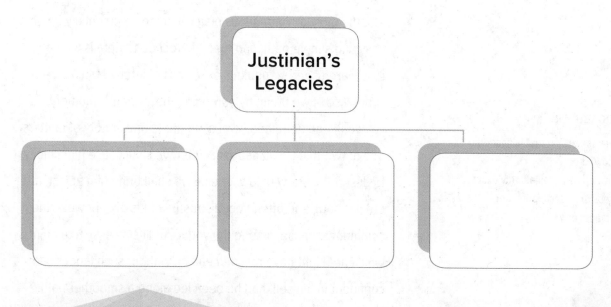

Justice and Law

ESSENTIAL QUESTION

Why do civilizations rise and fall?

DIRECTIONS: Read the excerpt and answer the accompanying questions.

EXPLORE THE CONTEXT: The Justinian Code is a collection of laws and legal interpretations created by a group of legal scholars under the direction of the Byzantine emperor Justinian, who ruled from 527 C.E. to 565 C.E. This code became the basis for legal systems in most of the Western countries for centuries.

PRIMARY SOURCE: LEGAL CODE

❝ Justice is the set and constant purpose which gives to every man his due.

1 Jurisprudence is the knowledge of things divine and human, the science of the just and the unjust.

2 Having laid down these general definitions, and our object being the exposition of the law of the Roman people, we think that the most advantageous plan will be to commence with an easy and simple path, and then to proceed to details with a most careful and scrupulous exactness of interpretation. Otherwise, if we begin by burdening the student's memory, as yet weak and untrained, with a multitude and variety of matters, one of two things will happen: either we shall cause him wholly to desert the study of law, or else we shall bring him at last, after great labour, and often, too, distrustful of his own powers (the commonest cause, among the young, of ill-success), to a point which he might have reached earlier, without such labour and confident in himself, had he been led along a smoother path. ❞

— Caesar Flavius Justinian, *The Institutes of Justinian,* c. 534 C.E.

VOCABULARY

due: something that is deserved or owed
scrupulous: painstakingly exact
exposition: description and explanation

1 **DETERMINING MEANING** The author writes that the purpose of the work is "the exposition of the law of the Roman people." What is the meaning of that phrase?

_____

_____

_____

2 **SUMMARIZING** What process does the Code recommend for studying the law? Why?

_____

_____

_____

_____

3 HISTORY What can you infer about the nature of Roman law based on this advice?

_____

_____

_____

4 **MAKING CONNECTIONS** Do you think the Justinian Code's statement "Justice is the set and constant purpose which gives to every man his due" is true today? Why or why not?

_____

_____

_____

_____

5 **INFERRING** How does a legal system contribute to the development of a civilization?

_____

_____

_____

Byzantine Mosaics

ESSENTIAL QUESTION
*Why do civilizations rise
and fall?*

DIRECTIONS: Examine the following image and answer the accompanying questions.

EXPLORE THE CONTEXT: Mosaics are part of the artistic legacy left by the Byzantine Empire. Mosaics like the one below created around the mid-500s C.E., used geometric patterns and often included images of daily life or images of religious figures.

PRIMARY SOURCE: MOSAICS

1 DESCRIBING What does this mosaic show about life in the Byzantine Empire?

_____

_____

_____

2 ECONOMICS What does the mosaic tell you about the Byzantine economy?

_____

_____

_____

_____

_____

_____

_____

3 **ASKING QUESTIONS** What questions could you ask to guide you to learn more about this mosaic?

_____

_____

_____

_____

_____

_____

_____

4 **MAKING CONNECTIONS** What kinds of art would future historians need to study to learn about daily life in the 2000s C.E.?

_____

_____

_____

_____

_____

_____

_____

1 Think About It

Review the supporting questions that you developed at the beginning of the chapter. Review the evidence that you gathered in the chapter. Were you able to answer each Supporting Question?

If there was not enough evidence to answer your Supporting Questions, what additional evidence do you think you need to consider?

_____

_____

_____

2 Organize Your Evidence

Use a chart like the one below to organize the evidence you will use to support your position statement. Think about the two empires you read about: the Roman Empire and the Byzantine Empire. What were the reasons for each empire's rise? What contributed to each empire's decline?

Fill in the chart with details from the chapter.

	Roman Empire	Byzantine Empire
Rise		
Fall		

❸ Write About It

Write a position statement for the ESSENTIAL QUESTION: *Why do civilizations rise and fall?* A position statement related to the Essential Question should reflect your conclusion about the evidence.

_____

_____

_____

_____

_____

_____

_____

_____

_____

_____

❹ Talk About It

Work in small groups to discuss your findings about the rise and fall of civilizations. Use the feedback from your classmates before you write a summary statement. You may choose to refine your position statement after you have discussed it with your classmates. Group members should listen to each other's arguments, ask questions, and offer constructive advice.

❺ Connect to the Essential Question

On a separate piece of paper or using a computer, create a graphic that explains the factors that contribute to the rise and fall of civilizations. The graphic should combine visual and text elements and reflect the evidence you've collected about the Roman and Byzantine Empires.

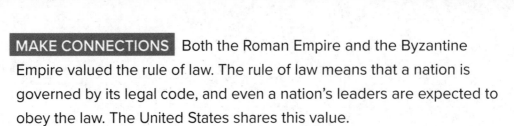

CITIZENSHIP
TAKING ACTION

MAKE CONNECTIONS Both the Roman Empire and the Byzantine Empire valued the rule of law. The rule of law means that a nation is governed by its legal code, and even a nation's leaders are expected to obey the law. The United States shares this value.

DIRECTIONS: With a partner or small group, create a public service announcement (PSA) explaining the importance of the rule of law. Perform your PSA as a skit or record it as a video and play it for your classmates.

CHAPTER
13

The Rise of Christianity

ESSENTIAL QUESTION

How do new ideas change the way people live?

Think about how this question might connect the practices important to early Christians with the practices of Christians today.

TALK ABOUT IT COLLABORATE

Discuss with a partner what type of information you would need to know to answer this question. For example, one question might be: How does understanding the ideas important in early Christianity relate to the ideas emphasized in different branches of modern Christianity?

DIRECTIONS: Now write down three additional questions you need to answer to explain how the practices of early Christians relate to Christianity today.

MY RESEARCH QUESTIONS

Supporting Question 1:

_____

_____

Supporting Question 2:

_____

_____

Supporting Question 3:

_____

_____

ESSENTIAL QUESTION

*How do new ideas change
the way people live?*

As you gather evidence to answer the
Essential Question, think about:

- the conflict between the Roman
  Empire and the Jewish people.

- the differences between Jewish
  practices and early Christian
  practices.

My Notes

_____

_____

_____

_____

_____

_____

_____

Early Christianity

DIRECTIONS: Search for evidence in Lesson 1 to help you
answer the following questions.

1 **ANALYZING** How did the Romans rule the Jewish
people? What was the outcome of these methods?

_____

_____

_____

_____

2 **CULTURE** In the graphic organizer below, write a summary
of each of Jesus' parables. Then describe the lesson he
was trying to teach his followers with each parable.

Parable	Lesson for Followers
The Good Samaritan	
The Prodigal Son	

3 DESCRIBING In the graphic organizer below, choose two Beatitudes and copy them into the first column. Then describe how each Beatitude can be interpreted in everyday language.

Beatitude	Interpretation

4 IDENTIFYING CAUSES Why do you think the Roman governor sentenced Jesus to death?

_____

_____

_____

_____

_____

5 ANALYZING INFORMATION How did the apostles contribute to the early growth of Christianity?

_____

_____

_____

_____

Jesus of Nazareth: Love Your Enemies

DIRECTIONS: Read the following excerpt and answer the accompanying questions.

EXPLORE THE CONTEXT: Unlike many early thinkers and philosophers, Jesus of Nazareth had different ideas about how to respond to persecution. In a violent time, he advocated for nonviolent means of interaction with those who would bring harm. The selection below was written by one of Jesus' apostles, Matthew.

PRIMARY SOURCE: HOLY BOOK

" 38 Ye have heard that it hath been said, An eye for an eye, and a tooth for a tooth:

39 But I say unto you, That ye resist not evil: but whosoever shall smite thee on thy right cheek, turn to him the other also.

40 And if any man will sue thee at the law, and take away thy coat, let him have thy cloak also.

41 And whosoever shall compel thee to go a mile, go with him twain.

42 Give to him that asketh thee, and from him that would borrow of thee turn not thou away.

43 Ye have heard that it hath been said, Thou shalt love thy neighbour, and hate thine enemy.

44 But I say unto you, Love your enemies, bless them that curse you, do good to them that hate you, and pray for them which despitefully use you, and persecute you. "

—from *The Holy Bible,* King James Version, Matthew 5:38–44

VOCABULARY

twain: two
despitefully: in spite
persecute: continually harm

1 INFERRING Matthew writes that Jesus of Nazareth tells his followers to turn the other cheek. What does Jesus mean by this phrase?

_____

_____

2 ANALYZING INFORMATION Which two verses tell followers to give up material things to people who ask for them? What is the underlying reason for this generosity?

_____

_____

_____

_____

_____

3 EVALUATING EVIDENCE What evidence in the text can you find for a departure from Jewish scripture? How does Jesus turn away from these rules in his recommendations to followers?

_____

_____

_____

_____

_____

4 ANALYZING How might these ideas have helped people who were poor or people who were suffering? Why did people believe what Jesus said?

_____

_____

_____

_____

_____

The Epistle of Paul to the Romans

DIRECTIONS: Read the following excerpt and answer the accompanying questions.

EXPLORE THE CONTEXT: Saul did not support Christianity and was on his way to Damascus to arrest followers of Jesus. According to Christian teaching, while traveling there, Saul was blinded by a bright light. He then heard a voice asking him why he was determined to persecute Jesus. After having this vision, Saul converted to Christianity and became Paul the Apostle. From this point he dedicated himself to sharing Christianity with others through journeys, preaching, and through letters. Paul was named a saint by the Church after his death. In this letter to believers of Christ who lived in Rome, Paul writes about those who love God.

ESSENTIAL QUESTION

How do new ideas change the way people live?

VOCABULARY

foreknow: know ahead of time
predestinate: decide a person's destiny before he or she is born
brethren: brothers

PRIMARY SOURCE: HOLY BOOK

❝28 And we know that all things work together for good to them that love God, to them who are called according to his purpose.

29 For whom he did foreknow, he also did predestinate to be conformed to the image of his Son, that he might be the firstborn among many brethren.

30 Moreover whom he did predestinate, them he also called: and whom he called, them he also justified: and whom he justified, them he also glorified.

31 What shall we then say to these things? If God be for us, who can be against us? . . .

38 For I am persuaded, that neither death, nor life, nor angels, nor principalities, nor powers, nor things present, nor things to come,

39 Nor height, nor depth, nor any other creature, shall be able to separate us from the love of God, which is in Christ Jesus our Lord. ❞

—from *The Holy Bible,* King James Version, Romans 8:28–31, 38–39

1 IDENTIFYING In the first line of the excerpt, for whom does Paul say that "all things work together for good"?

_____

_____

_____

2 INFERRING In the excerpt, what do you think Paul means by "If God be for us, who can be against us?"

_____

_____

_____

_____

3 IDENTIFYING Paul writes that nothing can separate believers "from the love of God, which is in Christ Jesus our Lord." What things does Paul list that cannot separate believers from the love of God?

_____

_____

_____

_____

4 ANALYZING Why do you think Paul wrote this letter to believers of Jesus who lived in Rome? Use what you have learned from Explore the Context as well as the passage.

_____

_____

_____

_____

_____

_____

ESSENTIAL QUESTION

How do new ideas change the way people live?

As you gather evidence to answer the Essential Question, think about:

- how the early Christian community was different from non-Christian communities in the Roman Empire.
- how the early Christian community spread its message.

My Notes

The Early Church

DIRECTIONS: Search for evidence in Lesson 2 to help you answer the following questions.

1   CIVICS   In the graphic organizer below, write three ways in which early Christian communities differed from other communities that followed the ancient Roman religion.

Roman Empire's Religion	Christianity

2 **ANALYZING EVENTS** How did the Romans treat the early Christians? How did that treatment affect the growth of Christianity?

_____

_____

_____

_____

3 **ANALYZING EVENTS** What did Constantine do to change the empire's position on Christianity? What effect did it have on the religion?

_____

_____

_____

_____

_____

_____

_____

4 **ECONOMICS** How did Christianity spread into East Africa?

_____

_____

_____

_____

_____

_____

_____

_____

5 **EXPLAINING** Why did early Christians eventually organize the church as a hierarchy?

_____

_____

_____

_____

_____

_____

_____

Second Letter from Paul to Timothy

DIRECTIONS: Read the following excerpt and answer the accompanying questions.

EXPLORE THE CONTEXT: In his second letter to the apostle Timothy, the apostle Paul explains how to spread the teachings of Christianity to nonbelievers. He tells Timothy to evangelize by explaining how any other way of life will lead people astray and increase their suffering.

PRIMARY SOURCE: HOLY BOOK

VOCABULARY

reprove: scold
rebuke: criticize
exhort: urge
doctrine: set of beliefs or stated principles

" 1 I charge thee therefore before God, and the Lord Jesus Christ, who shall judge the quick and the dead at his appearing and his kingdom;

2 Preach the word; be instant in season, out of season; reprove, rebuke, exhort with all longsuffering and doctrine.

3 For the time will come when they will not endure sound doctrine; but after their own lusts shall they heap to themselves teachers, having itching ears;

4 And they shall turn away their ears from the truth, and shall be turned unto fables.

5 But watch thou in all things, endure afflictions, do the work of an evangelist, make full proof of thy ministry. "

—from *The Holy Bible,* King James Version, 2 Timothy 1–5

1 **INFERRING** Based on the nature of these verses, what do you think Timothy is being instructed to do?

_____

_____

_____

_____

2 **DESCRIBING** According to this letter, what duty does an evangelist have?

_____

_____

_____

_____

_____

_____

3 **EVALUATING EVIDENCE** What evidence in the text can you find for Paul's worry that Christianity will not survive?

_____

_____

_____

_____

_____

4 **ANALYZING** Based on the text, does Paul expect Timothy's task to be easy?

_____

_____

_____

_____

Tertullian's Apology

Copyright © McGraw-Hill Education   Tertullian. n.d. The Writings Of The Fathers Down To A.D. 325: Latin Christianity: Its Founder, Tertullian. Vol. 3 of Ante-Nicene Fathers. Trans. Sydney Thelwall. Ed. Allan Menzies. Grand Rapids, Michigan: Wm. B. Eerdmans Publishing Company.

ESSENTIAL QUESTION

How do new ideas change the way people live?

DIRECTIONS: Read the following excerpt and answer the accompanying questions.

EXPLORE THE CONTEXT: This passage is from Tertullian, one of the teachers in the early Christian church. This style of writing is called an "apology." An apology in this style is not meant to apologize for a wrong done, but is meant to be a defense of something. In this case, it is Christianity. Here Tertullian explains to the Roman rulers the reasons why they should not hate Christians. When Tertullian wrote this piece, the rulers of the Roman Empire were against Christianity because they saw it as a threat to their power.

VOCABULARY

severities: actions that are severe

aggravates: makes worse

enmity: hatred

PRIMARY SOURCE: BOOK

❝Rulers of the Roman Empire, . . . if in this case alone you are afraid or ashamed to exercise your authority in making public inquiry with the carefulness which becomes justice; if, finally, the extreme severities inflicted on our people . . . stand in the way of our being permitted to defend ourselves before you, you cannot surely forbid the Truth to reach your ears by the secret pathway of a noiseless book. . . . We lay this before you as the first ground on which we urge that your hatred to the name of Christian is unjust. And the very reason which seems to excuse this injustice (I mean ignorance) at once aggravates and convicts it. For what is there more unfair than to hate a thing of which you know nothing[?] . . . The proof of their ignorance, at once condemning and excusing their injustice, is this, that those who once hated Christianity because they knew nothing about it, no sooner come to know it than they all lay down at once their enmity. From being its haters they become its disciples. ❞

—from *The Apology*, by Tertullian, c. 197 C.E.

1 EXPLAINING How does this text explain that the Roman hatred of Christians is unjust?

_____

_____

_____

_____

2 ANALYZING What is Tertullian offering to the Romans, and what does he want them to do with it?

_____

_____

_____

_____

_____

_____

_____

3 SUMMARIZING What is the lesson that the author is trying to teach?

_____

_____

_____

_____

_____

4 COMPARING How is this passage similar to Paul's letter to Timothy?

_____

_____

_____

_____

_____

_____

_____

ESSENTIAL QUESTION

How do new ideas change the way people live?

As you gather evidence to answer the Essential Question, think about:

- how the church established its authority in Rome.
- why the church eventually split into two factions.

My Notes

A Christian Europe

DIRECTIONS: Search for evidence in Lesson 3 to help you answer the following questions.

1 **ANALYZING IDEAS** How were the ideas of church organization different in the eastern church compared to the western church?

_____

_____

_____

_____

_____

_____

2 **DESCRIBING** How did the Benedictine rule bring the teachings of Jesus into the lives of monks?

_____

_____

_____

_____

_____

3 **ANALYZING EVENTS** What did Pope Gregory I do to encourage the spread of Christianity? Did it work and, if so, how?

_____

_____

_____

_____

_____

_____

④ **COMPARING AND CONTRASTING** In the graphic organizer below, write the similarities and differences between Pope Gregory I and Constantine.

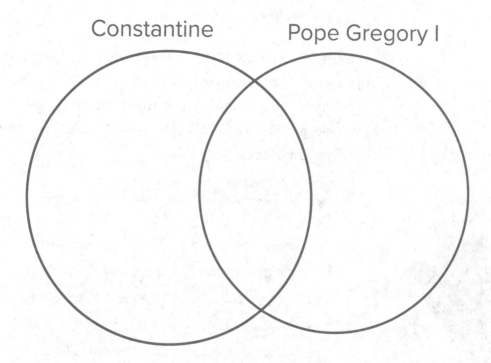

Constantine   Pope Gregory I

⑤ **DESCRIBING** In the graphic organizer below, describe missionaries and their methods in early Christianity. Then describe how missionaries work today.

Early Christian Missionaries	Modern Christian Missionaries

The Monk at Prayer

Morison, E. F. 1912. St. Basil And His Rule: A Study In Early Monasticism. London, Edinburgh, New York, Toronto, Melbourne, and Bombay: Henry Frowde Oxford University Press.

ESSENTIAL QUESTION

How do new ideas change the way people live?

DIRECTIONS: Read the following excerpt and answer the accompanying questions.

EXPLORE THE CONTEXT: The monk Basil formed the basis for the way that monks in the Eastern Christian Church live and pray. As the Benedictine rule directed Benedictine monks in Western Europe, the Basilian rule directed monks in Eastern Europe.

PRIMARY SOURCE: BOOK

66 Ought we to pray without ceasing? Is it possible to obey such a command? These are questions which I see you are ready to ask. I will endeavor, to the best of my ability, to prove my case. Prayer is a petition for good addressed by the pious to God. But we do not rigidly confine our petition to words. Nor yet do we imagine that God requires to be reminded by speech. He knows our needs even though we do not ask Him. . . .

Thus mayest thou pray without ceasing, not in words, but by the whole conduct of thy life, so uniting thyself to God that thy life is one long, unceasing prayer. 99

— Basil, *Homilies*, c. 306 C.E.

VOCABULARY

endeavor: attempt
pious: religious, obedient
unceasing: continuous, never-ending

1 **INFERRING** What does Basil mean when he says that God does not need to hear words?

_____

_____

_____

_____

2 IDENTIFYING What word does Basil use to describe the way that monks should pray, and what does it mean?

_____

_____

_____

_____

_____

_____

_____

3 EVALUATING EVIDENCE What evidence in the text can you find for the idea that God requires monks to do what they are told and follow certain rules?

_____

_____

_____

_____

_____

_____

_____

_____

4 ANALYZING How does this text explain the connection between monks and the public?

_____

_____

_____

_____

_____

_____

_____

Exposition of the Present State of the Churches

Copyright © McGraw-Hill Education   Basil. n.d. The Treatise De Spiritu Sancto: The Nine Homilies of the Hexaemeron and the Letters of Saint Basil the Great, Archbishop of Caesaria. Ser. 2, vol. 8 of Nicene And Post-Nicene Fathers Of The Christian Church Trans: Blomfield Jackson. Eds. Philip Schaff and Henry Wace. Grand Rapids, Michigan: Wm. B. Eerdmans Publishing Company.

ESSENTIAL QUESTION

How do new ideas change the way people live?

DIRECTIONS: Read the following excerpt and answer the accompanying questions.

EXPLORE THE CONTEXT: In this text, Basil explains the animosity between each of the factions of Christianity as the western and eastern churches experience a painful split.

PRIMARY SOURCE: BOOK

66 To what then shall I liken our present condition? It may be compared, I think, to some naval battle which has arisen out of time old quarrels, and is fought by men who cherish a deadly hate against one another, of long experience in naval warfare, and eager for the fight. Look, I beg you, at the picture thus raised before your eyes.

See the rival fleets rushing in dread array to the attack. With a burst of uncontrollable fury they engage and fight it out. Fancy, if you like, the ships driven to and fro by a raging tempest, while thick darkness falls from the clouds and blackens all the scenes so that watchwords are indistinguishable in the confusion, and all distinction between friend and foe is lost. . . . Jealousy of authority and the lust of individual mastery splits the sailors into parties which deal mutual death to one another. . . . They do not cease from their struggle each to get the better of the other, while their ship is actually settling down into the deep. 99

— Basil, *De Spiritu Sancto (The Book Of Saint Basil On The Spirit),* c. 375 C.E.

VOCABULARY

fleets: groups of ships
tempest: storm
watchwords: guiding principles

1 **INFERRING** What does the writer of this document mean by "all distinction between friend and foe is lost"?

_____

_____

_____

_____

2 **DESCRIBING** How does this document describe the argument between the two church factions?

_____

_____

_____

_____

3 **EVALUATING EVIDENCE** What evidence in the text can you find for the reasons that Basil thinks the churches are fighting?

_____

_____

_____

_____

4 **ANALYZING** How does Basil make arguments that are similar to the teachings of Jesus?

_____

_____

_____

_____

① Think About It

How do new ideas change the way people live?

Review the supporting questions that you developed at the beginning of the chapter. Review the evidence that you gathered in this chapter. Were you able to answer each Supporting Question? If there was not enough evidence to answer your Supporting Questions, what additional evidence do you think you need to consider?

② Organize Your Evidence

Use a chart such as the one below to organize the evidence you will use to support your position statement.

Source of information	Specific Evidence to Cite from the source	How Does the Evidence Support my Position Statement?

3 Write About It

A position statement related to the Essential Question should reflect your conclusion about the evidence. Write a position statement for the ESSENTIAL QUESTION: *How do new ideas change the way people live?*

_____

_____

_____

_____

4 Talk About It

Work in a small group to present your position statement and evidence. Gather feedback from your classmates before you write your final conclusion. You may choose to refine your position statement after you have discussed it with your classmates. Group members should listen to each other's arguments, ask questions, and offer constructive feedback to help create clear position statements.

_____

_____

_____

_____

5 Connect to the Essential Question

Create a poster comparing and contrasting how people in Europe and other parts of the Roman Empire lived before and after the birth of Christianity to answer the ESSENTIAL QUESTION: *How do new ideas change the way people live?*

_____

_____

_____

CITIZENSHIP
TAKING ACTION

MAKE CONNECTIONS Christianity spread across the Roman Empire because the empire's road network made it easy for Christians to travel and spread their message. Today, we do not need roads to help us communicate ideas across long distances. We have technology that can do that for us.

DIRECTIONS: Imagine you have a new idea that might improve your community. How would you spread that message? Write a three- to five-step plan to share your idea. Include which technologies or social media platforms you would use, how you would use each one, and why.

_____

_____

_____

_____

_____

_____

_____

_____

_____

_____

_____

_____

_____

_____

_____

Islamic Civilization

ESSENTIAL QUESTION

How do belief systems influence society and government?

Think about how this question might relate to the development of early Islamic civilization.

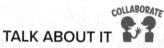

TALK ABOUT IT

Discuss with a partner what type of information you would need to know to answer this question. For example, one question might be: What are the most important teachings of the Quran?

DIRECTIONS: Now write down three additional questions that you need to answer to be able to explain why and how Islam developed.

MY RESEARCH QUESTIONS

Supporting Question 1:

_____

_____

Supporting Question 2:

_____

_____

Supporting Question 3:

_____

_____

ESSENTIAL QUESTION

How do belief systems influence society and government?

As you gather evidence to answer the Essential Question, think about:

- what life was like on the Arabian Peninsula.
- why people followed Muhammad.
- how the Arabs' tribal society changed with the rise of Islam.
- the teachings of the Quran.

My Notes

A New Faith

DIRECTIONS: Search for evidence in Lesson 1 to help you answer the following questions.

1 EXPLAINING What is the significance of Makkah to Islamic society?

_____

_____

_____

_____

2 CITING TEXT EVIDENCE How were the beliefs Arabs held prior to Islam carried over into this new religion?

_____

_____

_____

_____

_____

3 ECONOMICS How did trade between Arabs and other civilizations help Islam to develop?

_____

_____

_____

_____

_____

4 **IDENTIFYING CAUSES** Why was Muhammad inspired to preach to other Arabs?

_____

_____

_____

_____

5 **INTEGRATING VISUAL INFORMATION** Look at the photographs of the Kaaba. What do these photographs illustrate about Islam and Muslims?

_____

_____

_____

_____

6 **UNDERSTANDING CHRONOLOGY** Complete the graphic organizer below with the significant events that contributed to Muhammad's rise as a prophet and the development of the Quran.

Muhammad wins the support of the poor.		

		Islamic scholars then create a code of law called shari'ah.

The Song of Maisuna

ESSENTIAL QUESTION

How do belief systems influence society and government?

DIRECTIONS: Read the following poem and answer the accompanying questions.

EXPLORE THE CONTENT: A great deal of literature came from Muslim men and women of this era. This poem was written C. 661–680 C.E. by a woman named Maisuna, who was a wife of a leader of Islam after the death of Muhammad. The poem brings the reader into a typical moment of Arabian life.

PRIMARY SOURCE: POEM

"The russet suit of camel's hair,

With spirits light, and eye serene,

Is dearer to my bosom far

Than all the trappings of a queen.

The humble tent and murmuring breeze

That whistles thro' its fluttering wall,

My unaspiring fancy please

Better than towers and splendid halls.

Th' attendant colts that bounding fly

And frolic by the litter's side,

Are dearer in Maisuna's eye

Than gorgeous mules in all their pride.

The watch-dog's voice that bays whene'er

A stranger seeks his master's cot,

Sounds sweeter in Maisuna's ear

Than yonder trumpet's long-drawn note.

The rustic youth unspoilt by art,

Son of my kindred, poor but free,

Will ever to Maisuna's heart

Be dearer, pamper'd fool, than thee."

—Maisuna, wife to the Caliph Mowiah

VOCABULARY

russet: a shade of reddish-brown

serene: peaceful

trappings: decorations or ornaments

humble: plain

frolic: to play, skip, or romp

litter: a long seat with rods surrounded by curtains that is used to carry one person

kindred: family

1a **ANALYZING** Why does the author use phrases such as "Is dearer to my bosom far/Than all the trappings of a queen" and "Sounds sweeter in Maisuna's ear/Than yonder trumpet's long-drawn note"?

_____

_____

_____

_____

1b **COMPARING** What are some other comparisons the author uses to express her feelings about the world around her?

_____

_____

_____

_____

2 **DETERMINING CONTEXT** What words and phrases does the author use to help the reader understand the time and place?

_____

_____

_____

_____

3 **INFERRING** What is the theme of the poem?

_____

_____

_____

_____

Islam and Charity

ESSENTIAL QUESTION

How do belief systems influence society and government?

DIRECTIONS: Read the following excerpt and answer the accompanying questions.

EXPLORE THE CONTENT: The following text is from "The Five Principles of Islam and their Significance." It specifically explains Islam's final principle, zakat, or the giving of alms.

VOCABULARY

optional: voluntary

ultimate: essential

inclined: tend to take a particular action

institution: organization or society

fancies: desires or whims

systemize: to develop a method, order, or regularity

SECONDARY SOURCE: PERIODICAL

"Now I come to the last and fifth principle of Islam, which has been promulgated [declared] by the Holy Qur-an in the terms of Zakat (poor-rates) or Sadaquat (alms). Every Muslim is expected to take a stock of his savings every year and to disburse [hand out] 2 1/2 per cent. of this as "alms." Charity in Islam takes two different forms: one is optional and the other compulsory [required], which is also called zakat. When asked as to what was the ultimate object of zakat, the Holy Prophet replied that it was a means whereby the rich had to give something out of their wealth for the help of those who are in need. The Holy Qur-an has laid down eight different purposes for the expenditure [spending] of this zakat money. It says: 'Alms are only for the poor, the needy, the officials appointed over them, those whose hearts are made inclined to truth, the ransoming of captives, those in debt, in the way of Allah and the wayfarer.'

It is Islam that has given charity the prestige [respect] and form of an institution. Before the advent [founding] of Islam the followers of other religions used to do charitable deeds on their own personal fancies and had no organization. But the Holy Prophet, whose aim was to systemize the religion and make it a living force in the civilization of mankind, laid down rules and regulations for charity, so that the general welfare of the society may be achieved. . . . "

— from "The Five Principles of Islam and their Significance" by Maulvi Mustafakhan, The Islamic Review, Vol. IX No. 6 (June-July 1921)

Copyright © McGraw-Hill Education TEXT: Mustafakhan, Maulvi. 1921. The Five Principles of Islam and Their Significance. The Islamic Review, 9 (6):211-217.

1a CIVICS Who is expected to pay zakat?

_____

1b **INFERRING** Why do you think this group is singled out for observing this principle?

_____

_____

_____

_____

2 **DESCRIBING** What are some of the purposes of zakat?

_____

_____

_____

_____

3 CIVICS What is the larger benefit to paying zakat?

_____

_____

4 **ANALYZING** Explain why Mustafakhan believes "It is Islam that has given charity the prestige [respect] and form of an institution."

_____

_____

_____

5 **INFERRING** Why is zakat such an important principle in the Islamic faith?

_____

_____

_____

_____

The Spread of Islam

DIRECTIONS: Search for evidence in Lesson 2 to help you answer the following questions.

ESSENTIAL QUESTION

How do belief systems influence society and government?

As you gather evidence to answer the Essential Question, think about:

- how the practices of Islam spread throughout the region.
- how the various Islamic leaders treated non-Muslims.
- how the first four caliphs changed and improved Islamic culture.
- how an Islamic state changed under various dynasties.

1 EXPLAINING What was the goal of the first four caliphs?

_____

_____

_____

_____

_____

2 CITING TEXT EVIDENCE What evidence in the text supports the idea that Byzantine and Persian policies helped Muslims create a large empire?

_____

_____

_____

_____

_____

_____

_____

My Notes

_____

_____

_____

_____

_____

_____

_____

3 **COMPARING** Complete the Venn diagram.

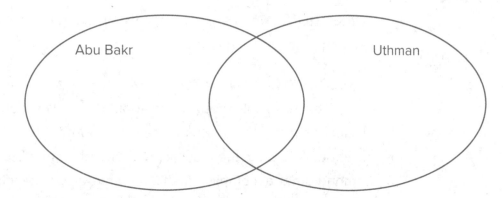

Abu Bakr   Uthman

4 **IDENTIFYING CAUSES** Why did Islam split into two similar but opposing groups?

_____

_____

_____

5 **DIFFERENTIATING** In the graphic organizer below, describe the major characteristics of each of the three Muslim empires.

Empire	Characteristics of the Empire			
Ottoman Empire				
Safavid Empire				
Mughal Empire				

Masu'di on the First Caliph

Copyright © McGraw-Hill Education TEXT: Home, Charles F., ed. 1917. Medieval Arabic, Moorish, and Turkish. Vol. 6 of The Sacred Books and Early Literature of the East. New York and London: Parke, Austin, & Lipscomb.

ESSENTIAL QUESTION

How do belief systems influence society and government?

DIRECTIONS: Read the following excerpt and answer the accompanying questions.

EXPLORE THE CONTENT: Abul Hasan Ali Al-Masu'di, author of this excerpt, collected stories about the early caliphs of Islam and published them in a series of books. This excerpt is about Abu Bakr, the first caliph after Muhammad's death. Among other accomplishments, he restored peace after Muhammad died and compiled verses of the Quran, the sacred text of Islam.

VOCABULARY

surpassed: went beyond
frugality: thriftiness
pious: holy; moral
gravity: seriousness
renounced: gave up

> **SECONDARY SOURCE: BOOK**
>
> ❝ Abu Bakr surpassed all the Muhammadans in his austerity, his frugality, and the simplicity of his life and outward appearance. During his rule he wore but a single linen garment and a cloak. In this simple dress he gave audience to the chiefs of the noblest Arab tribes and to the kings of Yemen. The latter appeared before him dressed in richest robes, covered with gold embroideries and wearing splendid crowns. But at sight of the Caliph, shamed by his mingling of pious humility and earnest gravity, they followed his example and renounced their gorgeous attire. ❞
>
> — Abul Hasan Ali Al-Masu'di, *The Book of Golden Meadows*, C. 940 C.E.

1a ANALYZING POINTS OF VIEW What is the author's opinion of Abu Bakr?

_____

_____

_____

1b **CITING TEXT EVIDENCE** What evidence in the excerpt supports your claim?

_____

_____

_____

_____

2 **ANALYZING INDIVIDUALS** Why does the author compare Abu Bakr to the chiefs?

_____

_____

_____

_____

3 **ANALYZING SOURCES** What phrase from the excerpt illustrates the author's claim that Abu Bakr was frugal?

_____

_____

_____

_____

4 **CIVICS** Why did the chiefs change the way they dressed?

_____

_____

_____

5 **INFERRING** What can you infer about Abu Bakr's character?

_____

_____

_____

_____

*How do belief systems
influence society and
government?*

Geography and the Ottoman Empire

DIRECTIONS: Look at the following map and answer the accompanying questions.

EXPLORE THE CONTEXT: Islamic civilization spread through Europe and the Middle East during the Ottoman Empire. The map below, made in 1898, shows the spread of Islamic civilization. Use this map, along with other maps in your Student Edition, to help you answer the questions.

PRIMARY SOURCE: MAP

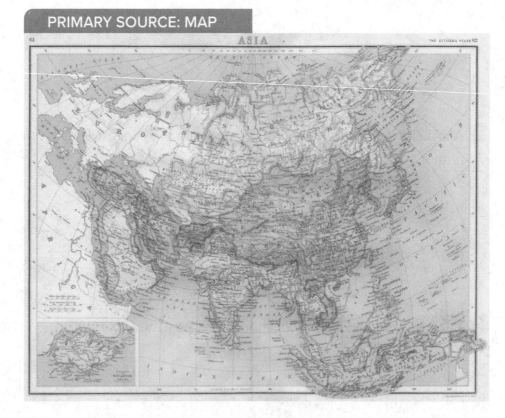

1 IDENTIFYING CAUSES Why did various rulers seeks to conquer neighboring regions?

_____

_____

_____

_____

2 USING MAPS How did the location of the empire assist in its expansion?

_____

_____

_____

_____

_____

_____

_____

3 GEOGRAPHY Why did Cairo and Baghdad likely grow into large cities?

_____

_____

_____

_____

_____

_____

_____

_____

ESSENTIAL QUESTION

How do belief systems influence society and government?

As you gather evidence to answer the Essential Question, think about:

- the development of trade in the region.
- how social groups were structured.
- contributions made by Muslims to mathematics, science, medicine, and the arts.

My Notes

Life in the Islamic World

DIRECTIONS: Search for evidence in Lesson 3 to help you answer the following questions.

1 EXPLAINING CAUSES What contributed to the success of Muslim traders?

_____

_____

_____

_____

_____

_____

2 CITING TEXT EVIDENCE How did mosques contribute to Islamic society?

_____

_____

_____

_____

3 COMPARING In the graphic organizer below, describe how life differed between cities and villages in the Muslim world.

Muslim City	Muslim Village

4 EXPLAINING ISSUES How did Islamic law protect enslaved people?

_____

_____

5 IDENTIFYING Complete the following chart to show the types of contributions Muslims made in the fields of medicine, science and mathematics, literature, and architecture.

Person	Field	Contribution
Al-Razi		
Mamun		
Omar Khayyam		
Shah Jahan		

The Poetry of Omar Khayyam

ESSENTIAL QUESTION

How do belief systems influence society and government?

DIRECTIONS: Read the following poem and answer the accompanying questions.

EXPLORE THE CONTENT: Omar Khayyam is one of the most famous authors of early Islam. In this poem, Khayyam explores a large topic—life—in very few sentences.

PRIMARY SOURCE: POEM

"Nothing in this world of ours
Flows as we would have it flow;
What avail, then, careful hours,
Thought and trouble, tears and woe?
Through the shrouded veil of earth,
Life's rich colors gleaming bright,
Though in truth of little worth,
Yet allure with meteor light.
Life is torture and suspense;
Thought is sorrow—drive it hence!
With no will of mine I came,
With no will depart the same."

— Omar Khayyam, "The Vanity of Regret," c. 1100

VOCABULARY

vanity: pride, conceit
avail: benefit
shrouded: covered

allure: lit up
depart: leave

1 **ANALYZING POINTS OF VIEW** Why does Khayyam most likely use the word "ours" in the first line of the poem?

_____

_____

_____

_____

_____

2 INFERRING What does the author mean by the lines "With no will of mine I came,/With no will depart the same."?

_____

_____

_____

_____

3 ANALYZING SOURCES Which pairs of lines from the poem suggests that people experience both good and bad times throughout their lives?

_____

_____

_____

_____

4a ANALYZING POINTS OF VIEW Overall, what is the speaker's opinion about life?

_____

_____

_____

_____

4b IDENTIFYING PERSPECTIVES What evidence from the poem supports that claim?

_____

_____

_____

_____

Art of the Muslim World

ESSENTIAL QUESTION

How do belief systems influence society and government?

DIRECTIONS: Look at the artwork and answer the accompanying questions.

EXPLORE THE CONTEXT: Early Muslims contributed greatly to the artwork of the era. Some of these pieces, such as this section of the Taj Mahal, built in the mid-1600s, still exist.

PRIMARY SOURCE: ART

1a DESCRIBING Describe the image shown in the artwork.

_____

_____

_____

_____

_____

_____

_____

1b **INFERRING** Why might no living creatures be shown in this artwork?

_____

_____

_____

_____

_____

2 **HISTORY** What does this artwork tell you about the artists of the time period?

_____

_____

_____

_____

_____

3 **DRAWING CONCLUSIONS** What does this artwork tell you about the principles of early Islam?

_____

_____

_____

_____

_____

_____

ESSENTIAL QUESTION

How do belief systems influence society and government?

1 Think About It

Review the supporting questions that you developed at the beginning of the chapter. Review the evidence that you gathered in this chapter. Were you able to answer each Supporting Question?

If there was not enough evidence to answer your Supporting Questions, what additional evidence do you think you need to consider?

_____

_____

_____

_____

_____

2 Organize Your Evidence

Use a chart like the one below to organize the evidence you will use to support your position statement.

Source of information	Specific evidence from the source to cite	How evidence helps support my position statement	Column Head Title

③ Write About It

A position statement related to the Essential Question should reflect your conclusion about the evidence. Write a position statement for the ESSENTIAL QUESTION: *How do belief systems influence society and government?*

_____

_____

_____

_____

_____

_____

④ Talk About It

Work in a small group to present your position statement and evidence. Gather feedback from your classmates before you write your final conclusion. You may choose to refine your position statement after you have discussed it with your classmates. Group members should listen to each other's arguments, ask questions, and offer constructive advice about the statement.

⑤ Connect to the Essential Question

Develop a visual essay to present your position statement and the evidence that supports it. Draw the images or choose photos and art from appropriate Web sites to illustrate the evidence. Include captions explaining how the evidence supports your position statement.

CITIZENSHIP
TAKING ACTION

MAKE CONNECTIONS The lessons of the Quran continue to guide Muslim beliefs, actions, society, and government. For example, every Muslim in the world today has the obligation of putting into practice the Five Pillars of Islam: belief, prayer, charity, fasting, and pilgrimage. Carrying out these practices, if at all possible, provides a framework for each Muslim's life.

DIRECTIONS: Think about life in the United States. What are the beliefs and practices that provide a framework and foundation for American life? Look to America's founding documents, such as the Declaration of Independence and the Constitution, for ideas. Think about the customs and routines of your life, your school, and your community. Then write and give a speech in which you propose a list of pillars of American life.

CHAPTER
15

African Civilizations

ESSENTIAL QUESTION

Why do people trade?

Think about how this question might relate to the cultural exchanges between African civilizations and other parts of the world during this time period.

TALK ABOUT IT

Discuss with a partner what type of information you would need to know to answer this question. For example, one question might be: How did the establishment of trade routes across the Sahara and Sahel regions impact African society?

DIRECTIONS: Now write down three additional questions that would help you explain how trade developed among African civilizations, as well as between Africa and other parts of the world.

MY RESEARCH QUESTIONS

Supporting Question 1:

_____

_____

Supporting Question 2:

_____

_____

Supporting Question 3:

_____

_____

ESSENTIAL QUESTION

Why do people trade?

As you gather evidence to answer the Essential Question, think about:

- the role of geography in the rise of civilizations.
- how trade encouraged cultural exchange.

My Notes

The Rise of African Civilizations

DIRECTIONS: Search for evidence in Lesson 1 to help you answer the following questions.

1A **IDENTIFYING CAUSE AND EFFECT** What elements of the landscape impacted where civilizations developed in Africa?

_____

_____

_____

_____

_____

_____

_____

_____

1B How did the Sahara and Sahel zones impact cultural exchange between East and West Africa?

_____

_____

_____

_____

2 GEOGRAPHY Why was the Niger River important to the rise of civilizations in West Africa?

_____

_____

_____

_____

3 **IDENTIFYING CAUSE AND EFFECT** The participation of West African civilizations in the Africa-Europe-Asia trade network between 400 B.C.E. and 1400 C.E. greatly impacted these societies. In the graphic below, identify why the following elements of trade were so important to the West African kingdoms.

ELEMENT OF TRADE	VALUE
CAMELS	
SALT	
GOLD	

4 **ECONOMICS** Complete the following chart to record the impact of how the development of trade and trade routes influenced the West African kingdoms.

Economic Impact of Trade

Equestrian Figure from the Mali Empire

DIRECTIONS: Examine the following image and answer the accompanying questions.

EXPLORE THE CONTEXT: The image below is a terra-cotta sculpture, created between 1200 and 1400 C.E. and found near the city of Djenne. This city became an important stop in the trans-Sahara trade route. The Mali warrior is depicted dressed in military gear and astride a horse. Some Arabic documents note that Mansa Musa had a cavalry of more than 100,000 during his reign in the early 1300s C.E. Horses were not native animals to Africa and required tremendous care and maintenance.

PRIMARY SOURCE: SCULPTURE

Copyright © McGraw-Hill Education   Werner Forman/Universal Images Group/Getty Images

1 **ANALYZING** What do the warrior and horse appear dressed to do in this sculpture?

_____

_____

_____

_____

_____

2 **HISTORY** How might the history of the rise of the Mali Empire be illustrated in this sculpture?

_____

_____

_____

3 **ANALYZING TEXT EVIDENCE** After referring to the text, describe the significance of this warrior being depicted on horseback.

_____

_____

_____

_____

_____

4 **DRAWING CONCLUSIONS** What important clues does this statue provide about the Mali Empire?

_____

_____

_____

The West African Griot

DIRECTIONS: Read the following excerpt and answer the accompanying questions.

EXPLORE THE CONTEXT: Griots served an important role in the royal courts of West African rulers. These artists were storytellers who relayed the history of the empires to the people.

PRIMARY SOURCE: BOOK

66 The bard, or griot, in West Africa, who used to relate the epic, was first and foremost an artist. His aim was to entertain the listeners who were fond of hearing about the prowess and exploits of the kings and warriors. The griot usually accentuated the superhuman dimensions of the hero. In order to make his tale more pleasant, he skillfully used his art, the literary form of his narrative, the beauty of this language and any other device which could strike the imagination of his listeners. He emphasized decisive moments such as fights, provocations, plots and magical scenes. . . . in order to make his narrative enjoyable, the griot was usually accompanied by a musical instrument. Indeed, in West Africa, the strong rhythm of the epic was almost always punctuated by a ngoni, a khalam, or a tam-tam, and the crowd participated by repeating the refrain in chorus. 99

—from *An Introduction to the African Prose Narrative*, 2004

VOCABULARY

prowess: skill, talent
exploits: heroic acts, adventures
accentuated: highlighted

decisive: significant
provocations: causes of anger

1 **CITING TEXT EVIDENCE** What was the goal of most griots?

_____

_____

_____

TEXT: Losambe, Lokangaka , ed. 2004. An Introduction to the African Prose Narrative. Trenton, NJ: Africa World Press.

Copyright © McGraw-Hill Education

2 DETERMINING MEANING What can you determine about the meaning of the words "ngoni, a khalam, or a tam-tam" based on this context?

_____

_____

_____

_____

3 ANALYZING TEXT EVIDENCE After referring to the text, describe what you know about the people of West Africa based on the role of the griot in this society. Think about the elements that unified the culture.

_____

_____

_____

_____

_____

_____

_____

_____

4 DRAWING CONCLUSIONS What point of view does this historian use when describing the griot?

_____

_____

_____

_____

_____

_____

ESSENTIAL QUESTION

Why do people trade?

As you gather evidence to answer the Essential Question, think about:

- the role of trade in the spread of Islam in Africa.
- the influence of Islam on African society and government.

My Notes

_____

_____

_____

_____

_____

_____

_____

Africa's Governments and Religions

DIRECTIONS: Search for evidence in Lesson 2 to help you answer the following questions.

1 INTERPRETING Why did some West African leaders originally accept Islam?

_____

_____

_____

_____

_____

2 CITING TEXT EVIDENCE Use the chart to describe how the elements of adopting Islam in African civilizations impacted their society.

ADOPTION OF ISLAM	IMPACT
Trade with Muslim merchants and civilizations	
Adoption of Islamic laws	
Teaching the Quran	

3 HISTORY Use the chart to identify some results that sprang from the introduction of Islam to the kingdoms in Africa.

RESULTS OF THE INTRODUCTION OF ISLAM TO AFRICAN KINGDOMS

West African Military and Trade

TEXT: Mendoza, Ruben G. "West African Empires, Dates: 400-1591 C.E., in Weapons & Warfare: Ancient and Medieval Weapons and Warfare (to c. 1500)., John Powell, ed. Vol. 1 of Weapons and Warfare. Ipswich, Massachusetts: Salem Press.

ESSENTIAL QUESTION

Why do people trade?

DIRECTIONS: Read the following excerpt and answer the accompanying questions.

EXPLORE THE CONTEXT: The historian John Powell describes the importance of the trans-Saharan trade route as a source of wealth. African rulers taxed the goods being traded and also raised funds by offering protection to travelers along trade routes.

SECONDARY SOURCE: BOOK

66 Ghana's emergence as the first of the West African empires ultimately set the stage for subsequent developments identified with the establishment of the kingdoms of Mali and Songhai. In each instance the intensification of trade along the trans-Saharan trade network was a critical factor underlying the expansion, influence and institutionalization of the military orders of the day. In fact, much of the wealth generated to support the maintenance of professional armies—documented by various Islamic writers to have ranged between 40,000 and 200,000 soldiers—was derived directly from the military and police protections afforded foreign travelers merchants on the trans-Saharan trade corridor. 99

— John Powell, *Weapons & Warfare: Modern Weapons and Warfare (since c. 1500),* 2010

VOCABULARY

ultimately: finally

subsequent: later

intensification: building up, strengthening

institutionalization: to establish as usual, or normal

derived: developed

1 **CITING TEXT EVIDENCE** According to John Powell, how did West African armies pay for their large armies?

_____

_____

_____

_____

2 **DETERMINING MEANING** What does Powell's description of the military tell you about the structure of West African governments?

_____

_____

_____

_____

_____

_____

_____

_____

3 **CITING TEXT EVIDENCE** Which phrase does Powell use to describe the relationship between trade and the size of the military? Underline the words he used.

_____

_____

_____

_____

_____

_____

4 HISTORY How does this perspective on African government influence our understanding of how trade impacted West African life?

_____

_____

_____

_____

_____

Rituals and Beliefs of the Nyakyusa

ESSENTIAL QUESTION

Why do people trade?

DIRECTIONS: Read the following excerpt and answer the accompanying questions.

EXPLORE THE CONTEXT: The Nyakyusa were a Bantu-speaking people who lived in the area north of Tanzania, in the Ngonde plain. Monica Wilson records the rituals and beliefs of this people in the following excerpt focused on the ruler called King Kyungu.

SECONDARY SOURCE: ANTHROPOLOGICAL STUDY

"Great precautions were taken to preserve his health. He lived in a separate house with his powerful medicines . . . When the Kyungu did fall ill he was smothered by the nobles who lived around him at Mbande, and buried in great secrecy, with a score or more of living persons—slaves—in the grave beneath him, and one or two wives and the sons of commoners above. And in the midst of all this slaughter the nobles brought a sheep to look into the grave that the dead Kyungu might be gentle (mololo) like the sheep! The living Kyungu was thought to create food and rain, and his breath and the growing parts of his body—his hair and nails and the constantly replaced mucus of his nose—were believed to be magically connected with the fertility of the Ngonde plain. When he was killed his nostrils were stopped so that he was buried 'with the breath in his body'; while portions of his hair and nails and of his nasal mucus were taken from him beforehand and buried by the nobles of Ngonde in the black mud near the river. This was 'to defend the country against hunger, to close up the land, to keep it rich and heavy and fertile as it was when he himself lived in it.'"

— Monica Wilson, *Communal Rituals of the Nyakyusa*, 1970

VOCABULARY

precautions: safety measures
nasal: having to do with the nose
beforehand: in advance

1 **ANALYZING** What is one of the primary roles of the Kyungu as described in this excerpt?

_____

_____

_____

_____

2 HISTORY What does the role of the Kyungu illustrate about the Bantu people's relationship with their environment?

_____

_____

_____

_____

3 **ANALYZING TEXT EVIDENCE** After referring to the text, describe what you know about the practices and beliefs of the Nyakyusa.

_____

_____

_____

_____

4 **DRAWING CONCLUSIONS** What can you determine about the Nyakyusa beliefs by examining how they treat the Kyungu when he falls ill?

_____

_____

_____

_____

ESSENTIAL QUESTION

Why do people trade?

As you gather evidence to answer the Essential Question, think about:

- the cultural traditions and ideas that many African societies share.
- the reasons for the origination of slavery in Africa.

My Notes

African Society and Culture

DIRECTIONS: Search for evidence in Lesson 3 to help you answer the following questions.

1A **IDENTIFYING CAUSE AND EFFECT** How did Bantu people spread their beliefs and ideas to large portions of Africa?

1B What role did families play in African society?

2 GEOGRAPHY How did geography determine which regions were most impacted by the Atlantic slave trade?

3 HISTORY Use the chart to identify some cultural results of the family serving as the central unit of African society.

CULTURAL RESULTS OF AFRICAN SOCIETY BASED ON FAMILY

4 INTERPRETING How did the capture and forced removal of enslaved people impact African societies?

_____

_____

_____

_____

_____

African Folktales

DIRECTIONS: Read the following excerpt and answer the accompanying questions.

EXPLORE THE CONTEXT: The Bantu people, a term that includes a large variety of ethnic groups, have common mythology and folklore. The following is typical of Bantu narratives that feature talking animals that are symbolic of different human attributes. These were most often used to educate the listener.

PRIMARY SOURCE: FOLKTALE

❝The hyena, for no apparent reason beyond ingrained ill-nature, put the tortoise up into the fork of a tree, where he could not get down. A leopard passed by and saw him: "Do you also climb trees, Tortoise?" "The hyena is the person who put me there, and now I can't get down if I try." The leopard remarked, "Hyena is a bad lot," and took the tortoise out of the tree. We are not told what the leopard looked like at this time, but he would seem to have been 'self-coloured,' for the tortoise, offering out of gratitude for his rescue to "make him beautiful, did so by painting him with spots, saying, as he worked, "Where your neighbour is all right, be you also all right [*makora*]." The leopard, when he went off, met a zebra, who admired him so much that he wanted to know who had made him beautiful, and himself went to the tortoise. In this way he got his stripes. This "Just-so" story accounts not only for the markings of the leopard and the zebra, but for their being creatures of the wild, for when the people, hoeing their gardens, saw them they exclaimed, "Oh! the big beauty! Catch it and let us domesticate it!" or words to that effect, so both of them fled into the bush, where they have remained ever since. ❞

—"How the Leopard Got His Spots" from *Myths and Legends of the Bantu* [Date unknown]

VOCABULARY

ingrained: deep-rooted
tortoise: a land-dwelling turtle
lot: sort
self-coloured: being of a single color
makora: Swahili word for "scamp" or "rascal"
domesticate: tame

1 CITING TEXT EVIDENCE How is the hyena portrayed here?

_____

_____

_____

2 DETERMINING MEANING What is the significance of this narrative and the belief, "Where your neighbour is all right, be you also all right?"

_____

_____

_____

_____

_____

_____

3 ANALYZING TEXT EVIDENCE After referring to the text, what do you know about the Bantu people? Why is a story featuring animals important to understanding this civilization?

_____

_____

_____

_____

_____

4 DRAWING CONCLUSIONS What can you determine about the Bantu culture based on this folktale?

_____

_____

_____

Copyright © McGraw-Hill Education   Conrad, David C. 2005. Empires of Medieval West Africa: Ghana, Mali, and Songhay. New York: Infobase Publishing.

ESSENTIAL QUESTION

Why do people trade?

VOCABULARY

currency: money
*commercial
transactions:* business
dealings

West African Money Cowries

DIRECTIONS: Read the following excerpt and answer the accompanying questions.

EXPLORE THE CONTEXT: Cowries functioned in African societies as currency, jewelry, and religious accessories. These shells symbolized strength, fertility, and wealth. Cowrie shells played an important role in the Atlantic trade of enslaved people, as well. Cowrie shell artifacts have been discovered in old enslaved peoples' quarters that were dug up for study in the United States.

SECONDARY SOURCE: BOOK

"In sub-Saharan West Africa, cowries were the most popular currency for centuries. These so-called "money cowries" are the shells of small snail-like creatures that live in the tropical waters of the Indian and Pacific Oceans. As early as the 13th century, Arab traders were carrying cowries from the Maldive Islands in the Indian Ocean to Egypt, then across the desert to the markets of sub-Saharan West Africa. Europeans were interested to find that in commercial transactions, Africans tended to prefer cowries to gold, and by the 16th century the shells were being imported in the ships of Dutch and English traders to the Guinea coast of West Africa. **"**

—from *Empires of Medieval West Africa: Ghana, Mali, and Songhay,* 2005

1 CITING TEXT EVIDENCE What role did cowries play in Atlantic trade?

_____

_____

_____

_____

_____

2 **DETERMINING POINT OF VIEW** What perspective does this author give on the value of cowries compared to gold in West African society?

_____

_____

_____

_____

_____

_____

_____

3 **CITING TEXT EVIDENCE** Which words serve as a clue to understanding why cowries might be so highly valued by West Africans? Underline the words, and explain why this is the best clue.

_____

_____

_____

_____

_____

_____

_____

_____

4 **DRAWING CONCLUSIONS:** Why do you think cowries were a good form of currency?

_____

_____

_____

_____

_____

_____

_____

ESSENTIAL QUESTION

Why do people trade?

1 Think About It

Review the Supporting Questions that you developed at the beginning of the chapter. Review the evidence that you gathered in this chapter. Were you able to answer each Supporting Question?

If there was not enough evidence to answer your Supporting Questions, what additional evidence do you think you need?

_____

_____

_____

_____

2 Organize Your Evidence

Use the chart below to organize the evidence you will use to support your position statement.

Central Idea

Supporting Details

❸ Write About It

A position statement related to the Essential Question should reflect your conclusion about the evidence. Write a position statement for the ESSENTIAL QUESTION: *Why do people trade?*

_____

_____

_____

_____

_____

_____

_____

_____

❹ Connect to the Essential Question

On a separate piece of paper, write a play about a trade caravan crossing the Saharan desert in the 1300s. Think about describing how the traders will make the journey, what goods they might be carrying, what religion they might practice, how long the journey will take, and what risks are involved.

Keep in mind the Essential Question about why people trade as you write about this journey.

CITIZENSHIP
TAKING ACTION

MAKE CONNECTIONS In this chapter, we have explored a folktale from Africa and what that story reveals about beliefs and cultural traditions. Folktales can be found around the world. In the United States, each region has different sets of folktales and fables that reflect the ethnic background and beliefs of the groups that initially settled these places. In some instances, these ideas no longer reflect the ideas and beliefs of the people.

DIRECTIONS: Research a folktale from the region where you live. Write an article for the school newspaper about what the folktale reveals about the beliefs and practices of the people who settled your region. Be sure and comment on how these beliefs and cultural traditions are similar to and different from those in your community today.

The Americas

ESSENTIAL QUESTION

What makes a culture unique?

Think about how this question might relate to natural resources and the rise and fall of early civilizations in the Americas.

TALK ABOUT IT COLLABORATE

Discuss with a partner what type of information you would need to know to answer this question. For example, one question might be: How did the natural world and competition for resources influence the daily lives and sacred beliefs of the early civilizations in the Americas?

DIRECTIONS: Now write down three additional questions that would help you explain how the natural world influenced the development of cultures and civilizations in the Americas.

MY RESEARCH QUESTIONS

Supporting Question 1:

_____

_____

Supporting Question 2:

_____

_____

Supporting Question 3:

_____

_____

The First Americans

DIRECTIONS: Search for evidence in Lesson 1 to help you answer the following questions.

ESSENTIAL QUESTION

What makes a culture unique?

As you gather evidence to answer the Essential Question, think about:

- how the early American cultures shifted from hunter-gathering to farming.
- the link between sacred beliefs and farming in the civilizations of Mesoamerica.

1A **EXPLAINING CAUSE AND EFFECT** How did the shift from hunting and gathering to farming relocate where unique civilizations thrived in Mesoamerica?

_____

_____

_____

1B **GEOGRAPHY** What role did sacred beliefs play in the lives of the first Americans?

_____

_____

_____

_____

My Notes

_____

_____

_____

_____

_____

_____

_____

_____

2 **GEOGRAPHY** How did the landscape of Mesoamerica influence the rise and fall of different civilizations?

_____

_____

_____

_____

3 **EXPLAINING CAUSE AND EFFECT** Fill in the chart below to describe how elements of the natural world impacted culture in the Americas.

Natural Elements	Impact on Culture
Weather	
Geography	
Animals	

4 ECONOMICS Use the chart below to record the ways that competition for resources impacted Mesoamerican civilizations.

Effects of Competition for Resources

An Olmec Figurine

DIRECTIONS: Analyze the artifact below and answer the accompanying questions.

EXPLORE THE CONTEXT: The Olmec were the earliest civilization to thrive in Mesoamerica near the Gulf of Mexico from c. 2700 b.c.e. to 900 b.c.e. Known for the colossal heads they carved from basalt with detailed faces of their rulers, the Olmec also created small figurines using basalt, jade, terracotta, and wooden materials. The image of the figurine below shows an example of the Olmec artistic tradition in sculpture. Figurines have been found at a variety of locations, including in everyday households and at burial sites. The subjects of these smaller figurines were often representations of Olmec Gods, like the "Rain Baby." They also include examples of people engaged in activities, such as playing a traditional Olmec ballgame. This ballgame was an important sport in the Olmec culture. It also had religious significance and became a feature of later cultures, including the Maya and the Aztec. Many elements of Mesoamerican art, including sculpture and ceramic traditions, can be traced back to the Olmec.

PRIMARY SOURCE: ARTIFACT

Copyright © McGraw-Hill Education   PHOTO: The Walters Art Museum; Gift of John G. Bourne, 2014

1 DESCRIBING Describe the figurine and the material you think might have been used to create it. How do you think this figurine was used by the Olmec people?

_____

_____

2 ANALYZING Why do you think Olmec figurines have been found at both common household sites and burial sites? Explain your answer.

_____

_____

3 ANALYZING SOURCES Does your analysis agree with the lesson text's description of what types of images were depicted in Olmec figurines and statues?

_____

_____

4 HISTORY How do you think the art of the Olmec represented their culture and impacted later civilizations?

_____

_____

_____

The Aztec Calendar

DIRECTIONS: Examine the following image and answer the accompanying questions.

EXPLORE THE CONTEXT: This image shows an Aztec calendar. Many elements of the Aztec culture, including the development of a calendar system, can be traced back to earlier civilizations in the Mesoamerican region, including the Maya. The Aztec calendar is a wheel with two distinct cycles. The first is a 365-day cycle that was based on the sun and used for agriculture. The second is a 260-day cycle that was used for religious rituals. Together, these cycles made up a 52-year unit of time similar to our century. In the center of the wheel is the representation of the sun God. In the next circle are 20 symbols for periods of time that are 13 days in length. The Aztec believed each 13-day period belonged to a different God and balance had to be maintained between each God in order for the people to thrive.

PRIMARY SOURCE: ARTIFACT

Copyright © McGraw-Hill Education   PHOTO: Newberry Library/SuperStock

1 **DESCRIBING** Do you recognize any of the figures depicted in the images on this calendar? Why do you think these images were used on this calendar?

_____

_____

_____

2 HISTORY How did the development of Aztec culture influence the development of this calendar?

_____

_____

_____

3 **ANALYZING SOURCES** Review the text and the image, and then describe what you know about the importance of the Aztec's sacred days.

_____

_____

_____

4 **DRAWING CONCLUSIONS** How do you think the natural world influenced the development of this calendar?

_____

_____

_____

_____

ESSENTIAL QUESTION

What makes a culture unique?

As you gather evidence to answer the Essential Question, think about:

- the importance of agriculture to civilizations in the Americas.

- how culture in the Americas evolved and was reflected in daily life and activities.

My Notes

_____

_____

_____

_____

_____

_____

_____

_____

_____

_____

_____

Life in the Americas

DIRECTIONS: Search for evidence in Lesson 2 to help you answer the following questions.

1 **HISTORY** Use the chart to identify the impact of agriculture on early American civilizations and culture.

IMPACT OF AGRICULTURE

Rise of Complex Societies

Sacred Practices and Beliefs

Innovation

Competition and War

2 EXPLAINING IDEAS Consider how the farming practices of the Maya were linked to their culture. What role did corn play in their sacred beliefs?

_____

_____

3 CITING TEXT EVIDENCE Use the chart to give examples of projects the Inca began in order to improve Inca society.

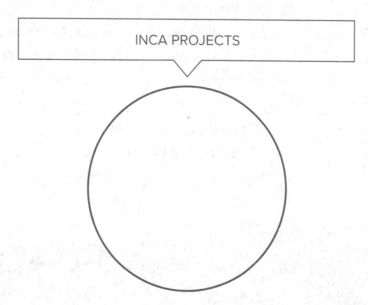

INCA PROJECTS

4 SUMMARIZING Use the chart to identify where each of the groups listed lived.

North American Peoples	
Inuit	
Tlingit	
Haida	
Chinook	
Chumash	
Pomo	
Zuni	

Nazca Pottery

DIRECTIONS: Examine the following image and answer the accompanying questions.

EXPLORE THE CONTEXT: This bowl is an example of Nazca pottery from the Andean region of present-day Peru. Early people in this region hunted animals and fished along the coast. Farming efforts in the inland region proved difficult due to dry, desert-like conditions. The Nazca created underground irrigation canals that enabled them to grow a variety of important staple crops such as corn, beans, and squash. Many of the colorful, painted decorations found on Nazca pottery reflect their growth as a civilization from farming. Rulers and common people alike used these ceramics bowls and vessels.

PRIMARY SOURCE: ARTIFACT

1 **ANALYZING** What do you think this piece of pottery was used for, based on its shape, size, and decoration?

_____

_____

_____

2 **DRAWING CONCLUSIONS** What does the decoration tell you about the Nazca?

_____

_____

_____

_____

3 **COMPARING** Compare the text information describing the Nazca pottery with this image. How does the image support what is said in the text?

_____

_____

_____

_____

4 **HISTORY** In what ways do you think the ability of the Nazca to create pottery reflects a complex society?

_____

_____

_____

_____

_____

A Conqueror's View of the Inca

VOCABULARY

quipu: the Inca system of counting by placing knots on lengths of rope or colored thread

Cuzco: a city situated in the Andean mountains of modern Peru that served as the center of the Inca Empire

fraud: deception

deceit: dishonesty

extent: size

allies: individuals associated by a common goal or purpose

provisions: supplies of food and resources

DIRECTIONS: Read the following excerpt and answer the accompanying questions.

EXPLORE THE CONTEXT: Pedro de Cieza de Léon was a Spanish conquistador who interviewed native people in the Andean region of what is now Peru. This excerpt gives us a view into the Inca system of record keeping and governance.

PRIMARY SOURCE: FIRST-HAND ACCOUNT

❝Soldiers, [I]n the time of the Kings Incas, orders were given through all the towns and provinces of Peru, that the principal lords and their lieutenants should take note, each year, of the men and women who had died, and also of the births. For as well for the assessment of tribute, as for calculating the number of men that could be called upon to serve as soldiers, and for the defence of the villages such information was needed. This was easily done, because each province, at the end of the year, was ordered to set down in the quipus, by means of the knots, all the men who had died in it during the year, as well as all who were born. In the beginning of the following year, the quipus were taken to Cuzco, where an account was made of the births and deaths throughout the empire. These returns were prepared with great care and accuracy, and without any fraud or deceit. When the returns had been made up, the lord and his officers knew what people were poor, the number of widows, whether they were able to pay tribute, how many men could be taken for soldiers and many other facts which were considered, among these people, to be of great importance. As this empire was of such vast extent, . . . there were a great number of storehouses for provisions and other necessaries for a campaign, and for the equipment of soldiers, if there was a war these great resources were used where the camps were formed, without touching the supplies of allies, or drawing upon the stores of different villages. If there was no war, all the great store of provisions was divided amongst the poor and the widows." **99**

—Pedro de Cieza de Léon, The Second Part of the Chronicle of Peru, 1540

1 **CITE TEXT EVIDENCE** What was the purpose of collecting information about the total number of births and deaths in each province and region?

_____

_____

_____

2 **DETERMINING MEANING** Examine how excess provisions were used by the Inca. How is the distribution of this resource important to understanding their culture?

_____

_____

_____

3 **CITING TEXT EVIDENCE** Which passage from Pedro de Cieza de Léon's account describes the Inca Empire as relying on a strong, central government? Underline the words he used.

_____

_____

4 HISTORY How does Pedro de Cieza de Léon's point of view affect the way that he describes the Inca system?

_____

_____

_____

_____

_____

ESSENTIAL QUESTION

What makes a culture unique?

1 Think About It

Review the Supporting Questions that you developed at the beginning of the chapter. Review the evidence that you gathered in this chapter. Were you able to answer each Supporting Question?

If there was not enough evidence to answer your Supporting Questions, what additional evidence do you think you need?

_____

_____

_____

_____

_____

2 Organize Your Evidence

Use a chart like the one below to organize the evidence you will use to support your position statement. You could also create a Web diagram with your position statement in the center and supporting evidence in the surrounding ovals.

Central and Supporting Ideas

➌ Write About It

A position statement related to the Essential Question should reflect your conclusion about the evidence. Write a position statement for the ESSENTIAL QUESTION: *What makes a culture unique?*

_____

_____

_____

_____

_____

➍ Connect to the Essential Question

On a separate piece of paper, create at least five good questions you would use if you were Pedro de Cieza de Léon interviewing someone who lived in the Inca Empire prior to the arrival of the Spanish. Questions might include why he or she settled where they did, what the advantages and disadvantages were, how he or she needed to adapt to the environment, or other similar questions.

Using the Essential Question as a guide, write an "interview" in which you answer the questions as an early Inca might have.

CITIZENSHIP
TAKING ACTION

MAKING CONNECTIONS Think about the ways that natural resources affect your home, family, and community. How do the use and conservation of natural resources affect the way you live?

DIRECTIONS: Working with a partner or a small group, think of a resource in your community that you believe is being wasted or that could be used more wisely. Collaborate with your partner or group to think of changes that could be made to help solve the problem. Then create a social media campaign to inform the public about the problem and to promote your solution.

_____

_____

_____

_____

_____

_____

_____

_____

_____

_____

_____

_____

_____

Imperial China

ESSENTIAL QUESTION

How do new ideas change the way people live?

Think about how this question might relate to the way people lived in Imperial China.

TALK ABOUT IT

Discuss with a partner what type of information you would need to know to answer this question. For example, one question might be: How did Imperial Chinese leaders react to the scientific and cultural progress happening around the world?

DIRECTIONS: Now write down three additional questions that would help you explain how new ideas changed the way of life for the people of Imperial China.

MY RESEARCH QUESTIONS

Supporting Question 1:

_____

_____

Supporting Question 2:

_____

_____

Supporting Question 3:

_____

_____

China Reunites

DIRECTIONS: Search for evidence in Lesson 1 to help you answer the following questions.

1 **IDENTIFYING CAUSE AND EFFECT** Use the cause-and-effect chart to list the factors that led to the major public works of the Sui dynasty, as well as the results of those projects.

Cause	Effect

ESSENTIAL QUESTION

How do new ideas change the way people live?

As you gather evidence to answer the Essential Question, think about:

- how traders and missionaries from other places change the way people think, worship, and live.
- how travel to faraway lands helps influence the way people live.

My Notes

2 **CONTRASTING** How did the Tang dynasty and the Song dynasty differ?

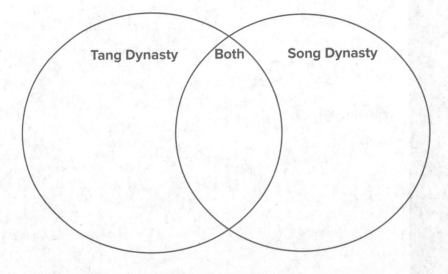

Tang Dynasty   Both   Song Dynasty

3 ANALYZING Confucianism and Buddhism both flourished during the Tang and Song dynasties. What evidence from the text helps explain the growth of these belief systems?

_____

_____

_____

_____

_____

_____

_____

_____

_____

_____

4 IDENTIFYING PERSPECTIVES Was the return of the civil service exam good or bad? Complete the chart below using information from the text.

Civil Service Exam Pro	Civil Service Exam Con

Tang Dynasty Artifact

DIRECTIONS: Examine the image below and answer the accompanying questions.

EXPLORE THE CONTEXT: The artifact shown in this image comes from the Tang dynasty, which was in power between 600 and 900 C.E. It is made of silver and hammered with a decoration. Its intricate pattern and fine craftsmanship indicate that it was probably an expensive tool used by a successful tradesperson. Trade grew during the rule of the Tang dynasty. The emperors restored the Silk Road, which allowed people to travel to other lands and learn about the way of life in other countries.

PRIMARY SOURCE: ARTIFACT

1 GEOGRAPHY What does this artifact tell us about the natural resources available in China during the Tang dynasty?

_____

_____

_____

_____

2 **HISTORICAL CONTEXT** How might the tool in the image be used? What does that tell you about the culture from which it came?

_____

_____

_____

_____

3 **HISTORICAL INFERENCE** What can you infer about the person who designed the tool? How does that help you understand the culture?

_____

_____

_____

_____

4 **DRAWING CONCLUSIONS** What can you conclude about the tool from the fact that it is preserved in a museum?

_____

_____

_____

_____

_____

A Buddhist Bible

ESSENTIAL QUESTION

How do new ideas change the way people live?

DIRECTIONS: Read the passage and answer the accompanying questions.

EXPLORE THE CONTEXT: The translator of the book titled *A Buddhist Bible,* Dwight Goddard, learned about Buddhism when he was 67 years old. He traveled to Asia and collected many texts about the religion, including both primary and secondary sources. He was fascinated by Buddhism and helped bring a greater understanding of it to the United States and elsewhere by translating these works into English.

VOCABULARY

Dharma: the teaching of the Buddha
non-dual: oneness or not separated

PRIMARY SOURCE: BOOK EXCERPT

"Under all circumstances you should free yourselves from attachment to objects; toward them your attitude should be neutral and indifferent. Let neither success nor failure, neither profit nor loss, worry you. Be ever calm and serene, modest and helpful, simple and dispassionate. The Dharma is non-dual as is the mind also. The Path is pure and above all 'form.' You are especially warned not to let the exercise for concentration of mind, fall into mere quiet thinking or into an effort to keep the mind in a blank state. The mind is by nature pure, there is nothing for us to crave or give up. "

— from *A Buddhist Bible,* Translated in 1932

1 HISTORY What type of document is this? How might it have been helpful to the people reading it?

_____

_____

_____

_____

2 **EXPLAINING IDEAS** What instructions does the passage offer as a way of life?

_____

_____

_____

_____

_____

_____

3 **HISTORY** What was happening in China during the rise of Buddhism that could have made its message especially important to the Chinese people?

_____

_____

_____

_____

_____

_____

_____

_____

4 **ECONOMICS** The text says that the reader should "free yourselves from attachment to objects." What economic impact would this have for its followers?

_____

_____

_____

_____

_____

Chinese Society

DIRECTIONS: Search for evidence in Lesson 2 to help you answer the following questions.

ESSENTIAL QUESTION

How do new ideas change the way people live?

As you gather evidence to answer the Essential Question, think about:

- how farm improvements affected the way people lived.
- how artistic expression changed the way people live.

My Notes

_____

_____

_____

_____

_____

_____

_____

_____

_____

1 ECONOMICS Some of the goods produced by Chinese tradespeople were traded all over the world. What were the characteristics of silk and porcelain that made them so economically valuable?

_____

_____

_____

_____

2 EXPLAINING EFFECTS Using the graphic organizer below, take notes on the effects of Chinese advancements. Use details from the book to complete the second column.

Advancement	Effect of Advancement
Irrigation Methods	
Coal and Steel	
Printing	
Gunpowder	
Ships	

3 HISTORY The printing press brought an age of literature to China. What did Chinese poetry reveal about the interests of the culture?

_____

_____

_____

_____

_____

_____

_____

_____

_____

_____

4 **ANALYZING** How did the Chinese style of landscape painting reveal the spiritual beliefs of the artists?

_____

_____

_____

_____

_____

_____

_____

_____

_____

_____

_____

Paper Artifact

*How do new ideas change
the way people live?*

DIRECTIONS: Study the following image and answer the
accompanying questions.

EXPLORE THE CONTEXT: The image shows a playing card
from early China's history. It was printed on paper using a
woodcut stamp, c. 1400 C.E.

PRIMARY SOURCE: ARTIFACT

1 HISTORY What type of artifact is this? What does the artifact suggest about the culture in which it was made?

_____

_____

_____

_____

2 **DETERMINING CONTEXT** What events in China's history help us understand this artifact?

_____

_____

_____

_____

_____

3 **ANALYZING SOURCES** Look closely at the artifact. What details are important in helping us understand it?

_____

_____

_____

_____

4 **CONNECT TO TODAY** What do the printed materials we use today tell about our modern culture?

_____

_____

_____

_____

_____

Xuanzang on Life in Magadha

DIRECTIONS: Study the following excerpt and answer the accompanying questions.

EXPLORE THE CONTEXT: Xuanzang [SHEE·AN·ZANG] was born during the Tang dynasty and studied Confucius as a young man. He grew interested in Buddhism and took a 16-year journey to India, traveling along the Silk Road. He wrote about what he learned and the places he saw in his book *Records of the Western Regions of the Great Tang Dynasty*. In this excerpt, he describes Magadha [MAH·guh·dah], a kingdom in northern India where the Buddha spent many years and where he achieved enlightenment.

ESSENTIAL QUESTION

How do new ideas change the way people live?

VOCABULARY

li: the Chinese mile; one *li* measures 1,640 feet

PRIMARY SOURCE: BOOK EXCERPT

"The country of Magadha is about 5000 li in circuit. The walled cities have but few inhabitants, but the towns are thickly populated. The soil is rich and fertile and the grain cultivation abundant. There is an unusual sort of rice grown here, the grains of which are large and scented and of an exquisite taste. It is specially remarkable for its shining colour. It is commonly called "the rice for the use of the great." As the ground is low and damp, the inhabited towns are built on the high uplands. After the first month of summer and before the second month of autumn, the level country is flooded, and communication can be kept up by boats. The manners of the people are simple and honest. The temperature is pleasantly hot; they esteem very much the pursuit of learning and profoundly respect the religion of Buddha. "

— Xuanzang, *Records of the Western Regions of the Great Tang Dynasty (Book Six)*, 629 C.E.

1 **DETERMINING CONTEXT** What information does Xuanzang record in his entry about Magadha?

_____

_____

_____

2 **ANALYZING POINTS OF VIEW** How does Xuanzang approach the people and culture of Magadha? What is his point of view about them?

_____

_____

3 **DRAWING CONCLUSIONS** Read Xuanzang's description of the rice product of Magadha. What conclusions can you draw about the author and the culture he is from?

_____

_____

_____

_____

4 **HISTORY** Based on the description of Magadha, what can you tell about the city in addition to the details that Xuanzang includes? Use evidence from the passage to support your answer.

_____

_____

_____

5 **IDENTIFYING EFFECTS** What effect do you think the details about Magadha would have on Xuanzang's readers after his return to China?

_____

_____

_____

ESSENTIAL QUESTION

How do new ideas change the way people live?

As you gather evidence to answer the Essential Question, think about:

- how the Mongol people affected the culture of China.
- how the strong Mongol leaders brought new ideas to Asia.
- how trade with faraway lands brought new ideas to China.

My Notes

The Mongols in China

DIRECTIONS: Search for evidence in Lesson 3 to help you answer the following questions.

1 **SEQUENCING** Use the text and the time line organizer below to record how the Mongol Empire grew and changed between 1200 and 1300.

1206:
1227:
1258:
1260:
1279:
1294:

2 **ANALYZING ISSUES** The Mongols damaged the land they conquered and destroyed many cities and towns. Yet they also brought stability. Analyze whether the Mongols were good or bad for China.

Positive	Negative

3 HISTORY How did the journey of Marco Polo bridge the cultural differences between east and west?

_____

_____

_____

_____

_____

_____

*How do new ideas change
the way people live?*

Artifacts from the Mongols

DIRECTIONS: Study the following image and answer the
accompanying questions.

EXPLORE THE CONTEXT: By the mid-1300s, the Mongols
ruled a vast empire of the Yuan dynasty. During that time,
China reached the height of its wealth and power. The
artifacts in this image represent some of the earliest tools
that Mongols created from bronze centuries before. They
are likely tools that helped people feed themselves.

PRIMARY SOURCE: ARTIFACTS

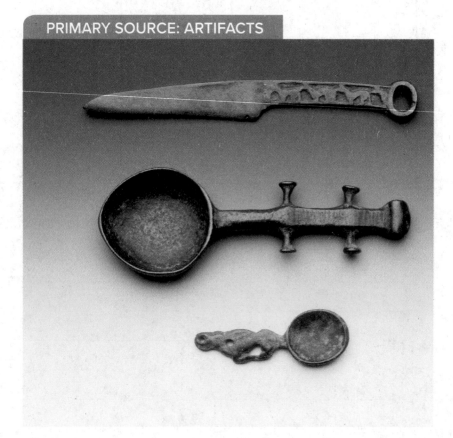

1 **DESCRIBING** Describe the tools shown in the image. Look for detail on the handles.

_____

_____

_____

_____

_____

2 **HISTORICAL INFERENCE** These artifacts were found in China. What can you infer about the area from these artifacts?

_____

_____

_____

_____

_____

3 **HISTORICAL CONTEXT** What do these artifacts tell you about the people who created them?

_____

_____

_____

_____

_____

4 **CONNECT TO TODAY** What instruments or tools from today are similar to the ones in this picture?

_____

_____

_____

_____

_____

Genghis Khan

Copyright © McGraw-Hill Education   TTEXT: Abbott, Jacob. 1901. Genghis Khan. Makers of History. New York and London: Harper & Brothers Publishers.

ESSENTIAL QUESTION

How do new ideas change the way people live?

VOCABULARY

inauguration: the act of placing someone in an official job

nominally: in name only

Tartars: nomadic people of northeastern Mongolia

pastoral: related to grazing sheep or cattle

grandeur: greatness

confined: limited

toil: hard work

roam: wander, travel

DIRECTIONS: Study the following passage and answer the accompanying questions.

EXPLORE THE CONTEXT: In the early 1800s, Jacob Abbot wrote a history of Genghis Khan. Abbot is known as an American children's book writer. The history of Genghis Khan is part of the *Makers of History* series.

SECONDARY SOURCE: BOOK EXCERPT

❝After the ceremonies of the inauguration were concluded, Genghis Khan returned, with the officers of his court and his immediate followers, to Karakorom. This town, though nominally the capital of the empire, was, after all, quite an insignificant place. . . .

The Monguls and Tartars led almost exclusively a wandering and pastoral life, and all their ideas of wealth and grandeur were associated with great flocks and herds of cattle, and handsome tents, and long trains of wagons loaded with stores of clothing, arms, and other movables, and vast encampments in the neighborhood of rich and extended pasture-grounds. Those who lived permanently in fixed houses they looked down upon as an inferior class, confined to one spot by their poverty or their toil, while they themselves could roam at liberty with their flocks.❞

— from *Genghis Khan, Makers of History,* 1901

1 **ASSESSING CREDIBILITY** Who wrote the passage? What was his occupation and background? How does this information help you understand the document?

_____

_____

_____

_____

_____

2 **COMPARING** What comparison(s) did the author make regarding the way of life of the Mongols?

_____

_____

_____

_____

_____

3 **DRAWING CONCLUSIONS** What can you conclude about the author's view of the Mongols ruled by Genghis Khan?

_____

_____

_____

_____

_____

4 **DESCRIBING** What details are important in understanding the Mongol culture?

_____

_____

_____

_____

_____

The Ming Dynasty

DIRECTIONS: Search for evidence in Lesson 4 to help you answer the following questions.

ESSENTIAL QUESTION

How do new ideas change the way people live?

As you gather evidence to answer the Essential Question, think about:

- how weak leaders and corruption ended Mongol rule.
- how the Ming dynasty restored peace and security.
- the impact of exploration on the ideas that entered China.

My Notes

1 **ANALYZING** Use the web below to take notes as you read the chapter about the Ming dynasty. Record the ways that the Ming emperors changed how people lived.

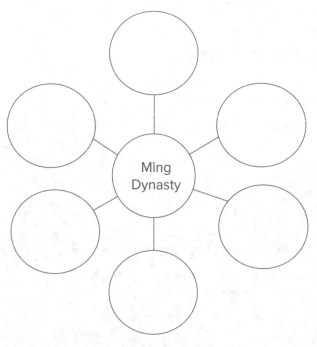

2 **SUMMARIZING** Summarize the details from your textbook to explain how the Ming gradually opened up China to Europeans and outside cultures.

3 RELATING EVENTS Use the chart below to integrate the information in the chapter about Zheng He and his travels.

Who was Zheng He?	
What did he do on his travels?	
When did he travel?	
Where did he go?	
Why did Chinese officials object to the travels?	
How did Zheng He travel?	

The Ming Census

ESSENTIAL QUESTION

How do new ideas change the way people live?

VOCABULARY

Revenue: income, usually taxes
secured: acquired
falsification: misrepresentation, deception

DIRECTIONS: Study the following excerpt and answer the accompanying questions.

EXPLORE THE CONTEXT: The Ming dynasty conducted a census of its subjects in order to help the government collect taxes. The Chinese historian Ping-ti Ho studied that process and the information collected. This passage translates instructions from the Ming Census.

PRIMARY SOURCE: BOOK EXCERPT

66 The officials of the Board of Revenue will take notice that although the country is now at peace the government has not yet secured accurate information about the population . . . The number of persons of each household must all be written down without falsification. Since my powerful troops are no longer going out on campaigns, they are to be sent to every county, in order to make a household-to-household check of the returns. If it is discovered in the course of checking that some local officials have falsified the returns, those officials are to be decapitated. Any common people who hide from the census will be punished according to the law and will be drafted into the army. 99

— Ping-ti Ho, *Studies on the Population of China, 1368–1953*

1 **ANALYZING SOURCES** What type of document is this? How does that help you understand the passage?

_____

_____

_____

_____

2 **EXPLAINING** What instructions does the emperor give in this passage?

_____

_____

_____

_____

_____

_____

_____

3 CIVICS What aspects of civil society during the Ming dynasty are evident in this passage?

_____

_____

_____

_____

_____

_____

4 **DETERMINING CONTEXT** What important events were happening at the time this document was created? How does that help us understand the purpose of the document?

_____

_____

_____

_____

_____

_____

_____

_____

Zheng He's Junks

DIRECTIONS: Study the following image and answer the accompanying questions.

EXPLORE THE CONTEXT: Zheng He's explorations in the early 1400s used about 300 ships and collected many goods, including animals, foods, and drinks foreign to China. These goods were collected on junks, or ships, such as this full-size replica and carried back to China.

PRIMARY SOURCE: ARTIFACT

1 HISTORY Based on its appearance, how do you think this structure was used? Why was it preserved?

_____

_____

_____

_____

_____

2 ECONOMICS What can you tell about the economy of the Ming dynasty from the source?

_____

_____

_____

_____

3 DETERMINING CONTEXT What do you know about the end of Zheng He's expedition that helps you understand this source?

_____

_____

_____

_____

4 INFERRING What inference can you make about the person or people who built this ship?

_____

_____

_____

_____

_____

ESSENTIAL QUESTION

How do new ideas change the way people live?

1 Think About It

Review the supporting questions you developed at the opening of the chapter. Review the evidence you found in this chapter. Were you able to answer each of your Supporting Questions?

If you didn't find enough evidence to answer your Supporting Questions, what do you think you need to consider?

_____

_____

_____

_____

2 Organize Your Evidence

Use a web like the one below to organize the evidence you will use to support your position statement.

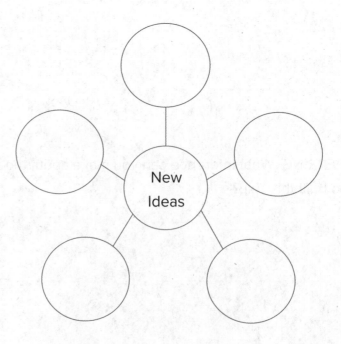

3 Talk About It

Discuss the evidence you have gathered with a small group or partner. Check your group's understanding of how ideas change the way people live, and answer any questions members may have. Consider any additional advice or input they may have.

4 Connect to the Essential Question

On a separate piece of paper, choose one invention or idea that emerged from early Chinese culture. Write a magazine article about how that invention or idea influenced the way people lived. Your article should give one example of how the ESSENTIAL QUESTION might be answered: *How do new ideas change the way people live?*

TAKING ACTION

MAKE CONNECTIONS At several points throughout Chinese history, emperors recruited workers to government jobs through a civil service exam. Young men (women were excluded from these jobs) would study for many years for the exam. They would memorize the works of Confucius and work closely with tutors to prepare for the test, which was designed to be very difficult. Just one out of five students passed it. Those who did pass were on a path to a comfortable and prestigious career helping to run the government. Those who failed might be able to work as a clerk or in a small office.

DIRECTIONS: Suppose that government jobs in the United States were the most prestigious jobs available. Consider what kind of test might be used to decide whether a person should be offered a government job. Work with a group of classmates to create an outline and four sample questions for an American civil service test that could be used today. Use what you know about the ideas that change the way people live to help you decide on the topics for the test. Would you test on math? History? Geography? Reading interpretation? Writing ability? Ethics? Combine the questions from every student in your class into a single test. Then, as a class, take the test, and decide whether it would result in the strongest civil servants.

Civilizations of Korea, Japan, and Southeast Asia

ESSENTIAL QUESTION

How do new ideas change the way people live?

Think about how this question might relate to the early civilizations of Korea, Japan, and Southeast Asia. What new ideas came about in government, warfare, and culture? How did these ideas affect people living in these societies?

COLLABORATE

TALK ABOUT IT

Discuss with a partner the type of information you would need to know to answer these questions. For example, one question might be: Do you recall or know any of the new ideas that came about during this time period in Asia?

DIRECTIONS: Now write down three additional questions that you need to answer to be able to explain how new ideas changed the way people lived.

MY RESEARCH QUESTIONS

Supporting Question 1:

_____

_____

Supporting Question 2:

_____

_____

Supporting Question 3:

_____

_____

Korea: History and Culture

DIRECTIONS: Search for evidence in Lesson 1 to help you answer the following questions.

ESSENTIAL QUESTION

How do new ideas change the way people live?

As you gather evidence to answer the Essential Question, think about:

- ideas from other countries that influenced Korean society.
- how new ideas changed Korean government, religion, system of writing, and culture.

1 **IDENTIFYING** From where did the early Korean kingdoms get their writing system?

_____

_____

2 HISTORY Whom did the three early Korean kingdoms model their governments after?

_____

_____

_____

3 GEOGRAPHY Why do you think Korean culture was influenced by China and Japan?

_____

_____

_____

_____

4 **SUMMARIZING** Use the graphic organizer below to list ideas that developed in Korea and their origins.

Ideas from Chinese Culture	Ideas Unique to Korea	Ideas from Japanese Culture

My Notes

_____

_____

_____

_____

_____

_____

_____

5 IDENTIFYING CAUSE AND EFFECT How did Korea transition from three kingdoms to one under the Koryo dynasty?

_____

_____

6 DESCRIBING What new ideas emerged during the Yi dynasty?

_____

_____

_____

_____

7 SUMMARIZING Complete the following chart.

Individual	Contribution to Korean Culture or Government
Wang Kon	
Yi Song-gye	
Sejong	
Yi-sun Shin	

Statue of the Buddha

DIRECTIONS: Examine the image below and answer the accompanying questions.

EXPLORE THE CONTEXT: This photograph shows a large Buddha statue from the Koryo dynasty c. 900 C.E. Buddhism arrived on the Korean peninsula in the fourth century, about five hundred years before the founding of the Koryo dynasty.

PRIMARY SOURCE: STATUE

1 **IDENTIFYING** What materials were used to make this statue? Why is this significant?

_____

_____

_____

_____

2 **ANALYZING** What does Buddha's posture in the statue suggest?

_____

_____

_____

_____

_____

_____

3 **HISTORY** Who was ruling Korea at the time this statue was built? What can you infer about their policies on religion from this image?

_____

_____

_____

_____

_____

4 **GEOGRAPHY** From where did the ideas represented by this statue come?

_____

_____

_____

_____

_____

5 **DRAWING CONCLUSIONS** What does this statue tell you about how new ideas changed the way Koreans lived?

_____

_____

_____

_____

_____

_____

ESSENTIAL QUESTION

How do new ideas change the way people live?

VOCABULARY

Monarch: king
adduce: offer or put forth
approprieties: qualities that are suitable or proper
reverentially: in a humble and respectful way

proclaim: announce
enact: make to be law
transmit: communicate
isolated: cut off or separate

Chŏng Inji on the Development of the Korean Alphabet

DIRECTIONS: Read the following excerpt and answer the accompanying questions.

EXPLORE THE CONTEXT: One of the greatest kings during the Yi dynasty in Korea was named Sejong. He was interested in scientific research, innovation, and spreading literacy. During his reign, Koreans used thousands of Chinese characters to read and write, so to simplify the writing system, he developed a phonetic alphabet called *hangul*. Chŏng Inji, one of the finest scholars of his day and an adviser to Sejong, wrote the following about the invention of the Korean alphabet.

SECONDARY SOURCE: BOOK

“In the winter of the year kye-hae (1443–1444), Our Monarch originated and designed the twenty-eight letters of the Correct Sounds, and he adduced in outline examples and approprieties by which to demonstrate them. He named them 'The Correct Sounds for the Instruction of the People.' . . . We note reverentially that under our Monarch, with his Heaven-loosed wisdom, the codes and measures that have been proclaimed and enacted exceed and excel those of a hundred kings. The making of the correct sounds is not something that has been transmitted by our ancestors; they have been perfected out of nature itself. Now since there is no place where the all-reaching Pattern is not found, this is certainly not a man-made, isolated thing.”

— From *The Korean Alphabet: Its History and Structure*

1 `HISTORY` What was Chŏng Inji's purpose in writing about the creation of the alphabet?

_____

_____

_____

_____

2 **ANALYZING** How do you think creating a new alphabet helped spread literacy in Korea?

_____

_____

_____

_____

3 **CITING TEXT EVIDENCE** From where does Chŏng Inji believe Sejong came up with the structure for the Korean alphabet? What evidence can you cite from the excerpt?

_____

_____

_____

_____

4 **MAKING CONNECTIONS** If each word in English had its own symbol, how many symbols do you think you would need to learn to be literate?

_____

_____

_____

_____

ESSENTIAL QUESTION

How do new ideas change the way people live?

As you gather evidence to answer the Essential Question, think about:

- the origins of Japan's different systems of government and how they influenced life for the Japanese people.

- how different religions and belief systems, such as Shinto, animism, and Buddhism, changed or flourished under different rulers.

My Notes

Early Japan

DIRECTIONS: Search for evidence in Lesson 2 to help you answer the following questions.

1 GEOGRAPHY Why did Japan develop a strongly independent civilization?

_____

_____

_____

_____

2 SUMMARIZING Complete the table with details about what characterized the following different periods of rule in early Japan.

The Yamato

Prince Shotoku

The Nara Period

3 **DESCRIBING** From where did early Japanese emperors claim their authority to rule?

_____

_____

_____

4 **MAKING CONNECTIONS** How does the practice of animism still influence Japanese culture today?

_____

_____

_____

5 CIVICS Why did Prince Shotoku create a constitution? On what did he base his ideas for some of the specific rules of the constitution?

_____

_____

6 **DETERMINING CENTRAL IDEAS** Fill in the graphic organizer with specific details of the following elements of life in early Japan.

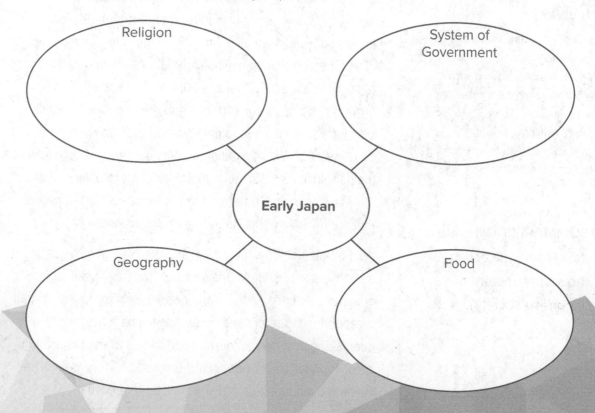

The Reform Edict of Taika

ESSENTIAL QUESTION

How do new ideas change the way people live?

DIRECTIONS: Read the following excerpt and answer the accompanying questions.

EXPLORE THE CONTEXT: Early Japan was divided by clans and ruled by emperors who believed they received the right to rule from heaven. Around 600 C.E., Prince Shotoku created the first constitution. After his death, the ruling Yamato clan enacted the Taika, or Great Change. These changes were decreed in the Reform Edict of Taika. The edict was written by two princes, one who later ruled as Emperor Tenchi. Japan was divided into districts that reported to the emperor and began to pay taxes to government officials. These changes created Japan's first strong central government.

PRIMARY SOURCE: IMPERIAL EDICT

❝I. Let the following be abolished: the titles held by imperial princes to serfs granted by imperial decrees (*koshiro*); the titles to lands held directly by the imperial court (*miyake*); and private titles to lands and workers held by ministers and functionaries (*omi*, *muraji*, and *tomo no miyatsuko*) of the court, by local nobles (*kuni no miyatsuko*), and by village chiefs (*mura no obito*). In lieu thereof, sustenance households shall be granted to those of the rank of Daibu (Chief of a bureau or of a ward) and upwards on a scale corresponding to their positions. Cloth and silk stuffs shall be given to the lower officials and people, varying in value. It is said that the duty of the Daibu is to govern the people. If they discharge their task diligently, the people will have trust in them. Therefore it is for the benefit of the people that the revenue of the Daibu shall be increased.

"II. For the first time, the capital shall be placed under an administrative system. In the metropolitan (or capital) region, governors (*kuni no tsukasa*) and prefects (*kori no tsukasa*) shall be appointed. Barriers and outposts shall be erected, and guards and post horses for transportation and communication purposes shall be provided. Furthermore, bell-tokens shall be made and mountains and rivers shall be regulated . . . The

VOCABULARY

administrative: governing or managing
outpost: military station
allocation: division or sharing out
redistribution: giving out in a new way
alderman: member of a local ruling body
cultivation: farming
prevention: action that stops something
requisition: demand for something

1 SUMMARIZING How did the reform edict change the main structure of Japanese society?

_____

_____

_____

metropolitan region shall include the area from the Yokogawa (river) in Nahari on the east, from (mount) Senoyama in Kii on the south, from Kushibuchi in Akashi on the west, and from (mount) Afusakayama in Sasanami in Omi on the north . . .

"III. It is hereby decreed that household registers, tax registers, and rules for allocation and redistribution of the land shall be established. Each fifty households shall be constituted into a village (*ri*), and in each village there shall be appointed an alderman. He shall be responsible for the maintenance of the household registers, the assigning of the sowing of crops and the cultivation of mulberry trees, the prevention of offenses, and the requisitioning of taxes and forced labor. All rice-fields shall be measured by a unit called a tan which is thirty paces in length by twelve paces in breadth. Ten tan make one cho. For each tan, the tax (*so* or *denso*) shall be two sheaves and two bundles of rice; for each cho, the tax shall be twenty-two sheaves of rice. "

— written by Prince Naka-no-ōe and Nakatomi-no Kamatari

2 DESCRIBING According to the edict, what was the duty of the Daibu, and how did they increase their earnings?

_____

_____

3 ANALYZING Why did Emperor Tenchi enact the Reform of Taika?

_____

4 MAKING CONNECTIONS What were the benefits and drawbacks of having a strong central government?

_____

_____

5 GEOGRAPHY How did the new central government mark the boundaries of the metropolitan region?

_____

The Kondei System

How do new ideas change the way people live?

DIRECTIONS: Read the following excerpt and answer the accompanying questions.

EXPLORE THE CONTEXT: In ancient Japan, the central government's military was usually made up of conscripted peasants required to serve as part of a labor obligation to the state. Emperor Kammu, who ruled from 782–806 C.E., questioned the effectiveness of a military made up of unorganized men from the countryside. In 792 C.E., Kammu decreed a series of military reforms including the Kondei System, sometimes translated as "stalwart youth" or "able-bodied young men."

PRIMARY SOURCE: IMPERIAL DECLARATION

"An Official Order of the Council of State on the matter relating to the recruitment of the kondei (physically able). Thirty people from the province of Yamato. Thirty people from the province of Kawachi. Twenty people from the province of Izumi.

1. . . . Previously [on the seventh day of this month], the Minister of the Right [Fujiwara Tsugunawa] declared that in obedience to the imperial command [all military divisions consisting of] conscript soldiers stationed in the provinces should be abolished with the exception of those in the important border areas. The munitions depots, outposts, and governmental offices which were previously defended by them should be defended by the kondei to be sent to those positions. We now order that you select those physically able from among the sons of the district chiefs (*kōri no tsukasa*), and place them to serve on these posts on a rotating basis.

Eleventh year of Enryaku (792), sixth month, 14th day."

VOCABULARY

official: formal, approved by government
council: people running local government
recruitment: enrolling into an army
conscripted: drafted, enlisted
munitions depots: places where arms are stored

1 **COMPARING** What does Emperor Kammu's decree have in common with the Reform Edict of Taika?

_____

_____

_____

2 **ANALYZING** How did the Reform Edict of Taika prepare the way for the Kondei System?

_____

_____

_____

_____

3 **IDENTIFYING** What is a draft? How was it changed by this official order?

_____

_____

_____

_____

4 **MAKING CONNECTIONS** Compare and contrast the system for recruiting soldiers under the Kondei System with the system used in the United States today.

_____

_____

_____

_____

Medieval Japan

DIRECTIONS: Search for evidence in Lesson 3 to help you answer the following questions.

ESSENTIAL QUESTION

How do new ideas change the way people live?

As you gather evidence to answer the Essential Question, think about:

- new ideas in Japanese culture and the different groups who contributed them.
- how Japanese culture is still influenced by beliefs and practices begun during the medieval period.

My Notes

_____

_____

_____

_____

_____

_____

_____

_____

1 **SUMMARIZING** What caused Japanese emperors to slowly lose power and influence?

_____

_____

2A **DETERMINING THE CENTRAL IDEA** Fill in the graphic organizer with specific details about the samurai.

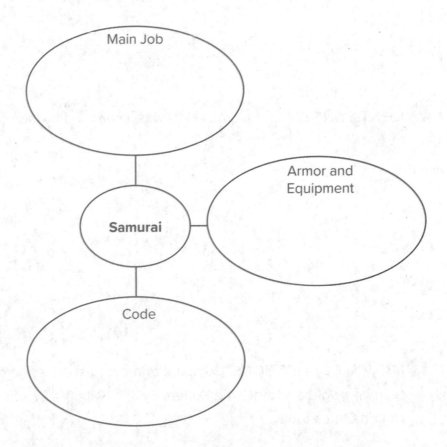

2B **ANALYZING** Why were the shoguns created?

_____

_____

_____

3 **ANALYZING** How did the creation of the position of shogun change the central government of Japan?

_____

_____

_____

4 **DESCRIBING** Who benefited the most from Japan's prosperity under the Ashikaga Shogunate?

_____

_____

5 **DESCRIBING** How is Shinto different from Buddhism?

_____

_____

6 **SUMMARIZING** Use the graphic organizer to list the main products or duties of the following roles in shogunate Japan.

Farmers	Artisans
Women	Writers
Architect Artisans	Creative Artisans

Samurai and Daimyo

DIRECTIONS: Examine the image below and answer the accompanying questions.

EXPLORE THE CONTEXT: This photograph shows a man standing, facing right, and a man wearing a sword kneeling before him, facing left, holding another sword as though offering it to the man standing in front of him. It is believed to depict a samurai kneeling before a daimyo around 1877.

PRIMARY SOURCE: PHOTOGRAPH

1 **IDENTIFYING** What was the role of a daimyo?

_____

_____

_____

_____

_____

2 CIVICS What was the likely relationship between the samurai and the daimyo depicted in this photograph? How is this relationship illustrated in the photograph?

_____

_____

_____

_____

_____

_____

3 **DESCRIBING** How did a samurai's loyalty to his daimyo change the way people lived in Japan?

_____

_____

_____

_____

_____

_____

4 **DETERMINING POINT OF VIEW** What do you think the photographer was trying to show by taking the picture of these two men in this position?

_____

_____

_____

_____

_____

_____

Hojo Shigetoki's Letter of Instruction to His Son Nagatoki

ESSENTIAL QUESTION

How do new ideas change the way people live?

DIRECTIONS: Read the excerpt below and answer the accompanying questions.

EXPLORE THE CONTEXT: Hojo Shigetoki was a leading samurai in Japan. In 1247, the Kamakura shoguns appointed his 18-year-old son to a key position. Shigetoki then wrote his son a letter instructing him in the ways of the warrior.

VOCABULARY

subordinates: those of lower rank
obvious: easy to see
distinction: difference
misdeeds: errors
circumstances: situations
provocation: baiting
haste: speed
remorse: regret, sorrow

PRIMARY SOURCE: LETTER

❝ . . . In dealing with subordinates do not make an obvious distinction between good and not-good. Use the same kind of language, give the same kind of treatment to all, and thus you will get the best out of the worst. But you yourself must not lose sight of the distinction between good character and bad character, between capable and incapable. You must be fair, but in practice you must not forget the difference between men who are useful and men who are not. Remember that the key to discipline is fair treatment in rewards and in punishments. But make allowances for minor misdeeds in young soldiers and others, if their conduct is usually good . . . Remember, however, that there are times when a commander must exercise his power of deciding questions of life or death. In those circumstances since human life is at stake you must give most careful thought to your action. Never kill or wound a man in anger, however great the provocation. Better get somebody else to administer the proper punishment. Decisions made in haste before your feelings are calm can only lead to remorse. Close your eyes and reflect carefully when you have a difficult decision to make. When accusations are brought to you, always remember that there must be another side to the question. Do not merely indulge in anger. To give fair decisions is the most important thing not only in commanding soldiers but also in governing a country. ❞

—Letter from Hojo Shigetoki to his son, Nagatoki, 1247

1 HISTORY How does this letter demonstrate aspects of the code of Bushido?

_____

_____

_____

_____

_____

_____

_____

2 **ANALYZING** What was Shigetoki's purpose in writing this letter? What do you think he meant by the phrase, "thus you will get the best out of the worst"?

_____

_____

_____

_____

_____

_____

_____

_____

3 **MAKING CONNECTIONS** If your parent or guardian were to write you a letter, what do you think he or she would say? What kind of a code do you think he or she would want you to live by?

_____

_____

_____

_____

_____

_____

_____

Southeast Asia: History and Culture

DIRECTIONS: Search for evidence in this lesson to help you answer the following questions.

ESSENTIAL QUESTION

What makes a culture unique?

As you gather evidence to answer the Essential Question, think about:

- how outside influences—particularly from China and India—affected the cultures of Southeast Asia.

- how geography helps shape the life and culture of a nation or region.

1 IDENTIFYING CONNECTIONS What are some of the main characteristics of Southeast Asia? Fill in the graphic organizer with your answers.

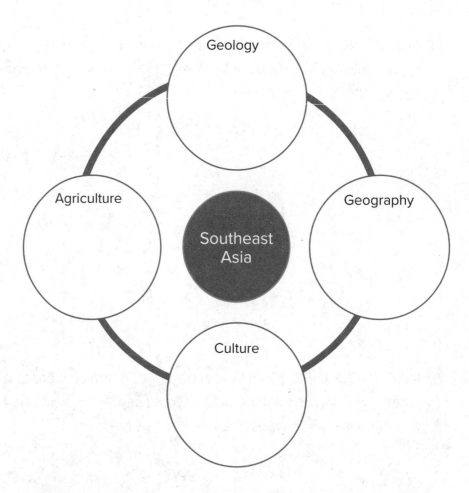

My Notes

_____

_____

_____

_____

_____

_____

_____

_____

_____

_____

_____

2 IDENTIFYING EFFECTS How did the arrival of Indian traders change the ancient culture of Southeast Asia?

_____

_____

3 **CONTRASTING** How were the ancient governments and religions of Vietnam and Cambodia different?

_____

_____

_____

_____

4 **DIFFERENTIATING** What were the different influences of China and India on Thailand?

_____

_____

_____

_____

5 **IDENTIFYING EFFECTS** What happened in the 1200s that weakened the culture of Burma?

_____

_____

6 **DESCRIBING** How do Malaysia and Indonesia differ geographically from the mainland nations of Southeast Asia?

_____

_____

_____

_____

7 **IDENTIFYING EFFECTS** What parts of Southeast Asia were the first to convert to Islam?

_____

_____

Description of Angkor Wat

ESSENTIAL QUESTION

What makes a culture unique?

DIRECTIONS: Study the excerpt below and answer the accompanying questions.

EXPLORE THE CONTEXT: Angkor Wat is one of the wonders of the world. The excerpt below discusses its origins and development. It also describes the uniqueness and beauty of Angkor Wat.

PRIMARY SOURCE: ARTICLE

" The 'temple which is a city,' or literally, 'city temple,' is the largest religious monument in the world. Including its moat and interior grounds, Angkor Wat covers almost 500 acres (203 ha). Though Suryavarman II (*r.* 1113–ca 1150) commissioned the temple at the beginning of his reign, it was not completed until after his death. . . . Since Suryavarman was a devotee of Vishnu, the temple likely was originally consecrated to him. Yet Angkor Wat derived its name from its conversion to a Buddhist sanctuary several hundred years later, after Theravada Buddhism became the established state religion. After the fall of Angkor in 1431, the city was abandoned as a capital, but Angkor Wat's grounds were continuously inhabited by Buddhist monks until the Khmer Rouge era.

. . . The temple only occupies a tenth of the area enclosed by the moat; the remaining land probably was occupied by the royal palace and other impermanent structures for the inhabitants of the capital city. Others believe Angkor Wat was more than just a temple to honor Vishnu and may have been built as a mausoleum or even a cosmic observatory. "

—Trevor Ranges, *Cambodia*, 2010

VOCABULARY

moat: a deep, wide trench, often filled with water, that surrounds and protects a castle

commissioned: ordered something to be made

devotee: an enthusiastic follower or supporter

consecrated: blessed and made sacred or holy

mausoleum: a building that contains tombs of the dead above ground

cosmic: relating to the universe

1 **CITING TEXT EVIDENCE** Why is Angkor Wat called a "city" according to the text?

_____

_____

2 **HISTORY** What can you conclude from the information in this article about how religious belief changed in Cambodia during this period? Cite information from the text about Angkor Wat to support your answer.

_____

_____

_____

_____

3 **INFERRING** What evidence stated in the text suggests that Cambodia might have been threatened by other empires or peoples in Southeast Asia?

_____

_____

_____

4 **EVALUATING TEXT EVIDENCE** What evidence stated in the text tells you that Angkor Wat was not just a temple but the seat of Cambodian government?

_____

_____

_____

_____

5 **IDENTIFYING PERSPECTIVES** What other function—aside from a temple—do some scientists think Angkor Wat might have had?

_____

_____

_____

The Tet Celebration

ESSENTIAL QUESTION
What makes a culture unique?

DIRECTIONS: Study the excerpt below and answer the accompanying questions.

EXPLORE THE CONTEXT: The festival of Tet is a feast celebrated every year by the people of Vietnam. The origins of the Tet festival are ancient, but the holiday reveals the cultural unity of the Vietnamese people.

SECONDARY SOURCE: BOOK

VOCABULARY

commemorating: marking the remembrance of something, as with a plaque or ceremony
lunar: referring to the moon
hearth: fireplace
carp: a type of freshwater fish

" The age-old customs and culture carried on by Vietnamese cooking are also reflected in the traditional holidays and festivals of Vietnam. . . . These events almost always include the preparation of special foods reflecting the nature of the occasion and the time of year. The most joyous and important of these celebrations is Tet Nguyen Dan (often simply called Tet), a festival commemorating the lunar new year and the birth of spring. . . .

. . . The beginning of the holiday season is marked by the departure of the Kitchen Gods. Vietnamese legends describe these three spirits as two men and a woman who watch over the hearth and home and observe all of the family's actions. On the twenty-third night of the twelfth lunar month, the Kitchen Gods leave earth—riding a horse . . . or a carp with golden scales—to report on the family's behavior during the past year. The family prepares special dishes and sends the gods on their way with a farewell feast in the hopes that their report will be a good one. "

—from *Cooking the Vietnamese Way* by Chi Nguyen and Judy Monroe, 2002

1 **CITING TEXT EVIDENCE** Which phrase in the text tells you that some Vietnamese cooking is based on ancient Vietnamese civilization?

_____

_____

2 **RELATING EVENTS** What does the festival of Tet commemorate or celebrate?

_____

_____

3 **ANALYZING INFORMATION** What information in the text seems to indicate that Tet is based on ancient religious beliefs and practices?

_____

_____

_____

4 **UNDERSTANDING CONTEXT** Why does the Vietnamese family prepare a feast for the Kitchen Gods during Tet? What is the feast intended to accomplish?

_____

_____

_____

_____

5 **HISTORY** Most Vietnamese today are Buddhists. Why do you think they still celebrate the ancient Kitchen Gods during the festival of Tet?

_____

_____

_____

_____

1 Think About It

ESSENTIAL QUESTION

How do new ideas change the way people live?

Review the Supporting Questions that you developed at the beginning of the chapter. Review the evidence that you gathered in this chapter. Were you able to answer each Supporting Question?

If there was not enough evidence to answer your Supporting Questions, what additional evidence do you think you need to consider?

2 Organize Your Evidence

Use a chart like the one below to organize the evidence you will use to support your position statement.

New Idea	Origin of the Idea	Influence on Korean, Japanese, or Southeast Asian Civilization	Source of Information to Cite as Evidence	How Evidence Helps Support My Position Statement

③ Write About It

A position statement related to the Essential Question should reflect your conclusion about the evidence. Write a position statement for the ESSENTIAL QUESTION: *How do new ideas change the way people live?*

_____

_____

_____

_____

_____

_____

_____

④ Talk About It

Work in a small group to present your position statement and evidence. Gather feedback from your classmates before you write your final conclusion. You may choose to refine your position statement after you have discussed it with your classmates. Group members should listen to one another's arguments, ask questions, and offer constructive advice about the statement.

⑤ Connect to the Essential Question

On a separate piece of paper, develop a written interview to answer the ESSENTIAL QUESTION: *How do new ideas change the way people live?* Choose one new idea that you learned about in this chapter and write an interview as if you were able to speak with someone who was involved in implementing the new idea. Through your interview, readers should be able to understand the idea and how it changed a specific society.

CITIZENSHIP
TAKING ACTION

MAKE CONNECTIONS New ideas often spread from culture to culture. Research some currently popular songs from Korea, Japan, or Southeast Asia. Do you see influences from other cultures in the song, or does the song influence other cultures?

DIRECTIONS: Popular music is often used to express people's feelings about their government and culture and to encourage people to take action. Choose an issue related to the chapter, such as styles of governance, warfare, class hierarchy, or geographical influence, and write your own song lyrics on that issue. Volunteers might want to perform their songs for the class.

CHAPTER
19

Medieval Europe

ESSENTIAL QUESTION

Why does conflict develop?

Think about how these questions might relate to the conflicts of the Middle Ages.

TALK ABOUT IT COLLABORATE

Discuss with a partner what type of information you would need to know to answer these questions. For example, one question might be: How were communities organized during the Middle Ages?

DIRECTIONS: Now write down three additional questions that would help you explain why conflict develops and how people act to create stability in their society.

MY RESEARCH QUESTIONS

Supporting Question 1:

_____

_____

Supporting Question 2:

_____

_____

Supporting Question 3:

_____

_____

The Early Middle Ages

DIRECTIONS: Search for evidence in Lesson 1 to help you answer the following questions.

ESSENTIAL QUESTION

Why does conflict develop?

As you gather evidence to answer the Essential Question, think about:

- the role that the Roman Catholic Church played in society.

- the way that cities and business leaders shaped the Middle Ages.

1 **GEOGRAPHY** Use the web organizer below to show how rivers and oceans influenced life in Europe.

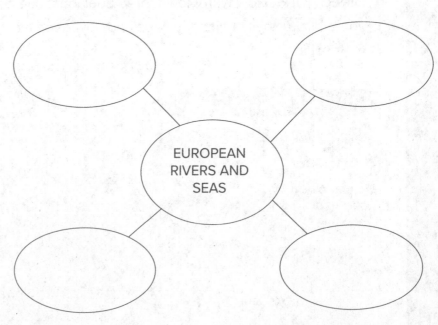

My Notes

2 **COMPARING AND CONTRASTING** How did the Franks differ from the Vikings?

_____

_____

_____

_____

_____

3 **IDENTIFYING CAUSE AND EFFECT** How did the growth of the communities of monks and nuns help spread Christianity?

_____

_____

_____

_____

4 **HISTORY** What was the conflict that led Pope Gregory VII to excommunicate the Holy Roman Emperor of Europe, Henry IV, and how was the conflict resolved?

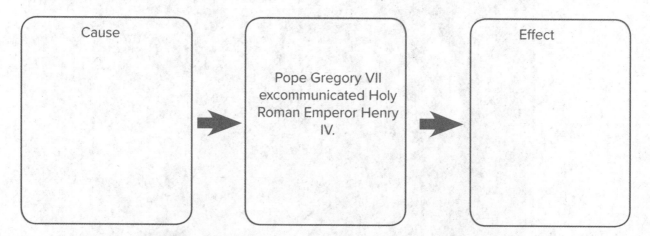

Cause → Pope Gregory VII excommunicated Holy Roman Emperor Henry IV. → Effect

Carolingian Denier

DIRECTIONS: Examine the image below and answer the accompanying questions.

EXPLORE THE CONTEXT: The coin in this image is called a denier. It is a French coin from the early 800s C.E. The denier was minted in silver rather than gold and is also known as the silver penny. The first deniers were minted in the 700s C.E. Some contained Charlemagne's image and title, while others contained images of other French leaders, temples, or religious symbols. Many coins were marked with letters that told where they were minted. For example, *C* stood for Cologne, *F* for Frankfurt, *M* for Mainz, and *V* for Worms.

PRIMARY SOURCE: MONEY

1 **EXPLORING CONTEXT** How do the letters on many deniers help you understand the society in which they were printed?

_____

_____

_____

_____

_____

2 **DETERMINING MEANING** Why might the detail of a temple or religious symbol be important on a coin of this period?

_____

_____

_____

_____

_____

3 **HISTORICAL INFERENCE** What inference can you make about a nation's ruler and land from a coin stamped with his image?

_____

_____

_____

_____

_____

4 **DRAWING CONCLUSIONS** What conclusions can you draw about a civilization that uses coins rather than a barter system for exchanging goods?

_____

_____

_____

_____

_____

The Oseberg Ship

DIRECTIONS: Look at the image and answer the accompanying questions.

EXPLORE THE CONTEXT: The oak vessel in this image is an actual Viking ship now displayed in a museum. It was used by the Vikings in the 700s to 800s C.E. The ship has oar holes for oarsmen so that it can be rowed. It also has a mast for a sail so that it can use wind power to navigate. The prows, or fronts, of many of these ships were carved with ornate decorations, one of the most common of which was a curled serpent. These beautiful carvings were likely the work of skilled artists, making them very expensive to create.

PRIMARY SOURCE: ARTIFACT

1 DETERMINING MEANING Who was the ship built for, and what evidence can you cite for your answer?

_____

_____

_____

_____

2 ANALYZING Why did the Vikings need to be able both to row and sail the ship? What evidence about their lifestyle and the geography of the region supports your answer?

_____

_____

_____

_____

_____

_____

3 IDENTIFYING CAUSE AND EFFECT What makes examples of these ships worthy of preservation to be in a museum?

_____

_____

_____

_____

4 GEOGRAPHY Based on the design and the size of the ship, what inference can you make about what the ship was used for?

_____

_____

_____

_____

ESSENTIAL QUESTION

Why does conflict develop?

As you gather evidence to answer the Essential Question, think about:

- the ties that bound a vassal to his lord.
- the people and workers who supported the operations of the manor or castle.
- the structures created by guilds in the cities and towns.

My Notes

_____

_____

_____

_____

_____

_____

_____

_____

_____

Feudalism and the Rise of Towns

DIRECTIONS: Search for evidence in Lesson 2 to help you complete the following items.

1 **COMPARE AND CONTRAST** Think about the differences between the manor and the cities. Consider how work life differed depending on where a person lived. Compare and contrast the work life of those living on a manor to the work life of people living in a town or city.

People Who Lived on a Manor	People in Towns and Cities

2 HISTORY What are the elements of a fief? Consider people, land, and jobs that make up a fief.

_____

_____

_____

_____

_____

3 **ANALYZING** Describe the lives of women in the feudal system. How did their role in society help create stability?

_____

_____

_____

_____

_____

Anglo-Saxon Early Law

DIRECTIONS: Study the following excerpt and answer the accompanying questions.

EXPLORE THE CONTEXT: This passage was written around the year 930 C.E. It comes from a collection of laws created by Anglo-Saxon government officials. These two paragraphs represent two of the laws that the people of England were required to follow.

VOCABULARY

Gemot: a meeting
Oferhyrnes: penalties for disobedience
Burh: a town or city
Both: debt
Burh-gemot: a town council meeting
Shire-gemot: a county meeting

PRIMARY SOURCE: EXTRACTS FROM EARLY LAWS OF THE ENGLISH

" If any one [when summoned] fail to attend the gemot thrice [three times], let him pay the king's 'oferhyrnes,' and let it be announced seven days before the gemot is to be. But if he will not do right, nor pay the 'oferhyrnes,' then let all the chief men belonging to the 'burh' ride to him, and take all that he has, and put him in 'both.' But if any one will not ride with his fellows, let him pay the king's 'oferhyrnes.' . . .

And let the hundred gemot be attended as it was before fixed; and thrice in the year let a burh-gemot be held; and twice, a shire-gemot; and let there be present the bishop of the shire and the ealdorman, and there both expound as well the law of God as the secular law from Select Charters and Other Illustrations of English Constitutional History from the Earliest Times to the Reign of Edward the First. "

—from *Select Charters and Other Illustrations of English Constitutional History from the Earliest Times to the Reign of Edward the First,* c. 930 C.E.

Copyright © McGraw-Hill Education   TEXT: Stubbs, William, comp. and ed. 1900. Select Charters, and Other Illustrations of English Constitutional History, from the Earliest Times to the Reign of Edward the First, 3rd ed. London: MacMillan and Co.

1 **ANALYZING SOURCES** What type of document is this? How does knowing this help you understand the document?

_____

_____

_____

_____

2 **IDENTIFYING EFFECTS** According to the law, what is the punishment for missing one of the king's meetings?

_____

_____

_____

_____

3 **HISTORY** What can you tell from the document about the system the king used to communicate with the people of his kingdom?

_____

_____

_____

_____

4 **EVALUATING EVIDENCE** What can you tell about civil society, or the relationship between government and citizens, from reading this document?

_____

_____

_____

_____

ESSENTIAL QUESTION
Why does conflict develop?

Richard of Ely on Tax Collection

DIRECTIONS: Study the following excerpt and answer the accompanying questions.

EXPLORE THE CONTEXT: Historians believe that this document was created in 1178. The author is Richard, son of Bishop Nigel of Ely. Both Richard and his father were important officials at the exchequer. Richard created the document as part of his work for the government. The "Conquest" he refers to is the conquest of England by William of Normandy in 1066 C.E. William is credited with introducing European feudalism to England.

SECONDARY SOURCE: BOOK

❝ VII. By whom, or for what purpose, the testing of silver was instituted.

In the primitive state of the kingdom after the Conquest, as we have learned from our fathers, not weights of gold or silver, but solely victuals were paid to the kings from their lands, from which the necessaries for the daily use of the royal household were furnished. And those who had been appointed for this purpose knew how much came from the separate estates. . . . This arrangement, however, continued during the whole time of King William I, and up to the time of King Henry, his son; so that I myself saw some people who had seen victuals carried at stated times from the estates of the crown to the court: and the officials of the royal household knew from which counties corn and from which different kinds of meat, or fodder for horses, or any other necessary things, were due. . . . But as time went on, when the same king was occupied across the channel and in remote places, in calming the tumults of war, it came about that the sum necessary for meeting these expenses was paid in ready money. ❞

—from *The Dialogue Concerning the Exchequer. First Book, Chapter VII,* 1178 C.E

VOCABULARY

Conquest: the triumph of William the Conqueror

victuals: food

tumults: chaos

exchequer: the government office responsible for collecting taxes and paying the king's bills

1 **DRAWING CONCLUSIONS** What economic system did the English use during most of the reign of King William I?

_____

_____

2 **CITING TEXT EVIDENCE** What change in society does the author record in the passage?

_____

_____

_____

3 **HISTORICAL CONTEXT** What were the likely causes and effects of the change to cash payments for taxes?

_____

_____

_____

_____

4 **HISTORICAL INFERENCE** How do the details in the document help you understand feudal England?

_____

_____

_____

_____

5 **CONNECT TO TODAY** Do you ever barter for goods? How is a barter system better or worse than exchanging money?

_____

_____

_____

_____

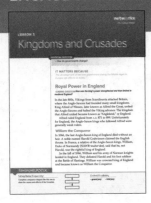

ESSENTIAL QUESTION

Why does conflict develop?

As you gather evidence to answer the Essential Question, think about:

- the influence of William the Conqueror on England.

- the reasons that a Parliament might change the king's power.

- the reasons that would lead people to take up arms against people of another religion.

My Notes

Kingdoms and Crusades

DIRECTIONS: Search for evidence in Lesson 3 to help you answer the following questions.

1 IDENTIFYING THE MAIN IDEA Use the table below to identify events leading to the rise and fall of the European kingdoms.

	England	France	Eastern States
Leaders			
Type of government and how it changed			

2 HISTORICAL INFERENCE How did William I change England, and what can you infer about the impact of that change among the people of England?

_____

_____

_____

_____

_____

_____

3 DRAWING CONCLUSIONS How did King Henry's advances in courts and common law lead to problems for his heir, King John?

_____

_____

_____

_____

_____

_____

_____

3 ECONOMICS What were the unintended economic consequences of the Crusades?

_____

_____

_____

_____

_____

Domesday Book

DIRECTIONS: Study the following excerpt and answer the accompanying questions.

EXPLORE THE CONTEXT: When William I conquered England, he set out to make a complete list of every person, animal, house, and farm that existed in England. This was a massive task and one that no government had undertaken before, during the Middle Ages. The Domesday Book helps us understand how people lived, what they owned, how wealthy they were, and what elements were part of a manor.

PRIMARY SOURCE: BOOK

❝ Hampshire: Andovere Hundred, which corresponds with the present Andover Hundred.

Andovere

The King holds Andover in demesne and King Edward held it. The number of hides is not mentioned. Here are 2 ploughlands in demesne, and 62 villeins, 36 borderers, 3 freemen and 6 servants with 24 ploughlands; also 6 mills worth 73s. 6d., 18 acres of meadow, and woods for the pennage of 100 hogs. The parish of Andover has an area of 7670 acres. ❞

—from *Domesday Book*, 1086

VOCABULARY

demesne: under the king's rule

ploughlands: land that is plowed for growing crops

villeins: a person who is subject to a lord

borderer: a person living near the border

pennage: act of keeping something in a pen

TEXT: Moody, Henry, trans. and ed. 1862. Hampshire In 1086: An Extension of the Latin And English Translation of the Domesday Book, As Far As it Relates to Hampshire. Winchester England: John T. Doswell; London: J. Russell Smith.

1 **ANALYZING SOURCES** How many people does Andovere contain? Include all of the people mentioned in the entry. What is the population density of the parish of Andover? Do some research and find out the population density of your town and compare that to medieval Andover.

_____

_____

_____

_____

_____

2 ECONOMICS How would you characterize the economy of Andover based on the details in the _Domesday Book_ entry for the area?

_____

_____

_____

3 **INFERRING** What do you think was William I's purpose for creating document?

_____

_____

_____

_____

4 **RELATING EVENTS** Can you think of how our government accounts for the people, property, and goods that exist in each town today? How is it similar to or different from the _Domesday Book?_

_____

_____

_____

_____

_____

Forgiveness of Sins

TEXT: Thatcher, Oliver J., and Edgar Holmes McNeal, eds. 1905. A Source Book for Medieval History: Selected Documents Illustrating the History of Europe in the Middle Age. New York: Charles Scribner's Sons.

ESSENTIAL QUESTION

Why does conflict develop?

VOCABULARY

Omnipotent: all-powerful, in this case, God

heathen: any non-Christian person

DIRECTIONS: Study the following passage and answer the accompanying questions.

EXPLORE THE CONTEXT: Pope Leo IV wrote this passage in 847 C.E. He issued the statement to the Frankish Army to encourage them to begin a Crusade to the Holy Land. Their enemy in the battle is the Muslims, who govern most of the lands of the Middle East.

PRIMARY SOURCE: PAPAL STATEMENT

66 Now we hope that none of you will be slain, but we wish you to know that the kingdom of heaven will be given as a reward to those who shall be killed in this war. For the Omnipotent knows that they lost their lives fighting for the truth of the faith, for the preservation of their country, and the defense of Christians. And therefore God will give then, the reward which we have named. 99

—from *Forgiveness of Sins for Those Who Dies in Battle With the Heathen,* 847 C.E.

1 **ANALYZING SOURCES** What is Pope Leo IV offering the soldiers who set out on a Crusade?

_____

_____

_____

_____

_____

_____

_____

_____

2 HISTORY   What was Pope Leo's role in the Crusade? How does that information help you understand the document?

_____

_____

_____

_____

_____

_____

3 IDENTIFYING CAUSE AND EFFECT What does Pope Leo IV want to happen as a result of writing this document?

_____

_____

_____

_____

_____

_____

4 INFERRING Who was the audience for the document? Who was it written for? How does that information help you understand the document?

_____

_____

_____

_____

_____

_____

_____

ESSENTIAL QUESTION

Why does conflict develop?

As you gather evidence to answer the Essential Question, think about:

- how education influenced society of the Middle Ages.
- how the practices of the Catholic Church created social stability.
- how the Church created conflict with secular leaders.

My Notes

_____

_____

_____

_____

_____

_____

_____

_____

_____

_____

_____

Culture and the Church

DIRECTIONS: Search for evidence in Lesson 4 to help you answer the following questions.

1 **IDENTIFYING CAUSE AND EFFECT** For each main idea below, write at least one way in which people created stability.

Architecture	Universities	Philosophy and Literature

2 ANALYZING KEY IDEAS AND DETAILS The Catholic Church was at the center of European medieval society. Use the web below to list the many ways that people's lives were influenced by the church.

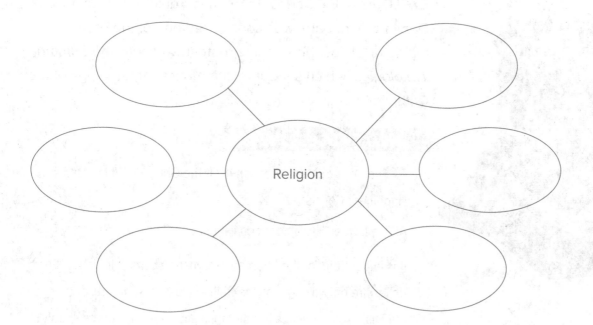

3 RELATING EVENTS Why did medieval society use Jews as a scapegoat for their problems? Have you seen similar behaviors toward certain groups in modern society?

_____

_____

_____

_____

Thomas Aquinas

Copyright © McGraw-Hill Education   TEXT: Acquinas, Thomas. 1892. Aquinas Ethicus: The Moral Teaching of St.Thomas; A Translation of the Principal Portions of the Second Part of the "Summa Theologica." Trans. Joseph Rickaby. London: Burns and Oates, Ltd.

ESSENTIAL QUESTION

Why does conflict develop?

DIRECTIONS: Study the following excerpt and answer the accompanying questions.

EXPLORE THE CONTEXT: Thomas Aquinas was an Italian Dominican friar and was considered one of the great medieval philosophers. His greatest work was the *Summa Theologica*, which set out to summarize the theology of the Catholic Church.

PRIMARY SOURCE: BOOK

❝Thomas Aquinas: Question II. Of the Object in Which Man's Happiness Consists

Article I. Does Happiness consist in riches?

It is impossible for the happiness of man to consist in riches. For riches are of two sorts, as the Philosopher says, natural and artificial. Natural riches are all those aids which go to the supply of natural wants, like meat and drink, clothing, means of transport, habitation, and the rest. Artificial riches take the form of money, something that is no aid to nature in itself, but is an invention of human contrivance for the convenience of exchange, as a measure of things saleable.❞

—Thomas Aquinas, *Summa Theologica, Question II Article I,* c. 1265-1273 C.E.

VOCABULARY

habitation: a place to live
contrivance: something produced with skill and cleverness

1 **DETERMINING CONTEXT** Who is the author of the passage and what is his background? How is this relevant to his point of view about whether riches can lead to happiness?

_____

_____

_____

_____

2 **IDENTIFYING PERSPECTIVES** What is the author's position on the idea that money can make you happy? Do you agree?

_____

_____

_____

_____

_____

_____

_____

3 **INFERRING** Who was the passage written for? How does that help you understand it?

_____

_____

_____

_____

_____

_____

_____

4 **HISTORY** The author describes money as an "invention of human contrivance for the convenience of exchange, as a measure of things saleable." How was money used during this time? Why could riches be easier to obtain with money than through the barter system?

_____

_____

_____

_____

_____

_____

Founding of the University of Heidelberg

VOCABULARY

theology or *divinity:* religious studies
canon law: laws of the Catholic Church
civil law: laws of the state

DIRECTIONS: Study the following excerpt and answer the accompanying questions.

EXPLORE THE CONTEXT: The German noble Rupert I founded the University of Heidelberg in 1386 with the blessing of the pope. The university helped Germany compete intellectually with France.

PRIMARY SOURCE: DECLARATION

"We, Rupert the elder, by the grace of God Count Palatine of the Rhine, elector of the Holy Empire and duke of Bavaria—lest we seem to abuse the privilege conceded to us by the apostolic see [the pope] of founding a place of study at Heidelberg like to that at Paris, and lest, for this reason, being subjected to the divine judgment, we should merit to be deprived of the privilege granted,—do decree . . . that the university of Heidelberg shall be ruled, disposed and regulated according to the modes and matters accustomed to be observed in the university of Paris. Also that, as a handmaid of the Parisian institution—a worthy one, let us hope,—the latter's steps shall be imitated in every way possible; so that, namely, there shall be four faculties in it: the first, of sacred theology or divinity; the second, of canon and civil law, which, by reason of their similarity, we think best to comprise under one faculty; the third, of medicine; the fourth, of liberal arts—of the threefold philosophy, namely, primal, natural and moral, three mutually subservient daughters. "

—from *The Foundation of the University of Heidelberg, 1386 C.E.*

TEXT: Henderson, Ernest F., trans. and ed. 1903. Select Historical Documents of the Middle Ages. London: George Bell and Sons.

1 **ANALYZING SOURCES** How is the University of Paris connected to the University of Heidelberg?

_____

_____

_____

2 **DRAWING CONCLUSIONS** What are the four schools within the University of Heidelberg? What can you tell about the culture from this structure?

_____

_____

_____

_____

3 **HISTORY** What historical factors might have led Rupert to model the University of Heidelberg after the existing University of Paris?

_____

_____

_____

4 **IDENTIFYING EFFECTS** How will the structure of the university directly impact Germany?

_____

_____

The Late Middle Ages

DIRECTIONS: Search for evidence in Lesson 5 to help you complete the following items.

1 Complete the chart about the Black Death.

ESSENTIAL QUESTION

Why does conflict develop?

As you gather evidence to answer the Essential Question, think about:

- how government responsibilities change during times of crisis.

- the ways that communities create scapegoats when things go wrong.

- how war changes the interactions between nations and religions.

My Notes

_____

_____

_____

_____

_____

_____

_____

_____

_____

_____

Who was impacted by the Black Death?	
What happened to wages as a result of the plague?	
When did the plague hit Europe the worst?	
Where did the plague begin? How did the plague get to Europe?	
How many people died in Asia and Europe from the plague?	

2 ECONOMICS What were some of the economic consequences of the bubonic plague?

_____

_____

_____

3 **ANALYZING KEY IDEAS AND DETAILS** How did the Great Schism weaken the leadership of the Church?

_____

_____

_____

4 **IDENTIFYING CAUSE AND EFFECT** Complete the organizer to show factors that led to the Spanish Inquisition and its effects.

CAUSE		EFFECT
	SPANISH INQUISITION	

Jacques Lenfant on the Council of Constance

DIRECTIONS: Study the following excerpt and answer the accompanying questions.

EXPLORE THE CONTEXT: The Council of Constance was the official meeting that ended the Great Schism. It occurred from 1414 until 1418. The outcome of the council was to have all the rival popes step down and for the bishops to elect one pope that all of them could agree upon. The meeting put to rest the leadership conflict in the Roman Catholic Church.

SECONDARY SOURCE: BOOK

❝Historical Dissertation on the Fifth Edition of the ACTS of the Council of Constance

The Curious Art of Printing was unknown at the Time of the Council of Constance; for it was not till twenty or thirty Years after, that all Europe was oblig'd for this Present to Germany. Therefore 'tis no wonder that Acts of such Importance, as those of this famous Council, were bury'd in the Dust of publick and private Libraries. Nor was it till the latter End of the 15th Century, that any body took it into their Heads to bring them out to the Light. ❞

—Jacques Lenfant, *The History of the Council of Constance*, 1714

VOCABULARY

oblig'd: grateful

Copyright © McGraw-Hill Education   TEXT: Lenfant, Jacques. 1730. The History of the Council of Constance, vol. 1. Trans. Stephen Whatley. London: printed for A. Bettesworth [etc.].

1 **IDENTIFYING CAUSES** According to the author, why had the details of the Council not been shared before this writing?

_____

_____

_____

_____

2 **ASSESSING CREDIBILITY** Who is the author of the passage? Why is his identity important to understanding the passage?

_____

_____

_____

_____

3 **ANALYZING SOURCES** What type of document is this? What details in the passage help you identify when the passage was written?

_____

_____

_____

4 **INFERRING** The _History of the Council of Constance_ was written in 1765, while the Council occurred in 1414–1418. Why did it take so long for someone to write this history?

_____

_____

_____

_____

Statutes of the Realm

ESSENTIAL QUESTION

Why does conflict develop?

DIRECTIONS: Study the following excerpt and answer the accompanying questions.

EXPLORE THE CONTEXT: The passage is a law from *Statutes of the Realm*, written in England in 1351.

PRIMARY SOURCE: LEGAL DOCUMENT

Statute of Laborers; 1351

❝ Because a great part of the people and especially of the workmen and servants has now died in that pestilence [plague], some, seeing the straights of the masters and the scarcity of servants, are not willing to serve unless they receive excessive wages, and others, rather than through labour to gain their living, prefer to beg in idleness: We, . . . ordain that every man and woman of our kingdom of England, . . . whether bond or free, who is able bodied and below the age of sixty years, not living from trade nor carrying on a fixed craft, . . . and not serving another, if he, considering his station, be sought after to serve in a suitable service, he shall be bound to serve him who has seen fit so to seek after him; and he shall take only the wages liveries, meed or salary which, in the places where he sought to serve, were accustomed to be paid in the twentieth year of our reign of England, or the five or six common years next preceding. ❞

—From *Select Historical Documents of the Middle Ages*

VOCABULARY

statute: law
straights: difficulties
idleness: laziness or unemployment
ordain: order
liveries: the business of vehicles for hire
meed: a share or reward

1 **ANALYZING SOURCES** What does the Statute of Laborers require?

_____

_____

_____

2 **DETERMINING CONTEXT** When was the law written? What events were happening in Europe at that time that help you understand the law?

_____

_____

_____

3 **ECONOMICS** What specific item does the statute demand related to wages? From this detail, what can you tell about how the Black Death impacted the labor market?

_____

_____

_____

_____

4 **INFERRING** What detail in the passage suggests that the Black Death had given serfs greater power to change their station in society?

_____

_____

_____

Why does conflict develop?

① Think About It

Review the supporting questions you developed at the opening of the chapter. Review the evidence you found in this chapter. Were you able to answer each of your Supporting Questions?

If you didn't find enough evidence to answer your Supporting Questions, what do you think you need to consider?

_____

_____

_____

_____

② Organize Your Evidence

Use charts like the one below to organize the evidence you will use to support your position statement.

Conflict	Evidence

❸ Talk About It

Discuss the evidence you have gathered with a small group or partner. Check your group's understanding of the structures in the Middle Ages that led to conflict and answer any questions members may have. Consider any additional advice or input they may have.

❹ Connect to the Essential Questions

On a separate piece of paper, write an expository essay that answers the Essential Question: *Why does conflict develop?* In your essay, explain how kingdoms, the Church, as well as the social structures of feudalism and guilds, contributed to conflict in Europe.

CITIZENSHIP
TAKING ACTION

MAKE CONNECTIONS Ideas about citizenship changed during the Middle Ages. For the first time, rights of citizens were recognized. Townspeople were given the right to buy and sell property. In England, the Magna Carta protected rights such as the right to a trial by jury. In the United States, the Bill of Rights lists specific rights guaranteed to all U.S. citizens. Some of these rights came from the Magna Carta.

DIRECTIONS: Look up the rights protected by the Bill of Rights. Choose the three you believe are most important and create a "Know Your Rights" campaign poster explaining those three rights. On your poster, use a combination of text and graphics to identify each right and explain what it means.

Renaissance and Reformation

ESSENTIAL QUESTION

How do new ideas change the way people live?

Think about how this question might relate to the Renaissance and the Reformation.

TALK ABOUT IT

Discuss with a partner what type of information you would need to know to answer this question. For example, one question might be: Why are the events and ideas that occurred during these eras so significant?

DIRECTIONS: Now write down three additional questions that you need to answer to be able to explain the importance of these eras and their ideas.

MY RESEARCH QUESTIONS

Supporting Question 1:

_____

_____

Supporting Question 2:

_____

_____

Supporting Question 3:

_____

ESSENTIAL QUESTION

How do new ideas change the way people live?

As you gather evidence to answer the Essential Question, think about:

- how secular ideas changed European society.
- the importance of trade to the Italian city-states.
- how exploration led to new ideas and behavior.
- why certain individuals had significant influence in Italy and over the changes that occurred.
- the art, architecture, and writing that developed during these eras.

My Notes

The Renaissance Begins

DIRECTIONS: Search for evidence in Lesson 1 to help you answer the following questions.

1 EXPLAINING How did the shift to a more secular way of life influence the Renaissance?

_____

_____

_____

_____

_____

2 IDENTIFYING EFFECTS In the graphic organizer below, describe how each characteristic of Italy influenced the Renaissance.

Characteristic of Italy	Influence on the Renaissance
Italian cities were wealthy.	
Italy was the heart of the old Roman Empire.	
Many Italians lived in cities instead of in rural areas.	
Stronger economies developed.	

3 ECONOMICS Why were the Italian states able to remain independent and prosper during the Middle Ages?

_____

_____

_____

_____

4 GEOGRAPHY How did Italy's location affect it during the Renaissance?

_____

_____

_____

_____

5 CIVICS Complete the chart.

Individual	How He Changed Italian Society and Ideas During the Renaissance
Marco Polo	
Lorenzo de' Medici	
Niccolò Machiavelli	

Niccoló Machiavelli on How to Gain a Ruler's Favor

DIRECTIONS: Read the following excerpt and answer the accompanying questions.

EXPLORE THE CONTEXT: Lorenzo de' Medici was one of the most influential people in Italy's history. Rather than governing Italy as an all-powerful ruler, de' Medici surrounded himself with others who could assist him in his governance. Niccolò Machiavelli dedicated his political treatise on power, *The Prince*, to de' Medici's grandson and ruler at the time, Lorenzo di Piero de' Medici.

PRIMARY SOURCE: BOOK

VOCABULARY

favor: approval, support
eminence: importance, reputation
symbolize: represent
contemporary: modern-day
the classics: classic literature
summarized: to give a short report on a subject

❝Those who wish to acquire favor with a ruler most often approach him with those among their possessions that are most valuable in their eyes, or that they are confident will give him pleasure. So rulers are often given horses, armor, cloth of gold, precious stones, and similar ornaments that are thought worthy of their social eminence. Since I want to offer myself to your Magnificence, along with something that will symbolize my desire to give you obedient service, I have found nothing among my possessions that I value more, or would put a higher price upon, than an understanding of the deeds of great men, acquired through a lengthy experience of contemporary politics and through an uninterrupted study of the classics. Since I have long thought about and studied the question of what makes for greatness, and have now summarized my conclusions on the subject in a little book, it is this I send your Magnificence. ❞

— Niccoló Machiavelli, *The Prince*, 1513

1 CIVICS Why does Machiavelli refer to Lorenzo di Peiro de' Medici as "your Magnificence?"

_____

_____

_____

_____

_____

_____

2 ANALYZING What is the purpose of Machiavelli's letter?

_____

_____

_____

_____

_____

3A IDENTIFYING What does Machiavelli offer de' Medici?

_____

_____

_____

_____

_____

3B ANALYZING Why does Machiavelli offer this in place of "horses, armor, cloth of gold, precious stones, and similar ornaments?"

_____

_____

_____

_____

_____

Lorenzo De' Medici on How a Cardinal Should Live

DIRECTIONS: Read the following excerpt and answer the accompanying questions.

EXPLORE THE CONTEXT: Due to the high-ranking position of the de' Medici family, Lorenzo de' Medici's nephew, Giovanni, became a cardinal in the Roman Catholic Church when he was only 13 years old. The letter below is from Lorenzo to Giovanni after his nephew became a cardinal.

PRIMARY SOURCE: LETTER

66 A handsome house and a well-ordered family will be preferable to a great retinue and a splendid residence. Endeavor to live with regularity, and gradually bring your expenses within those bounds which in a new establishment cannot perhaps be expected. Silk and jewels are not suitable for persons in your station. Your taste will be better shown in the acquisition of a few elegant remains of antiquity, or in the collecting of handsome books, and by your attendants being learned and well-bred rather than numerous. 99

— Letter from Lorenzo de' Medici to Giovanni de' Medici, 1491

VOCABULARY

retinue: servants, attendants
residence: home
endeavor: try, attempt
station: level in society
acquisition: gaining
antiquity: ancient times
learned: educated

1A IDENTIFYING What is the purpose of Lorenzo's letter?

_____

_____

_____

1B **DESCRIBING** What is Lorenzo's opinion about the acquisition of possessions?

_____

_____

_____

_____

_____

2 **CIVICS** Why does Lorenzo write that "Silk and jewels are not suitable for persons in your station"?

_____

_____

_____

_____

3 **EXPLAINING** Explain why Lorenzo believes that his nephew's "taste will be better shown in the acquisition of a few elegant remains of antiquity, or in the collecting of handsome books, and by your attendants being learned and well-bred rather than numerous."

_____

_____

_____

_____

4 **DETERMINING CONTEXT** Why might it have been important for Giovanni to follow his uncle's advice?

_____

_____

_____

_____

ESSENTIAL QUESTION

How do new ideas change the way people live?

As you gather evidence to answer the Essential Question, think about:

- how new technology helped to spread ideas.
- the significant art and literature that came from the Renaissance.
- how other countries were affected by the changes occurring in Italy.

My Notes

_____

_____

_____

_____

_____

_____

_____

_____

New Ideas and Art

DIRECTIONS: Search for evidence in Lesson 2 to help you answer the following questions.

1A EXPLAINING What is humanism?

_____

_____

_____

_____

_____

1B CITING TEXT EVIDENCE What role did humanism play in the Renaissance?

_____

_____

_____

_____

_____

2 UNDERSTANDING CHRONOLOGY Complete the graphic organizer below to explain how Francesco Petrarch contributed to the Renaissance.

Francesco Petrarch travels to old monasteries.

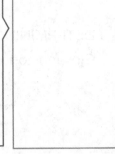

3 **IDENTIFYING EFFECTS** The graphic organizer below includes names of individuals who were important to the Renaissance. Identify where each person was born, list a significant contribution made by each individual, and explain how that contribution influenced the Renaissance.

Individual	Country of Origin	Contribution to the Renaissance	How This Contribution Influenced the Renaissance
Dante Alighieri			
Geoffrey Chaucer			
Johannes Gutenberg			
Giotto			

4 GEOGRAPHY How did Italy's location help to expand the art of the Renaissance?

_____

_____

_____

_____

_____

Giotto's *The Lamentation*

How do new ideas change the way people live?

DIRECTIONS: Study the image and answer the accompanying questions.

EXPLORE THE CONTEXT: This painting by Giotto is entitled *The Lamentation*, or *Mourning of Christ*. It was painted between 1305 and 1306. In it, the deceased body of Jesus, referred to as "Christ" in the title, is surrounded by various people. Included are figures significant to the Roman Catholic Church, such as Mary Magdalene and John, as well as angels. Giotto has set apart the religious figures by painting them with halos.

PRIMARY SOURCE: PAINTING

Copyright © McGraw-Hill Education   ART Collection/Alamy Stock Photo

1 DESCRIBING Describe the scene shown in the image.

_____

_____

_____

_____

2 ANALYZING How are the figures in the painting depicted?

_____

_____

_____

_____

3A DESCRIBING Describe the colors used in the painting.

_____

_____

_____

_____

3B ANALYZING What mood do these colors create?

_____

_____

_____

_____

4 INFERRING Why did Giotto most likely include religious figures and angels in this painting?

_____

_____

_____

_____

Jan Van Eyck's *The Annunciation*

ESSENTIAL QUESTION
How do new ideas change the way people live?

DIRECTIONS: Study the image and answer the accompanying questions.

EXPLORE THE CONTEXT: This Northern Renaissance painting, entitled *The Annunciation*, is a masterpiece created by Jan van Eyck, an artist from the Netherlands. The painting was created around 1434. It depicts an important story from the beliefs of the Roman Catholic Church: The Virgin Mary (on the right) is told by the angel Gabriel (on the left) that she will give birth to the son of God, Jesus.

PRIMARY SOURCE: PAINTING

1 **INFERRING** How is the scene significant to the Renaissance?

_____

_____

_____

_____

2 **DESCRIBING** What are some aspects about the painting that stand out to you and why?

_____

_____

_____

_____

_____

3 **COMPARING** How is this van Eyck painting similar to that of Giotto's _The Lamentation_?

_____

_____

_____

_____

_____

4 **COMPARING** How is _The Annunciation_ similar to van Eyck's other masterpiece, _The Arnolfini Portrait, which can be found in the textbook?_

_____

_____

_____

_____

The Reformation Begins

DIRECTIONS: Search for evidence in Lesson 3 to help you answer the following questions.

ESSENTIAL QUESTION

How do new ideas change the way people live?

As you gather evidence to answer the Essential Question, think about:

- how criticism of the Catholic Church inspired the Reformation.
- the political implications of the Protestant Reformation in Europe.

My Notes

1A **IDENTIFYING CAUSE AND EFFECT** What were the criticisms of the Catholic Church at the time of the Reformation?

_____

_____

_____

_____

_____

1B How had respect for the leaders of the Catholic Church, including the pope, weakened over time?

_____

_____

_____

_____

2 GEOGRAPHY How did location impact the divide between Protestants and Catholics in Germany?

_____

_____

_____

_____

_____

3 **IDENTIFYING CAUSE AND EFFECT** As the ideas of the Reformation gained popularity and spread across Europe, these ideas influenced the way that people thought about government. In the graphic below, identify the political influence of certain religious ideas.

IDEAS OF THE REFORMATION	IDEAS ABOUT GOVERNMENT
THE ELECTION OF CLERGY	
OBEDIENCE TO THE CHURCH	
PAYING INDULGENCES	

4 **ECONOMICS** Complete the following chart to record the impact of rulers who decided to embrace Protestant Christianity.

ECONOMIC IMPACT OF REFORMATION

Criticism of the Catholic Church

ESSENTIAL QUESTION

How do new ideas change the way people live?

DIRECTIONS: Read the following excerpt and answer the accompanying questions.

EXPLORE THE CONTEXT: Desiderius Erasmus was a priest, humanist, and dedicated scholar who found himself caught between the Church and the spirit of the Reformation. A prolific writer, Erasmus wrote to people at all levels within the Church, including the following letter to the Bishop of Augsburg, in Germany.

PRIMARY SOURCE: DIARY

❝ The state of the Church distracts me. My own conscience is easy; I was alone in saying from the first that the disorder must be encountered in its germs; I was too true a prophet; the play, which opened with universal hand clapping, is ending as I foresaw that it must. The kings are fighting among themselves for objects of their own. The monks instead of looking for a reign of Christ, want only to reign themselves. The theologians curse Luther and in cursing him curse the truth delivered by Christ and the Apostles and . . . alienate with their foul speeches many who would have returned to the Church or but for them would have never left it. No fact is plainer than that this tempest has been sent from heaven by God's anger, as the frogs and locusts and the rest were sent on the Egyptians; but no one remembers his own faults, and each blames the other. It is easy to see who sowed the seed and who ripened the crop. ❞

—Erasmus to the Bishop of Augsburg, August 26, 1528 in *Life and Letters of Erasmus: Lectures Delivered at Oxford 1893-4*

VOCABULARY

encountered: come across; met with
universal: worldwide
theologians: people who study God and religion
alienate: turn away

1 **CITING TEXT EVIDENCE** How does Erasmus describe the theologians' response to Martin Luther's ideas?

_____

_____

_____

_____

2 **DETERMINING MEANING** Examine the language that Erasmus uses to describe the conflict between the Church and the ideas of Martin Luther. What can you determine about his concern for the future based on this context?

_____

_____

_____

_____

3 **ANALYZING TEXT EVIDENCE** After referring to the text, describe how ideas of the Reformation related to power in the government and in the Church.

_____

_____

_____

_____

4 **DRAWING CONCLUSIONS** What is Erasmus's point of view about the Reformation and the Church's response to it?

_____

_____

_____

_____

The German Peasant Rebellion

Copyright © McGraw-Hill Education TEXT: Robinson, James Harvey, ed. 1906. From the Opening of the Protestant Revolt to the Present Day. Vol. 2 of Readings in European History. Boston, New York, Chicago and London: Ginn & Company.

ESSENTIAL QUESTION

How do new ideas change the way people live?

DIRECTIONS: Read the following excerpt and answer the accompanying questions.

EXPLORE THE CONTEXT: The German Peasants' Rebellion was a series of uprisings among German-speaking people in Central Europe between 1524 and 1525. Their demands were listed in a document entitled "The Twelve Articles." Some of these demands were inspired by ideas of the Reformation.

VOCABULARY

petition: request
depose: remove from office
doctrine: set of guidelines
ordinance: rule

PRIMARY SOURCE: PETITION

❝The First Article. First, it is our humble petition and desire, as also our will and resolution, that in the future we should have power and authority so that each community should choose and appoint a pastor, and that we should have the right to depose him should he conduct himself improperly. The pastor thus chosen should teach us the gospel pure and simple, without any addition, doctrine, or ordinance of man. ❞

—from "The Twelve Articles," Demands from the German Peasants, 1524

1 **CITING TEXT EVIDENCE** According to this except, what change do the people want in how their religious leaders are appointed?

_____

_____

_____

_____

_____

2 DETERMINING MEANING What does the phrase, "The pastor thus chosen should teach us the gospel pure and simple, without any addition, doctrine, or ordinance of man" refer to?

_____

_____

_____

_____

_____

3 CITING TEXT EVIDENCE Which words best show the desire of the people to appoint their own religious leaders? Underline the words that best demonstrate what is demanded.

_____

_____

_____

_____

_____

_____

4 DRAWING CONCLUSIONS What can you determine about the importance of selecting religious leaders based on where it appears in "The Twelve Demands"?

_____

_____

_____

_____

_____

Catholics and Protestants

DIRECTIONS: Search for evidence in Lesson 4 to help you answer the following questions.

ESSENTIAL QUESTION

How do new ideas change the way people live?

As you gather evidence to answer the Essential Question, think about:

- how the Catholic Church attempted reform.
- why the Edict of Nantes was important.

1 | HISTORY | Use the chart to identify some results that sprang from the conflict between Catholics and Protestants.

RESULTS OF CONFLICT BETWEEN CATHOLICS AND PROTESTANTS

2 **INTERPRETING** Consider how religious conflict was more likely in certain geographic regions and countries.

_____

_____

_____

_____

My Notes

_____

_____

_____

_____

_____

_____

_____

3 CITING TEXT EVIDENCE The Thirty Years' War was a period of violent religious conflict. Use the chart to describe the impact of the conflict on the strength of the major empires in Europe.

EMPIRE	IMPACT
France	
Spain	
Holy Roman	

4 DESCRIBING How did the role of women change after the end of the Reformation?

_____

_____

_____

_____

_____

_____

Criticism of the Pope

ESSENTIAL QUESTION

How do new ideas change the way people live?

DIRECTIONS: Read the following excerpt and answer the accompanying questions.

EXPLORE THE CONTEXT: Raimon de Cornet was a French priest, troubadour, and poet who opposed the clergy and the pope.

VOCABULARY

prebend: payment to the clergy
abbacy: office of abbot or abbess in the Church
miter: bishop's hat

PRIMARY SOURCE: POEM

"I see the pope his sacred trust betray,

For while the rich his grace can gain alway,

His favors from the poor are aye withholden.

He strives to gather wealth as best he may,

Forcing Christ's people blindly to obey,

So that he may repose in garments golden.

The vilest traffickers in souls are all

His chapmen, and for gold a prebend's stall

He'll sell them, or an abbacy or miter.

And to us he sends clowns and tramps who crawl

Vending his pardon briefs from cot to hall—

Letters and pardons worthy of the writer,

Which leaves our pokes, if not our souls, the lighter."

—Raimon de Cornet, c. 1324–1340

Copyright © McGraw-Hill Education   J. H. Robinson, Readings in European History (Boston: 1904), pp. 375-377 https://archive.org/details/readingsineurope005820mbp

1 **CITING TEXT EVIDENCE** What are the criticisms of the pope in this poem?

_____

_____

_____

_____

2 **DETERMINING MEANING** How does the description of indulgences in this poem reinforce the ideas the writer is trying to communicate?

_____

_____

_____

_____

_____

_____

_____

3 **CITING TEXT EVIDENCE** Which words does the author use to convey his ideas about the corruption that the pope has spread to the clergy? Underline the words he used.

_____

_____

_____

4 HISTORY How does this perspective inform our understanding of the religious conflicts in France during this time?

_____

_____

_____

_____

A Huguenot on St. Bartholomew's Day

DIRECTIONS: Examine the following image and answer the accompanying questions.

EXPLORE THE CONTEXT: The painting by Sir John Everett Millais in 1852 depicts a couple embracing on St. Bartholomew's Day in 1572 when Catholics in Paris massacred Protestants. The woman in this painting is attempting to tie a white scarf around the arm of her beloved. The white scarf was a marker of Catholicism and would have shielded the man from the massacre. The man is refusing this protection. He is a Huguenot, a French protestant persecuted by the Catholic Church leaders for their faith. The moment in this painting symbolizes the choice between physical safety and spiritual devotion.

SECONDARY SOURCE: PAINTING

1 **ANALYZING** Describe the figures and the setting in this painting.

_____

_____

_____

_____

_____

2 **HISTORY** This painting dates from 1851, but it depicts an event in France from 1572. In what ways does this inform your understanding of the impact of the religious wars during this time period?

_____

_____

_____

_____

_____

3 **ANALYZING TEXT EVIDENCE** After referring to the text, describe what you know about the significance of the white scarf around the man's arm.

_____

_____

_____

_____

_____

4 **DRAWING CONCLUSIONS** What important statement is the artist making in this painting making about an individual's responsibility to their ideas?

_____

_____

_____

ESSENTIAL QUESTION

How do new ideas change the way people live?

1 Think About It

Review the Supporting Questions that you developed at the beginning of the chapter. Review the evidence that you gathered in this chapter. Were you able to answer each Supporting Question?

If there was not enough evidence to answer your Supporting Questions, what additional evidence do you think you need?

2 Organize Your Evidence

Use the chart below to organize the evidence you will use to support your position statement.

Central Idea

Supporting Details

③ Talk About It

A position statement related to the Essential Question should reflect your conclusion about the evidence. Write a position statement for the ESSENTIAL QUESTION: *How do new ideas change the way people live?*

_____

_____

_____

_____

_____

_____

_____

_____

④ Connect to the Essential Question

On a separate piece of paper, develop an expository essay to answer the ESSENTIAL QUESTION: *How do new ideas change the way people live?*

CITIZENSHIP
TAKING ACTION

MAKE CONNECTIONS The ideas of the Reformation have shaped the world in which we live. Many people during the Reformation spoke out against the power of the Church and some of its practices. Their arguments against a single religious authority changed the lives of many people. In addition, these same ideas, in a similar way, began to change the way people thought about the power of government.

DIRECTIONS: Find something you would like to change in your school or community. Write a school newspaper article, an editorial for your local newspaper, or a community education pamphlet, or create a Web page that supports the change you would like to make. Include an explanation of why you would like to make this change, as well as ways in which this change could be implemented.

Age of Exploration and Trade

ESSENTIAL QUESTION

Why do civilizations rise and fall?

Think about how this question might relate to early European explorers, trade, and the impact on the cultures these explorers encountered.

COLLABORATE

TALK ABOUT IT

Discuss with a partner what type of information you would need to know to answer this question. For example, one question might be: What factors contributed to the fall of the Taino civilization on the island of Hispaniola?

DIRECTIONS: Now write three additional questions that would help you explain some of the reasons why civilizations rise and fall.

MY RESEARCH QUESTIONS

Supporting Question 1:

_____

_____

Supporting Question 2:

_____

_____

Supporting Question 3:

_____

_____

The Age of Exploration

DIRECTIONS: Search for evidence in Lesson 1 to help you answer the following questions.

1 ECONOMICS What economic choices affected the Europeans' decision to explore?

_____
_____
_____
_____
_____
_____

2 **SEQUENCING** Trace the interactions of the European nations, their explorers, and what they discovered. Use the graphic organizer to show the interactions among the three groups. When sent out, what did the explorers find, and what did they do with what they discovered?

Sending Country	Explorers	Discoveries
Spain		
Portugal		
France		

ESSENTIAL QUESTION

Why do civilizations rise and fall?

As you gather evidence to answer the Essential Question, think about:

- the effect of technology on European overseas exploration.
- the rise of kingdoms in Europe and its impact on overseas exploration.

My Notes

_____
_____
_____
_____
_____
_____
_____
_____
_____
_____
_____

3 EXPLAINING CAUSE AND EFFECT What were some factors that caused Europeans to begin exploring? Use the chart to organize your information.

_____

_____

_____

_____

_____

_____

_____

_____

_____

4 ANALYZING How did Vasco da Gama landing on India's coast change the world?

_____

_____

_____

_____

_____

_____

_____

_____

_____

_____

_____

_____

Magellan's Voyage

Why do civilizations rise and fall?

DIRECTIONS: Study the excerpt below and answer the accompanying questions.

EXPLORE THE CONTEXT: *Magellan; or The First Voyage Round the World,* by George M. Towle, was written as one in a series of history books. The story provides insights into what early explorers encountered in their quest to discover unknown lands and seas.

SECONDARY SOURCE: BOOK EXCERPT

"What made the heat still more unendurable, the supply of fresh water was now almost exhausted; what remained had become so filthy and nauseous that the wanderers could not drink it without shuddering, and it often made them ill. Then Magellan was grief-stricken to be forced to reduce the rations of his brave and suffering comrades. The only food left consisted of course biscuit and these were, as one who was on board says, "reduced to powder, and full of worms." They had been gnawed and defiled by rats, and were scarcely eatable. But even such food was a rich and rare luxury compared to that to which the poor fellows were at last reduced. In no long time not a biscuit, not a crumb remained. Then they were obliged to do the very thing that Magellan had spoken of, when he said he would go forward, "even if they had to eat the leather off the yards." This miserable apology for food was now, indeed, all that was left. The gaunt and famished sailors tore off the ox-hides under the main yard, which had been placed there to protect the rigging from the strain of the yard. The leather was so tough that the hungry teeth could make no impression upon it. They attached pieces of it to strong cords, and let them trail in the sea for four or five days. When they were thus soaked through, the sailors made a poor pretense of cooking the leather. They placed it over the fire, until it was singed, and then ate it greedily. "

—from *Magellan; or The First Voyage Round the World,* 1879

VOCABULARY

unendurable: not able to tolerate

comrades: members of the same group

defiled: ruined, made filthy

obliged: felt the responsibility to do it

gaunt: bony, thin

famished: starving

rigging: the lines and wires that support the masts on sailing vessels

pretense: to act as if something were true; pretending

singed: charred, scorched, blackened

1 **COMPARING AND CONTRASTING** Reread the "Voyage of Magellan" in Lesson 1 and compare the information with this excerpt.

_____

_____

_____

_____

_____

2 **IDENTIFYING PERSPECTIVES** What does this excerpt lead you to believe about Magellan's character?

_____

_____

_____

_____

3 HISTORY What does this excerpt illustrate about the perils of sailing in the age of European exploration?

_____

_____

_____

_____

4 **SUMMARIZING** Write a brief summary of this excerpt. Analyze the details supporting the central idea before beginning to summarize.

_____

_____

_____

_____

Vasco da Gama Reaches India

Copyright © McGraw-Hill Education   TEXT: Correia, Gaspar. 1869. *The Three Voyages of Vasco da Gama, and His Viceroyalty; From the Lendas de India of Gaspar Correa, Accompanied by Original Documents.* Trans. Henry E. J. Stanley. London: Printed for the Hakluyt Society.

ESSENTIAL QUESTION
Why do civilizations rise and fall?

DIRECTIONS: Study the excerpt below and answer the accompanying questions.

EXPLORE THE CONTEXT: This excerpt is a narrative of the voyages of Vasco da Gama. Some historians believe it is more accurate than other accounts. Gaspar Correa traveled to India only a few years after the land was discovered. Correa found the diary of a priest, Joam Figueira, who reportedly had accompanied da Gama on his voyages. To preserve everything he had learned about the events in India, Correa began writing. This passage has been translated from the Portuguese.

VOCABULARY

Cananor: a monarchy-ruled region in old India
thatched: a roof covering of leaves, straw, etc.
skiffs: small boats to sail or row
rigging: the ropes that attached to sails on the masts and yards

SECONDARY SOURCE: BOOK EXCERPT

❝ . . . this was a great mountain which is on the coast of India, in the kingdom of Cananor, which the people of the country in their language call the mountain Delielly, and they call it "of the rat," and they call it Mount Dely, because in this mountain there were so many rats that they never could make a village there. . . . and they went on approaching the land until they saw the beach, and they ran along it and passed within sight of a large town of thatched houses inside a bay, which the pilots said was named Cananor, where many skiffs were going about fishing; and several came near to see the ships and were much surprised, and went ashore to relate that these ships had so much rigging and so many sails and white men; which having been told to the King he sent some men of his own to see, but the ships had already gone far, and they did not go. **❞**

—from *The Three Voyages of Vasco da Gama and His Viceroyalty,* 1525

1 **ANALYZING** From this description, how were the explorers greeted when they were first sighted? Explain.

_____

_____

_____

_____

2 **COMPARING AND CONTRASTING** How is the excerpt similar to or different from the lesson text describing Vasco da Gama's discovery? Explain which one helps you understand the human interaction best and why you think so.

_____

_____

_____

_____

3 ECONOMICS How would Vasco da Gama's discovery of India's coast have an economic impact on both countries?

_____

_____

_____

_____

4 **INFERRING** In Lesson 1, you read of the early European explorers and their discovery of new lands and cultures. What do you believe were the motivations that caused explorers and monarchies to risk lives and fortunes to accomplish these great explorations? What was often the impact to the cultures found? Explain your views, citing text evidence to support them.

_____

_____

_____

_____

Spain's Conquests in the Americas

DIRECTIONS: Search for evidence in Lesson 2 to help you answer the following questions.

ESSENTIAL QUESTION

Why do civilizations rise and fall?

As you gather evidence to answer the Essential Question, think about:

- Spain's invasions of Cuba and Mexico in search of gold and power.
- the conquest of Peru, allowing Spain to have access to most of South America.

1 **COMPARING AND CONTRASTING** Look closely at the interactions between Cortés and the Aztec rulers and Cortés and some of the Maya people. Use the Venn diagram below to show the similarities and differences.

Differences

Cortés and the Aztec rulers

Similarities

Differences

Cortés and the Maya

My Notes

_____

_____

_____

_____

_____

_____

_____

_____

_____

2 **RELATING EVENTS** Create a 5Ws map to integrate the information in the lesson about how Spain conquered Peru.

_____

_____

_____

_____

_____

_____

_____

_____

_____

_____

3 **ECONOMICS** The Spanish monarchs decided to invest in exploration of the America's. What did their investment yield for Spain?

_____

_____

_____

_____

_____

_____

4 **SUMMARIZING** What is the central idea in Lesson 2? Cite the most relevant supporting details as you explain.

_____

_____

_____

_____

_____

_____

The Execution of Vasco Núñez de Balboa

Copyright © McGraw-Hill Education   TEXT: Ober, Frederick A. 1906. Vasco Nunez de Balboa. New York and London: Harper and Brothers Publishers.

ESSENTIAL QUESTION

Why do civilizations rise and fall?

DIRECTIONS: Study the excerpt below and answer the accompanying questions.

EXPLORE THE CONTEXT: Vasco Núñez de Balboa is well known as a Spanish explorer, but his life and journeys are not discussed as much as other Spanish explorers. In this excerpt from his biography, Balboa has been charged with treason, imprisoned, and brought out to his execution.

SECONDARY SOURCE: BIOGRAPHY

❝ But the day had arrived, Balboa's last on earth. The hot afternoon wore away and the sun sank towards the mountains which the prisoner had been the first to explore, and touched with its rays the roofs of the dwellings he himself had erected. The dungeon door was thrown open, and forth came Balboa, preceded by his jailer and loaded with clanking chains. But the burden of the chains was as naught to the armor he had carried in the days of his great deeds, and he bore himself erect, dauntless in mien as of yore. . . . Preceding the prisoner walked the public crier, who announced: "This is the punishment inflicted by command of the king and his lieutenant, Don Pedrarias de Avila, governor of this colony, upon this man, as a traitor, and usurper of lands belonging to the crown." "Nay, nay," exclaimed the still loyal Balboa when he heard this lie proclaimed; "It is false! You, my former comrades, know it is false. Never hath thought of such a crime entered my mind. I have ever served my king with truth and loyalty, and ever sought to augment his dominions! ❞

— from *Vasco Núñez de Balboa,* by Frederick A. Ober, 1906

VOCABULARY

naught: nothing

dauntless: fearless

mien: facial expression

yore: days in the past

public crier: someone from the court who announces

usurper: one who uses force to take what is not his or hers

augment: to increase in size

dominions: government territory

1 **COMPARING AND CONTRASTING** How does the description of Balboa's conviction of wrongdoing in Lesson 2 compare with the excerpt? Does one support the other, and if so, how?

_____

_____

_____

_____

2 **DESCRIBING** Balboa calls the charges against him false. Underline the words that are used to describe Balboa that appear to support his claim of innocence.

_____

_____

_____

_____

_____

3 **CIVICS** What civic virtues, or dedication to the monarchy at his own expense, are found in Balboa's statements?

_____

_____

_____

_____

4 **HISTORY** What were the effects of the charge of treason against Balboa? Cite evidence from Lesson 2.

_____

_____

_____

_____

_____

A Chronicle of the Spanish Conqueror Cortés

DIRECTIONS: Study the excerpt below and answer the accompanying questions.

EXPLORE THE CONTEXT: The excerpt jumps into a description of the conflict between Spanish explorer Hernán Cortés and the Aztec ruler, Montezuma II. Based on an Aztec legend, a God who opposed human sacrifice said he would someday return. Because of this, Montezuma did not act aggressively toward Cortés when the Spanish landed.

VOCABULARY

grave: serious or solemn

Grijalva: another explorer (from Cuba) who visited the coast of Mexico

expedition: journey

raiment: clothing

sway: to have power over something or someone

visage: the appearance or expression of a person's face

bestriding: putting a leg on either side of something, such as a horse

---

SECONDARY SOURCE: BOOK

❝In the mind of Montezuma, meanwhile, the grave question has been: Can these Spaniards, these strangers of the sunrise, be gods? When Grijalva's expedition appeared off the coast in 1518, it had been reported to Tenochtitlan that in the 'waters of heaven,' as the open sea was called, 'floating towers' had appeared, from which had descended beings with white faces and hands, with beards and long hair, and wearing raiment of brilliant colors and 'round headcoverings.' Could these beings be priests or heralds of the Fair God Quetzalcoatl, come, according to the Maya-Nahua tradition, to resume sway over his people? Before proof could be adduced, Grijalva had departed; and then, shortly, had come swift messengers with news of Cortés and with pictures of his 'floating towers' and of his fair-visaged, yet bearded attendants, handling the thunder and bestriding fierce creatures . . . ❞

—from *The Spanish Conquerors, a Chronicle of the Dawn of Empire Overseas*, 1919

1 `HISTORY` How is the reaction of Montezuma to the strangers in his land related to another event in recent history for the Aztec? Use details from the excerpt to support your response.

_____

_____

_____

_____

2 **COMPARING AND CONTRASTING** Examine the description of Montezuma's reaction to Cortés in Lesson 2 and see whether the excerpt corresponds. Describe whether the ideas are in agreement, and support your claim with evidence from the text.

_____

_____

_____

_____

_____

3 **ANALYZING** What words are used to describe a possible danger to the Aztec? Underline the vocabulary that applies and explain what you think the words represent. Cite evidence of something similar in Lesson 2.

_____

_____

_____

_____

_____

4 **DRAWING CONCLUSIONS** How does Montezuma's religious belief affect his strategies to defeat the Spanish? Cite evidence from the excerpt and the lesson.

_____

_____

_____

ESSENTIAL QUESTION

*Why do civilizations
rise and fall?*

As you gather evidence to answer
the Essential Question, think about:

- the establishment of European
  empires in the Americas.
- the global exchange of trade
  known as the Columbian
  Exchange.

My Notes

Exploration and Worldwide Trade

DIRECTIONS: Search for evidence in Lesson 3 to help you answer the following questions.

1 IDENTIFYING In the 1600s, what areas did Spain, Portugal, France, England, and the Netherlands control in the Americas? In the chart below, identify the areas where each country established settlements.

Country	Areas of Settlements in the Americas
Spain	
Portugal	
France	
England	
The Netherlands	

2 ECONOMICS What was the French goal for colonizing North America? Cite text evidence to explain your answer.

3 DESCRIBING What steps did England take to establish North American settlements?

_____

_____

_____

_____

_____

4 EXPLAINING As Europeans established empires in the Americas, world trade changed in many ways. Three results of those changes in world trade were mercantilism, the Commercial Revolution, and the Columbian Exchange. In the chart below, explain what each of those was.

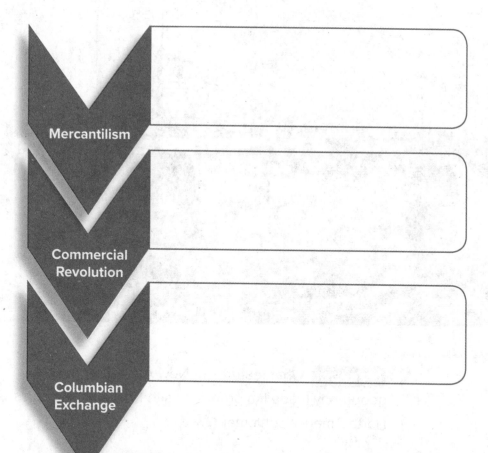

Mercantilism

Commercial Revolution

Columbian Exchange

New Amsterdam

DIRECTIONS: Examine the image below and answer the accompanying questions.

EXPLORE THE CONTEXT: This image shows a harbor scene in New Amsterdam, now known as New York City, in 1667. The original illustration was created c. 1700s.

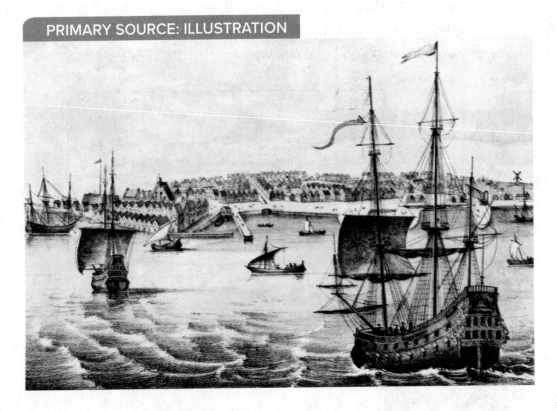

PRIMARY SOURCE: ILLUSTRATION

1   GEOGRAPHY   What features of New Amsterdam's geography made it a promising site for Henry Hudson's North America settlement?

_____

_____

_____

_____

2 **DESCRIBING** Describe the modes of transportation shown. After referring to the text, what can you infer about the larger sailing vessels in the New Amsterdam harbor?

_____

_____

_____

_____

_____

_____

_____

3 **INFERRING** What might the image reveal about the Dutch settlement on Manhattan Island that is _not_ found in the text?

_____

_____

_____

_____

_____

_____

4 **HISTORY** What was happening globally that may have motivated the Dutch to begin overseas explorations? Cite details from the text that support your claim.

_____

_____

_____

_____

_____

The Fur Trade

DIRECTIONS: Examine the image below and answer the accompanying questions.

EXPLORE THE CONTEXT: The French who explored and settled in North America established trade relationships with many Native American groups. The French were especially interested in trading or trapping for furs to send back to Europe. Deer hide, known as buckskin, was important in this trade. This engraving shows the Native Americans trapping deer. This piece was originally a wood engraving made c. 1600 by Samuel de Champlain, an explorer hired by the French. During his explorations he wrote journals and sketched images of what he saw and found.

PRIMARY SOURCE: ENGRAVING

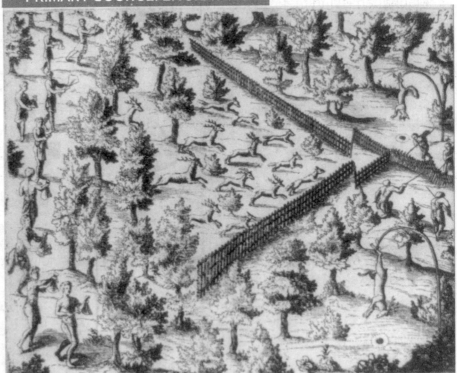

1 **ANALYZING** How are the Iroquois depicted in this image? Describe their actions and what they are doing behind the deer.

_____

_____

_____

_____

2 **DRAWING CONCLUSIONS** Using the visual information in the image, explain why Native Americans might build fencing in the woods.

_____

_____

_____

3 **ECONOMICS** How might the actions of the Iroquois impact them economically?

_____

_____

_____

_____

_____

_____

4 **ANALYZING SOURCES** Using the text from Lesson 3, how might this image relate to European colonies?

_____

_____

_____

_____

_____

ESSENTIAL QUESTION

Why do civilizations rise and fall?

1 Think About It

Review the Supporting Questions that you developed at the beginning of the chapter. Review the evidence that you gathered in the chapter. Were you able to answer each Supporting Question?

If there was not enough evidence to answer your Supporting Questions, what additional evidence do you think you need?

2 Organize Your Evidence

Use the chart to organize the evidence you will use to support your position statement. Remember to cite the source of each piece of evidence.

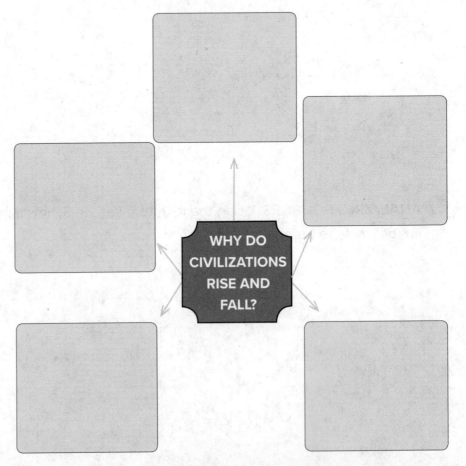

WHY DO CIVILIZATIONS RISE AND FALL?

3 Talk About It

Work with a partner or small group to discuss your position statement and the evidence you have gathered. Before you write your final conclusion, gather ideas from your classmates. Group members should take turns sharing their ideas, asking questions, and offering insights. Use your lesson readings to guide you as you support your ideas.

4 Write About It

Write your position statement for the ESSENTIAL QUESTION, using your gathered information: *Why do civilizations rise and fall?*

_____

_____

_____

5 Connect to the Essential Question

With your partner or group, create a slide show presentation about why civilizations rise and fall, using what you've learned in this chapter about civilizations. In developing your presentation, use the evidence you gathered to answer the Supporting Questions. Find images on the Internet to enhance your presentation to make it more visually interesting.

TAKING ACTION

MAKE CONNECTIONS Think about civilization in North America and in the United States in particular and what you have learned from the text about making a nation strong. List some important elements you feel will keep America thriving.

DIRECTIONS: Choose one element you believe is essential for a nation or civilization to thrive. Then compose a speech that you might deliver to students your age about the future of the United States. In your speech, list the important elements that you think will help America thrive, and emphasize the one element that you think is most important. Use the space here to make an outline of your speech.

_____

_____

_____

_____

_____

_____

_____

_____

_____

_____

_____

_____

The Scientific Revolution and the Enlightenment

ESSENTIAL QUESTION

How do new ideas change the way people live?

Think about how this question might relate to the Scientific Revolution and the Enlightenment.

TALK ABOUT IT

Discuss with a partner what type of information you would need to know to answer this question. For example, one question might be: Why are the events and ideas that occurred during these eras so significant?

DIRECTIONS: Now write down three additional questions that you need to answer to be able to explain the importance of these eras and their ideas.

MY RESEARCH QUESTIONS

Supporting Question 1:

_____

_____

Supporting Question 2:

_____

_____

Supporting Question 3:

_____

ESSENTIAL QUESTION

How do new ideas change the way people live?

As you gather evidence to answer the Essential Question, think about:

- the significance of the Scientific Revolution.
- the scientists who changed the way people thought about Earth and the wider universe.
- how new ideas were able to spread throughout Europe.
- how the discoveries during this era are linked to today's ideas and knowledge.

My Notes

_____

_____

_____

_____

_____

_____

_____

The Scientific Revolution

DIRECTIONS: Search for evidence in Lesson 1 to help you answer the following questions.

1 UNDERSTANDING CHRONOLOGY Complete the graphic organizer below to explain how geographic exploration influenced the development of science.

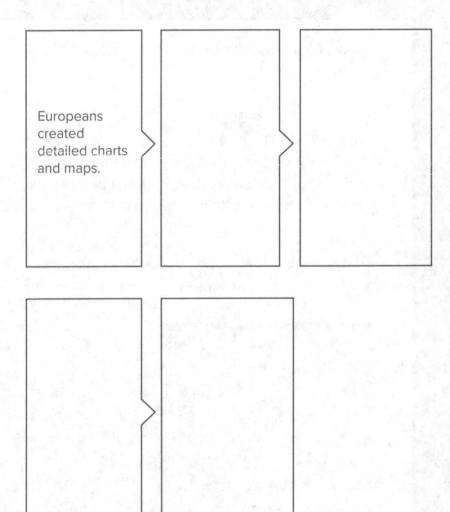

Europeans created detailed charts and maps.

2 EXPLAINING ISSUES What prompted English thinker Francis Bacon to develop the scientific method?

_____

3 **COMPARING** Complete the Venn diagram.

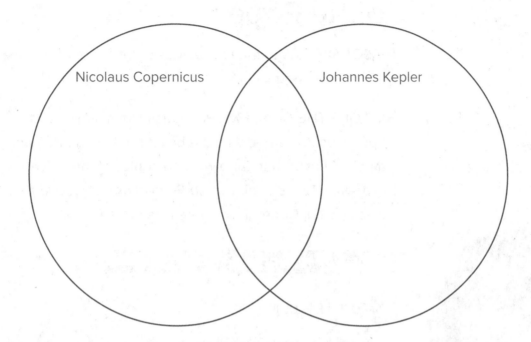

Nicolaus Copernicus

Johannes Kepler

4 **IDENTIFYING EFFECTS** Complete the following chart about Italian scientist Galileo Galilei.

Contribution	Contribution's Purpose or Result
Designed and built his own telescope	
Improved how clocks operated	
Invented a water thermometer	
Conducted experiments with weight and objects	

5 **EXPLAINING** How did dissection affect the Scientific Revolution?

_____

_____

_____

Copernicus's Explanation to the Pope

ESSENTIAL QUESTION

How do new ideas change the way people live?

DIRECTIONS: Read the following excerpt and answer the accompanying questions.

EXPLORE THE CONTEXT: Polish astronomer Nicolaus Copernicus disagreed with the belief held by the Roman Catholic Church that Earth was the center of the universe. In the preface to his book *On the Revolutions of Heavenly Bodies* (1543), Copernicus addresses Pope Paul III.

PRIMARY SOURCE: BOOK PREFACE

❝TO POPE PAUL III

I can easily conceive, most Holy Father, that as soon as some people learn that in this book which I have written concerning the revolutions of the heavenly bodies, I ascribe certain motions to the Earth, they will cry out at once that I and my theory should be rejected. For I am not so much in love with my conclusions as not to weigh what others will think about them, and although I know that the meditations of a philosopher are far removed from the judgment of the laity, because his endeavor is to seek out the truth in all things, so far as this is permitted by God to the human reason, I still believe that one must avoid theories altogether foreign to orthodoxy. Accordingly, when I considered in my own mind how absurd a performance it must seem to those who know that the judgment of many centuries has approved the view that the Earth remains fixed as center in the midst of the heavens, if I should, on the contrary, assert that the Earth moves. ❞

— Nicolaus Copernicus, *On the Revolutions of Heavenly Bodies*, 1543

VOCABULARY

conceive: imagine

ascribe: assign

meditations: thoughts

laity: church congregation

foreign: not related to

orthodoxy: custom

assert: declare, defend

1 **SUMMARIZING** What does Copernicus think the reaction of most people will be to his theory?

_____

_____

_____

_____

2 **DETERMINING CONTEXT** What does Copernicus mean when he says his thoughts are "far removed from the judgment of the laity?"

_____

_____

_____

_____

3 **IDENTIFYING PERSPECTIVES** Why is the phrase "so far as this is permitted by God to the human reason" significant?

_____

_____

_____

_____

4 **PREDICTING** How do you think the Roman Catholic Church reacted to Copernicus's book?

_____

_____

_____

_____

Kepler's Prayer

ESSENTIAL QUESTION

How do new ideas change the way people live?

DIRECTIONS: Read the following excerpt written by German astronomer Johannes Kepler and answer the accompanying questions.

EXPLORE THE CONTEXT: Using mathematics, Kepler supported Copernicus's theory that the planets revolved around the sun, not Earth. He also proposed other ideas regarding planets and how they moved. Devoted to his work, Kepler's efforts are considered the beginning of modern astronomy.

PRIMARY SOURCE: BOOK

❝It now remains that at last, with my eyes and hands removed from the tablet of demonstrations and lifted up towards the heavens, I should pray, devout and supplicating, to the Father of lights: O Thou Who dost by the light of nature promote in us the desire for the light of grace, that by its means Thou mayest transport us into the light of glory, I give thanks to Thee, O Lord Creator, Who hast delighted me with Thy makings and in the works of Thy hands have I exulted. Behold! now, I have completed the work of my profession, having employed as much power of mind as Thou didst give to me. . . . ❞

— Johannes Kepler, *Harmonies of the World,* 1619

VOCABULARY

devout: serious, heartfelt

supplicating: praying, appealing, begging

dost: does

promote: encourage

exulted: rejoice

1 **ANALYZING** Who is Kepler speaking to in this excerpt? What message does he share?

_____

_____

_____

_____

2 DESCRIBING Describe the mood of the excerpt.

_____

_____

_____

_____

_____

_____

_____

3 EXPLAINING How does Kepler link God and the natural world?

_____

_____

_____

_____

_____

_____

_____

4 COMPARING In addition to their theories, what do Kepler and Copernicus have in common? Use the excerpt from Copernicus's _On the Revolutions of Heavenly Bodies_ to help you.

_____

_____

_____

_____

_____

_____

ESSENTIAL QUESTION

How do new ideas change the way people live?

As you gather evidence to answer the Essential Question, think about:

- how great thinkers both agreed and disagreed about ideas.
- how books of the era promoted nontraditional beliefs and change.
- how the Enlightenment helped the lives of serfs.
- how different rulers chose to treat their subjects during the Enlightenment.

My Notes

The Enlightenment

DIRECTIONS: Search for evidence in Lesson 2 to help you answer the following questions.

1   **CIVICS**   How did the Age of Enlightenment affect ideas of government?

2 IDENTIFYING CAUSES What events caused England to become a constitutional monarchy?

3 EXPLAINING Explain how the monarchy of France's King Louis XIV differed from the constitutional monarchy of England.

4 CONTRASTING Complete the chart.

Individual	Published Work	How It Affected the Enlightenment
Baron Montesquieu		
Denis Diderot		
Mary Wollstonecraft		
Jean-Jacques Rousseau		

5 COMPARING How were Frederick II of Prussia, Maria Theresa of Austria, and Joseph II of Austria similar?

_____

_____

6 IDENTIFYING EFFECTS What was the result of the Russian serf revolt?

_____

_____

_____

_____

Thomas Hobbes on Man's Worth

ESSENTIAL QUESTION

How do new ideas change the way people live?

DIRECTIONS: Read the following excerpt and answer the accompanying questions.

EXPLORE THE CONTEXT: Thomas Hobbes, an English writer, wrote his book *Leviathan* in 1651. Hobbes had strong feelings about human behavior, essentially believing that people had a natural instinct to be selfish and violent toward others. In the excerpt below, he writes about a person's value, or worth.

PRIMARY SOURCE: BOOK

❝ The Value, or WORTH of a man, is as of all other things, his Price; that is to say, so much as would be given for the use of his Power: and therefore is not absolute; but a thing dependant on the need and judgement of another. An able conductor of Souldiers, is of great Price in time of War present, or imminent; but in Peace not so. A learned and uncorrupt Judge, is much Worth in time of Peace; but not so much in War. And as in other things, so in men, not the seller, but the buyer determines the Price. For let a man (as most men do,) rate themselves as the highest Value they can; yet their true Value is no more than it is esteemed by others.

The manifestation of the Value we set on one another, is that which is commonly called Honouring, and Dishonouring. To Value a man at a high rate, is to Honour him; at a low rate, is to Dishonour him. But high, and low, in this case, is to be understood by comparison to the rate that each man setteth on himselfe. ❞

— Thomas Hobbes, *Leviathan*

VOCABULARY

absolute: complete
Souldiers: Soldiers
imminent: pending, about to occur
learned: educated
uncorrupt: honest
esteemed: valued, admired
manifestation: expression
setteth: sets

1 **ANALYZING TEXT** Hobbes uses the example of a soldier in discussing what a person is worth. He says that a soldier has a "great Price in time of War . . . but in Peace not so." What is Hobbes saying about how a change in circumstances can change what soldiers are worth?

_____

_____

_____

_____

2 **ANALYZING POINTS OF VIEW** Describe the tone of the excerpt.

_____

_____

_____

_____

3 **INFERRING** How does Hobbes believe that a person's value is determined?

_____

_____

_____

_____

4 **CONTRASTING** Compare this sentence with the one in question 3: "But high, and low, in this case, is to be understood by comparison to the rate that each man setteth on himselfe." According to Hobbes, what role do individuals take regarding their own worth?

_____

_____

_____

John Locke on the Different Types of Laws

DIRECTIONS: Read the following excerpt and answer the accompanying questions.

EXPLORE THE CONTEXT: John Locke wrote his book *Two Treatises of Government* in 1690. In it, he focused on several ideas of the Glorious Revolution.

VOCABULARY

annexted: annexed, seized

inforce: enforce, impose

conformable: able to follow or obey

fundamental: basic

sanction: restriction

valid: legal, official

PRIMARY SOURCE: BOOK

❝The obligations of the law or nature cease not in society, but only in many cases are drawn closer, and have by human laws known penalties annexted to them, to inforce their observation. Thus the law of nature stands as an eternal rule to all men, legislators as well as others. The rules that they make for other men's actions, must, as well as their own and other men's actions, be conformable to the law of nature, i.e. to the will of God, of which that is a declaration, and the fundamental law of nature being the preservation of mankind, no human sanction can be good, or valid against it. ❞

— John Locke, *Two Treatises of Government*

1 **IDENTIFYING** What law does Locke believe everyone must obey?

_____

_____

_____

_____

_____

_____

2 **ANALYZING TEXT** What does Locke mean when he says that the rules, or laws, legislators make must be "conformable to the law of nature"?

_____

_____

_____

_____

_____

_____

_____

_____

3 CIVICS How does Locke view the behavior of legislators compared with otherindividuals in society?

_____

_____

_____

_____

_____

_____

_____

4 **EXPLAINING** Explain the role Locke believes God plays in society.

_____

_____

_____

_____

_____

_____

_____

*How do new ideas change
the way people live?*

1 Think About It

Review the supporting questions that you developed at
the beginning of the chapter. Review the evidence that
you gathered in this chapter. Were you able to answer
each Supporting Question?

If there was not enough evidence to answer your
Supporting Questions, what additional evidence do you
think you need to consider?

_____

_____

_____

_____

_____

2 Organize Your Evidence

Use a chart like the one below to organize the evidence
you will use to support your position statement.

Central Idea

Supporting Details

③ Write About It

A position statement related to the Essential Question should reflect your conclusion about the evidence. Write a position statement for the ESSENTIAL QUESTION: *How do new ideas change the way people live?*

_____

_____

_____

_____

_____

_____

_____

_____

_____

_____

_____

④ Talk About It

Work in a small group to present your position statement and evidence. Gather feedback from your classmates before you write your final conclusion. You may choose to refine your position statement after you have discussed it with your classmates. Group members should listen to each other's arguments, ask questions, and offer constructive advice about the statement.

⑤ Connect to the Essential Question

On a separate piece of paper, develop an interview with one of the scientists described in this chapter to answer the ESSENTIAL QUESTION: *How do new ideas change the way people live?*

CITIZENSHIP
TAKING ACTION

MAKING CONNECTIONS The Scientific Revolution had a profound effect on how people began to think differently about nature and the world around them. People began using the scientific method to help them test theories. Science could be used to make people's lives better.

DIRECTIONS: Think about the role of science today. With a partner, discuss how science influences the way people think and make decisions about the environment, health care, and other issues. How does today's science help to make people's lives better? Create a poster, mural, or slide show that shows examples of how science is, or could be, used to improve the way people live in your community.

Political and Industrial Revolutions

ESSENTIAL QUESTIONS

- ## Why does conflict develop?
- ## Why is history important?
- ## How do governments change?
- ## How does technology change the way people live?
- ## How do new ideas change the way people live?

Think about the events and attitudes that have led to revolutionary changes throughout history.

COLLABORATE

TALK ABOUT IT

With a partner, talk about the kinds of information you will need to answer these Essential Questions.

DIRECTIONS: Now write three additional questions that will help you explain why conflict develops and why people strive for changes in society and in government.

MY RESEARCH QUESTIONS

Supporting Question 1:

_____

_____

Supporting Question 2:

_____

_____

Supporting Question 3:

_____

_____

ESSENTIAL QUESTION

Why does conflict develop?

As you gather evidence to answer the Essential Question, think about:

- the events and conditions in the American colonies that led the colonists to revolt.

- the actions taken by the British government that enraged the colonists.

- how the government created by the colonists after the American Revolution fit their civic needs and desires.

My Notes

_____

_____

_____

_____

_____

_____

_____

_____

_____

The American Revolution

DIRECTIONS: Search for evidence in this lesson to help you answer the following questions.

1 **CITING TEXT EVIDENCE** How did early colonists exert their desire for freedom and independence from European influence?

_____

_____

_____

_____

_____

2 ECONOMICS How did trade create conflict between the colonists and Britain?

_____

_____

_____

_____

_____

_____

3 CIVICS How did the government created by newly independent states differ from that under British rule?

_____

_____

_____

_____

_____

4 IDENTIFYING CAUSES Use the following chart to show the events and actions that caused the American colonists to revolt against British rule.

Causes

→

Effect: REVOLUTION

5 DRAWING CONCLUSIONS How was the Declaration of Independence vital to justifying the conflict and uniting the colonists?

_____

_____

6 ANALYZING INFORMATION Why did it seem unlikely that the Americans would win the war for independence?

_____

_____

7 CONTRASTING How did the Articles of Confederation differ from the U.S. Constitution that replaced it?

_____

_____

_____

_____

Speech to the Continental Congress

ESSENTIAL QUESTION

Why does conflict develop?

DIRECTIONS: Study the excerpt below and answer the accompanying questions.

EXPLORE THE CONTEXT: In 1774, conflict between the American colonies and Britain was brewing, and delegates to the Continental Congress convened to discuss the issues. In this speech given in 1774, Joseph Galloway, a delegate from Pennsylvania, outlines some of the reasons why the colonists were angry with the actions of the British government.

VOCABULARY

incursion: invasion or intrusion
commencement: beginning
levied: imposed
actuated: motivated
oppressive: burdensome
grievances: complaints

PRIMARY SOURCE: SPEECH

❝ [W]e must take into consideration a number of facts which led the Parliament to pass the acts complained of, since the year 1763, and the real state of the Colonies. . . . I will therefore call your recollection to the dangerous situation of the Colonies from the intrigues of France, and the incursions of the Canadians and their Indian allies, at the commencement of the last war. None of us can be ignorant of . . . the cheerfulness with which Great-Britain sent over her fleets and armies for their protection, of the millions she expended in that protection, and of the happy consequences which attended it.

In this state of the Colonies it was not unreasonable to expect that Parliament would have levied a tax on them proportionate to their wealth. . . . But what was the conduct of the Colonies on this occasion . . . ? [N]one gave equitably in proportion to their wealth, and all that did give were actuated by partial and self-interested motives, and gave only in proportion to the approach or remoteness of the danger. . . .

To remedy these mischiefs, Parliament was naturally led to exercise the power which had been, by its predecessors, so often exercised over the Colonies, and to pass the Stamp Act. . . .

As to the tax, it is neither unjust or oppressive, . . . but it is want of constitutional principle in the authority that passed it, which is the ground for complaint. . . . [T]his only, is the source of American grievances. Here, and here only, is the defect; and if this defect were removed, a foundation would be laid for the relief of every American complaint. . . . **"**

—from Speech to the Continental Congress by Joseph Galloway, 1774

1 **IDENTIFYING CAUSES** What conflict is mentioned in this speech that convinced the British to pass the Stamp Act?

_____

_____

2 CIVICS What is Galloway's primary political issue regarding the way the Stamp Act was imposed?

_____

_____

3 **RELATING EVENTS** Why did Britain send large numbers of troops to North America?

_____

_____

4 **INFERRING** According to Galloway, how might the problem described have been avoided if taxes had been levied proportionately?

_____

_____

_____

5 **PREDICTING** What defect described by Galloway can you predict will help shape the government of the United States?

_____

_____

_____

Common Sense

Copyright © McGraw-Hill Education   Paine, Thomas. Common Sense. Girard, Kans.: Haldeman-Julius Company, 1920, 38.

ESSENTIAL QUESTION

Why does conflict develop?

VOCABULARY

fallacious: false, wrong; illogical

precedent: earlier example

DIRECTIONS: Study the excerpt below and answer the accompanying questions.

EXPLORE THE CONTEXT: Thomas Paine was an influential writer who argued that it was necessary and good for the people of the American colonies to rebel against British rule. This excerpt reflects his writing style and his talent to persuade through reason.

PRIMARY SOURCE: PAMPHLET

❝I have heard it asserted by some, that as America has flourished under her former connection with Great Britain, the same connection is necessary towards her future happiness, and will always have the same effect. Nothing can be more fallacious than this kind of argument. We may as well assert that because a child has thrived upon milk, that it is never to have meat, or that the first twenty years of our lives is to become a precedent for the next twenty. But even this is admitting more than is true; for I answer roundly that America would have flourished as much, and probably much more, had no European power taken any notice of her. The commerce by which she hath enriched herself are the necessaries of life, and will always have a market while eating is the custom of Europe. ❞

— from *Common Sense* by Thomas Paine, 1776

---

1 DETERMINING MEANING What fallacy, or error, does Paine argue against in this paragraph?

_____

_____

_____

2 **CITING TEXT EVIDENCE** What metaphor does Paine use in his argument?

_____

_____

_____

_____

_____

3 ECONOMICS What can you infer about what type of goods the colonies would have traded with Europe?

_____

_____

_____

_____

_____

4 **IDENTIFYING PERSPECTIVES** What is Paine's perspective on European interference with the American colonies?

_____

_____

_____

_____

_____

5 **IDENTIFYING CAUSES** According to Paine's argument in this excerpt, what is the main source of conflict between the colonists and the British?

_____

_____

_____

_____

_____

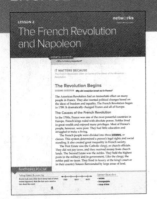

The French Revolution and Napoleon

DIRECTIONS: Search for evidence in this lesson to help you answer the following questions.

ESSENTIAL QUESTION

Why is history important?

As you gather evidence to answer the Essential Question, think about:

- ways in which the French Revolution was similar to and different from the American Revolution.

- whether Napoleon's rule benefited or damaged the aspirations of the French people.

- how the Congress of Vienna changed Europe for the good and the bad.

My Notes

1 **IDENTIFYING CAUSES** Use the following diagram to identify causes of the French Revolution.

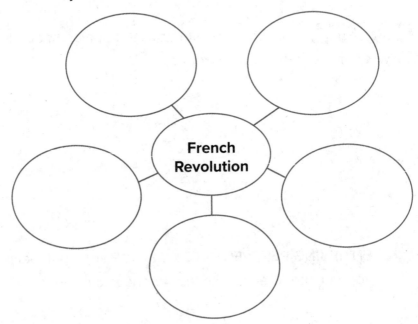

2 **UNDERSTANDING CHANGE** How was France governed in the early 1700s? How did this change after the French Revolution?

3 **COMPARING** How was the Declaration of the Rights of Man and of the Citizen like the Declaration of Independence?

_____

_____

4 **EVALUATING** Did the French Revolution have a positive or a negative impact on the French people? Explain.

_____

_____

_____

_____

_____

5 **IDENTIFYING CAUSES** How did Napoleon rise to power?

_____

_____

_____

_____

6 HISTORY What two situations led to Napoleon's downfall? Explain.

_____

_____

_____

7 **SUMMARIZING** How did Europe change after Napoleon's defeat?

_____

_____

_____

Declaration of the Rights of Man and of the Citizen

Copyright © McGraw-Hill Education   Van Kley, Dale. ed., The French Idea of Freedom: The Old Regime and the Declaration of Rights of 1789. Stanford, California: Stanford University Press, 1994. 1.

ESSENTIAL QUESTION

Why is history important?

DIRECTIONS: Study the excerpt below and answer the accompanying questions.

EXPLORE THE CONTEXT: Partly inspired by the success of the American Revolution, the oppressed people of France rose up to overthrow their monarchy. They created in its place a government of the people that helped the poor, promoted equality, and gave them justice. This excerpt is from the founding document that sets out the principles of the new revolutionary government.

VOCABULARY

constituted: organized

resolved: determined, decided

inalienable: inherent; not able to be denied or taken away

incontestable: unable to be challenged

PRIMARY SOURCE: SPEECH

"The representatives of the French people, constituted as the National Assembly, considering that ignorance, disregard, or contempt for the rights of man are the sole causes of public misfortunes and the corruption of governments, have resolved to set forth, in a solemn declaration, the natural, inalienable, and sacred rights of man, so that the constant presence of this declaration may ceaselessly remind all members of the social body of their rights and duties; so that the acts of the legislative power and those of the executive power may be the more respected, since it will be possible at each moment to compare them against the goal of every political institution; and so that the demands of the citizens, grounded henceforth on simple and incontestable principles, may always be directed to the maintenance of the constitution and to the welfare of all. "

—from *The Declaration of the Rights of Man and of the Citizen*, 1789

1 INFERRING What can you infer from the text about the members of the new French National Assembly?

_____

2 CIVICS What principles does the declaration state will guide the new revolutionary government of France?

_____

_____

_____

3 CONTRASTING How does the revolutionary government, as described here, differ in its attitude toward the people from the monarchy the people rebelled against?

_____

_____

4 DRAWING CONCLUSIONS According to this document, who determines what the new revolutionary government does?

_____

5 SUMMARIZING In one sentence, describe why the principles of the new government likely arose from the way the monarchy had ruled France.

_____

_____

_____

6 IDENTIFYING CAUSES How do you think the American Revolution of 1776 affected the rising of the French in their revolution?

_____

_____

_____

Napoleon's Diary

DIRECTIONS: Study the excerpt below and answer the accompanying questions.

EXPLORE THE CONTEXT: As government in the aftermath of the French Revolution seemed to lose its way, the French military gained power and influence. Napoleon Bonaparte's immense military talent boosted him to the rank of general. He led French troops in the conquest of large parts of Europe. Then in a markedly unrevolutionary move, Napoleon declared himself emperor in 1804. By 1817, however, Napoleon had lost his empire and his power.

PRIMARY SOURCE: SPEECH

❝ March 3, 1817

In spite of all the libels, I have no fear whatever about my fame. Posterity will do me justice. The truth will be known; and the good I have done will be compared with the faults I have committed. I am not uneasy as to the result. Had I succeeded, I would have died with the reputation of the greatest man that ever existed. As it is, although I have failed, I shall be considered as an extraordinary man: my elevation was unparalleled, because unaccompanied by crime. I have fought fifty pitched battles, almost all of which I have won. I have framed and carried into effect a code of laws that will bear my name to the most distant posterity. I raised myself from nothing to be the most powerful monarch in the world. Europe was at my feet. I have always been of opinion that the sovereignty lay in the people. In fact, the imperial government was a kind of republic. Called to the head of it by the voice of the nation, my maxim was, *la carrière est ouverte aux talens* without distinction of birth or fortune, and this system of equality is the reason that your oligarchy hates me so much. ❞

—from *The Corsican: A Diary of Napoleon's Life in His Own Words*
by Napoleon I, Emperor of the French, 1817

VOCABULARY

libels: lies or accusations that damage one's reputation
posterity: future generations
sovereignty: rule or power, as of a national government or its leader
maxim: fundamental principle or general truth
la carrière est ouverte aux talens: "the career is open to the talented"
oligarchy: rule by a small group of the rich, powerful, and often corrupt

Napoleon I. The Corsican: A Diary of Napoleon's Life in His Own Words. Boston and New York: Houghton Mifflin Company, 1910. 492.

1 ANALYZING INDIVIDUALS How does Napoleon view himself, his life, and his accomplishments?

_____

_____

_____

_____

_____

2 IDENTIFYING PERSPECTIVES When Napoleon writes, "I am not uneasy as to the result," what is he referring to? What does it reveal about Napoleon?

_____

_____

_____

_____

_____

3 GEOGRAPHY Which region of the world did Napoleon rule over that convinced him to call himself "emperor," or ruler over an empire and not just one nation?

_____

_____

4 EVALUATING TEXT EVIDENCE What does Napoleon explain in this text that makes his rise to power so remarkable? In what way does his personal history reflect a value most Americans admire?

_____

_____

_____

_____

_____

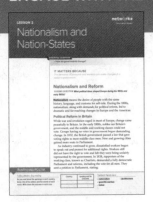

ESSENTIAL QUESTION

How do governments change?

As you gather evidence to answer the Essential Question, think about:

- how political and social reform in Britain differed from how it was achieved in many other countries of Europe.
- ways in which nationalism brought change to the United States.
- how Latin America faced many challenges even after winning its fight for independence.

My Notes

Nationalism and Nation-States

DIRECTIONS: Search for evidence in this lesson to help you answer the following questions.

1 RELATING EVENTS Use the following sequence chart to show the order of some of the events that brought social and political reform to Britain.

Date:	Event:

Date:	Event:

Date:	Event:

Date:	Event:

Date:	Event:

2 SUMMARIZING Why did the Irish want home rule? Why didn't they achieve it?

3 DETERMINING CENTRAL IDEAS How did Bismarck unite Germany?

_____

_____

_____

4 GEOGRAPHY How did the belief in Manifest Destiny drive the U.S. expansion all the way to the Pacific Ocean?

_____

_____

_____

5 COMPARING AND CONTRASTING What advantages did the North have over the South during the Civil War? What disadvantages did it have?

_____

_____

_____

6 COMPARING How was the effect of nationalism in Latin America similar to the effect of nationalism in Europe?

_____

_____

_____

7 EXPLAINING ISSUES Why didn't independence bring prosperity and peace to Latin America?

_____

_____

_____

_____

The "Corner Stone" Speech

Copyright © McGraw-Hill Education   Stephens, Alexander H.   "Corner Stone Speech." 1861 In Brewer, David J. Ed., The World's Best Orations. St. Louis: Ferd. P. Kaiser, 1900.

ESSENTIAL QUESTION

How do governments change?

DIRECTIONS: Study the excerpt below and answer the accompanying questions.

EXPLORE THE CONTEXT: After the South seceded, its new government—the Confederacy—wrote its own constitution in which slavery was upheld. Alexander Stephens, who was vice president of the Confederacy, delivered the speech from which this excerpt is taken. It offers an insight into the Southerners' justifications for slavery.

PRIMARY SOURCE: SPEECH

“African slavery . . . was the immediate cause of the late rupture and present revolution. Jefferson, in his forecast, had anticipated this, as the 'rock upon which the old Union would split.' He was right. . . . But whether he fully comprehended the great truth upon which that rock stood and stands may be doubted. The prevailing ideas entertained by him and most of the leading statesmen at the time of the formation of the old Constitution were that the enslavement of the African was in violation of the laws of nature; that it was wrong in principle, socially, morally, and politically. It was an evil they knew not well how to deal with; but the general opinion of the men of that day was that, somehow or other, in the order of Providence, the institution would be evanescent and pass away. . . . The Constitution, it is true, secured every essential guarantee to the institution while it should last, and hence no argument can be justly urged against the constitutional guaranties thus secured, because of the common sentiment of the day. Those ideas, however, were fundamentally wrong. They rested upon the assumption of the equality of races. This was an error. It was a sandy foundation, and the government built upon it fell when the 'storm came and the wind blew.'”

—from *On the Confederate Constitution* by Alexander Stephens, 1861

VOCABULARY

Providence: divine guidance in human affairs; God
evanescent: vanishing; not substantial
sentiment: attitude or judgment

1 ANALYZING TEXT According to Stephens, how did Jefferson and others like him foresee the end of slavery in the United States?

_____

_____

_____

_____

2 INTERPRETING TEXT Why couldn't those opposed to slavery use the U.S. Constitution to support their point of view?

_____

_____

_____

3 CITING TEXT EVIDENCE What reason does Stephens give for the failure of antislavery arguments and principles at the time that the Constitution was written? Cite the text in your answer.

_____

_____

_____

_____

4 INTERPRETING According to Stephens, which government fell because it was based on a "sandy foundation"?

_____

_____

5 HISTORY What evidence does Stephens present that supports his argument in favor of slavery?

_____

_____

_____

_____

Copyright © McGraw-Hill Education   Pankhurst, Emeline. Votes for Women – Letter to Members of Women's Social and Political Union (WSPU), January 10, 1913. Reprinted by The National Archives (UK) website. 1913.

Emmeline Pankhurst's Letter to Suffragettes

ESSENTIAL QUESTION

How do governments change?

DIRECTIONS: Study the excerpt below and answer the accompanying questions.

EXPLORE THE CONTEXT: Emmeline Pankhurst campaigned for women's right to vote in Great Britain. In this letter, she describes her view of the role of women in the fight for the right to vote if the Women's Amendments bill fails to pass.

VOCABULARY

militancy: dedicated aggressive action in pursuit of a goal

militant: one who is aggressive or fierce in pursuit of a goal

PRIMARY SOURCE: LETTER

66 Dear Friend,

The Prime Minister has announced that in the week beginning January 20th the Women's Amendments to the Manhood Suffrage Bill will be discussed and voted upon. This means that within a few short days the fate of these Amendments will be finally decided. . . .

But every member of the W.S.P.U. recognises that the defeat of the Amendments will make militancy more a moral duty and more a political necessity than it has ever been before. We must prepare beforehand to deal with that situation!

. . . Some women are able to go further than others in militant action and each woman is the judge of her own duty so far as that is concerned. To be militant in some way or other is, however, a moral obligation. It is a duty which every woman will owe to her own conscience and self-respect, to other women who are less fortunate than she herself is, and to all those who are to come after her.

If any woman refrains from militant protest against the injury done by the Government and the House of Commons to women and to the race, she will share the responsibility for the crime. Submission under such circumstances will be itself a crime. . . .

We must, as I have said, prepare to meet the crisis before it arises. . . .

Yours sincerely,

(Signed) E. Pankhurst 99

—Letter to Members of Women's Social and Political Union by Emmeline Pankhurst, 1913

1 CIVICS How do you know from the text that Emmeline Pankhurst is discussing British suffrage, not American?

_____

_____

_____

_____

2 **IDENTIFYING CAUSES** What political event does Pankhurst say will make it necessary for women to work even harder to gain the right to vote?

_____

3 **ANALYZING CENTRAL IDEAS** How does Pankhurst describe the lack of action in support of woman suffrage? How does this compare to her reasonable words about doing what you can for the cause?

_____

_____

_____

4 **DETERMINING CENTRAL IDEAS** When does Pankhurst believe that militant action should be prepared? Why do you think she advocates for this timely action?

_____

_____

_____

5 **INFERRING** What can you infer from this letter about what Pankhurst believes the outcome of the Women's Suffrage Bill will be? Support your answer with evidence from the text.

_____

_____

_____

_____

ESSENTIAL QUESTION

How does technology change the way people live?

As you gather evidence to answer the Essential Question, think about:

- how advances made during the Industrial Revolution benefited individuals and society.

- how changes in society created opportunities for industrial growth.

- how inventions fed the pace of industrialization.

My Notes

The Industrial Revolution

DIRECTIONS: Search for evidence in this lesson to help you answer the following questions.

1 **ECONOMICS** Where did the capital necessary for fostering the Industrial Revolution come from? Explain.

2 **IDENTIFYING CAUSES** Use the following diagram to identify causes behind the emergence of the Industrial Revolution in Britain.

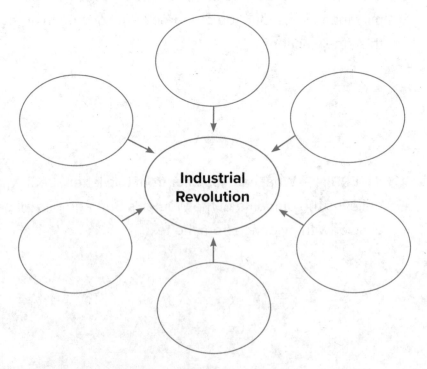

3 **IDENTIFYING CAUSES** Why did factories develop?

_____

_____

_____

_____

4 **DETERMINING CENTRAL IDEAS** How did the Industrial Revolution spread to other lands from Britain?

_____

_____

_____

_____

5 **IDENTIFYING CAUSES** How did improvements in transportation contribute to industrial development?

_____

_____

_____

_____

6 **SUMMARIZING** Why were inventors so important to the Industrial Revolution?

_____

_____

_____

_____

_____

How New Technology Changed an Industry

ESSENTIAL QUESTION
How does technology change the way people live?

DIRECTIONS: Study the excerpt below and answer the accompanying questions.

EXPLORE THE CONTEXT: Cloth weaving on a loom was an important industry in Britain in the 1700s. In this excerpt, Edward Baines describes how a simple idea improved the production of cloth during these early days of industrialization.

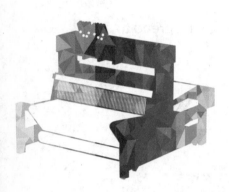

SECONDARY SOURCE: BOOK

> ❝In the year 1738, Mr. John Kay, a native of Bury, in Lancashire, then residing at Colchester, where the woollen manufacture was at that time carried on, suggested a mode of throwing the shuttle, which enabled the weaver to make nearly twice as much cloth as he could make before. The old mode was, to throw the shuttle with the hand, which required a constant extension of the hands to each side of the warp. By the new plan, the lathe (in which the shuttle runs) was lengthened a foot at either end; and, by means of two strings attached to the opposite ends of the lathe, and both held by a peg in the weaver's hand, he, with a slight and sudden pluck, was able to give the proper impulse to the shuttle. The shuttle thus impelled was called the *flying-shuttle*, and the peg was called the *picking-peg* (i.e. the *throwing* peg). This simple contrivance was a great saving of time and exertion to the weaver, and enabled one man to weave the widest cloth, which had before required two persons.❞

—from *The History of the Cotton Manufacture in Great Britain* by Edward Baines, 1835

VOCABULARY

Lancashire: a region in northwest England

shuttle: a weaving device that holds the thread and moves it through threads to weave cloth

warp: yarns extending lengthwise in a weaving loom

lathe: supporting stands at either side of a loom

contrivance: clever plan or setup

1 **DIFFERENTIATING** How did the flying-shuttle differ from the older style of shuttle?

_____

_____

_____

_____

2 **UNDERSTANDING CHANGE** How did the flying-shuttle make working at the loom easier for weavers?

_____

_____

_____

_____

3A **ECONOMICS** What text evidence supports the idea that the owners of cloth-making factories were happy to adopt the flying-shuttle in the manufacturing process?

_____

_____

_____

_____

3B **ECONOMICS** What economic benefits would the flying-shuttle have for industry owners?

_____

_____

_____

_____

James Watt's Breakthrough

Copyright © McGraw-Hill Education   Smiles, Samuel. Lives of the Engineers: Boulton and Watt. London: John Murray, 1904. 88-89.

ESSENTIAL QUESTION

How does technology change the way people live?

VOCABULARY

inquiries: questions, studies, or experiments

Newcomen model: an early steam engine, invented by Thomas Newcomen in 1712, that used atmospheric pressure to move parts of the engine

ignis fatuus: a misleading objective or hope

DIRECTIONS: Study the excerpt below and answer the accompanying questions.

EXPLORE THE CONTEXT: This excerpt describes James Watt's experience as he worked to perfect his invention—the steam engine. Watt didn't begin from scratch. Rather, he began by studying Thomas Newcomen's earlier, less-efficient steam engine, which was developed sometime before 1712.

> **SECONDARY SOURCE: BOOK**
>
> ❝Watt continued to pursue his studies as before. Though still occupied with his inquiries and experiments as to steam, he did not neglect his proper business, but was constantly on the look-out for improvements in instrument making. . . .
>
> Above all other subjects, however, the improvement of the steam-engine continued to keep the fastest hold upon his mind. He still brooded over his experiments with the Newcomen model, but did not seem to make much way in introducing any practical improvement in its mode of working. . . . He continued, to use his own words, 'to grope in the dark, misled by many an *ignis fatuus*.' It was a favourite saying of his that 'Nature has a weak side, if we can only find it out;' and he went on groping and feeling for it, but as yet in vain. At length light burst upon him, and all at once the problem over which he had been brooding was solved. ❞
>
> —from *Lives of the Engineers* by Samuel Smiles, 1904

1 **SUMMARIZING** What were the two main pursuits that Watt was engaged in?

_____

_____

2 DETERMINING MEANING What do you think Watt meant by seeking "Nature's weak side" to design a better steam engine?

_____

_____

_____

3 CITING TEXT EVIDENCE According to the author, how did Watt finally figure out how to improve on the steam engine?

_____

_____

_____

_____

4 IDENTIFYING CONNECTIONS How might Watt's business of improving the manufacture of instruments have helped him in his invention of an improved steam engine?

_____

_____

_____

_____

5 ECONOMICS How would the improvements in the steam engine change the lives of peoples and societies in the 1700s and 1800s?

_____

_____

_____

_____

_____

_____

ESSENTIAL QUESTION

How do new ideas change the way people live?

As you gather evidence to answer the Essential Question, think about:

- how industry changed society and political ideas.

- how the art movements reflected people's views and attitudes.

- why scientific breakthroughs occurred and how they changed people's lives.

My Notes

Society and Industry

DIRECTIONS: Search for evidence in this lesson to help you answer the following questions.

1 IDENTIFYING EFFECTS How did industrialization affect cities? Explain.

_____

_____

_____

_____

2 ECONOMICS What effect did industrial growth have on the working class?

_____

_____

_____

_____

3 IDENTIFYING CAUSES Why did people turn to labor unions? How did unions try to help workers?

_____

_____

_____

_____

4 CONTRASTING How was romanticism different from realism?

_____

_____

_____

_____

5 **IDENTIFYING CONNECTIONS** How have the scientific advances made in the 1800s affected people's lives today?

_____

_____

_____

_____

_____

_____

6 **CIVICS** How did the liberals, the socialists, and Karl Marx seek to solve problems created by industrialization? What were the basic beliefs of each? Use the chart below to record your answers.

Comparing Political Views		
Liberals	Socialists	Karl Marx

The Bitter Cry of the Children

How do new ideas change the way people live?

VOCABULARY

breakers: mechanisms in a coal plant that break pieces of coal into small chunks and remove some of the noncoal material mixed with the coal
consumption: a term used for the lung disease tuberculosis
pellucid: clear and very light or sunny
expectorating: spitting
anthracite: a high-grade type of coal

DIRECTIONS: Study the excerpt below and answer the accompanying questions.

EXPLORE THE CONTEXT: Before child labor laws were passed in the 1900s, many children worked in factories and mines. This excerpt describes in some detail the dangerous work young boys did in coal-processing plants.

PRIMARY SOURCE: BOOK

❝The coal is hard, and accidents to the hands, such as cut, broken, or crushed fingers, are common among the boys. Sometimes there is a worse accident: a terrified shriek is heard, and a boy is mangled and torn in the machinery, or disappears in the chute to be picked out later smothered and dead. Clouds of dust fill the breakers and are inhaled by the boys, laying the foundations for asthma and miners' consumption. I once stood in a breaker for half an hour and tried to do the work a twelve-year-old boy was doing day after day, for ten hours at a stretch, for sixty cents a day. The gloom of the breaker appalled me. Outside the sun shone brightly, the air was pellucid, and the birds sang in chorus with the trees and the rivers. Within the breaker there was blackness, clouds of deadly dust enfolded everything, the harsh, grinding roar of the machinery and the ceaseless rushing of coal through the chutes filled the ears. I tried to pick out the pieces of slate from the hurrying stream of coal, often missing them; my hands were bruised and cut in a few minutes; I was covered from head to foot with coal dust, and for many hours afterwards I was expectorating some of the small particles of anthracite I had swallowed.❞

—from *The Bitter Cry of the Children* by John Spargo, 1915

1 **IDENTIFYING CONNECTIONS** Steam engines are fueled by coal. How did the new steam technology affect the lives of young boys such as those described in this text?

_____

_____

_____

_____

2 **ANALYZING INFORMATION** How much was a breaker boy paid for one hour of hard work in the coal plant?

_____

_____

3 **CITING TEXT EVIDENCE** What text evidence leads you to conclude that the daily exposure to coal dust could cause diseases?

_____

_____

_____

4 **ANALYZING POINTS OF VIEW** What is the author's purpose in writing this description of breaker boys?

_____

_____

_____

5 **EVALUATING ARGUMENTS** What does the author do personally to support his argument about the horrors of child labor in coal plants?

_____

_____

_____

_____

_____

Einstein's Warning

ESSENTIAL QUESTION

How do new ideas change the way people live?

VOCABULARY

formidable: overwhelming, awesome
harassed: bothered
desist: stop
slacken: relax, slow down
trustees: those who oversee and administer something for the benefit of all

DIRECTIONS: Study the excerpt below and answer the accompanying questions.

EXPLORE THE CONTEXT: Albert Einstein was a scientist whose work helped lay the foundation for the design and creation of the atomic bomb. After the bomb was used at the end of World War II (in 1945), Einstein became concerned about how people would use this powerfully destructive weapon. In this excerpt, Einstein discusses his concerns.

PRIMARY SOURCE: ESSAY

66 Today, the physicists who participated in forging the most formidable and dangerous weapon of all times are harassed by an equal feeling of responsibility, not to say guilt. And we cannot desist from warning, and warning again, we cannot and should not slacken in our efforts to make the nations of the world, and especially their governments, aware of the unspeakable disaster they are certain to provoke unless they change their attitude toward each other and toward the task of shaping the future. We helped in creating this new weapon in order to prevent the enemies of mankind from achieving it ahead of us, which, given the mentality of the Nazis, would have meant inconceivable destruction and the enslavement of the rest of the world. We delivered this weapon into the hands of the American and the British people as trustees of the whole of mankind, as fighters for peace and liberty. But so far we fail to see any guarantee of peace. . . . The war is won, but the peace is not. 99

—from *The Einstein Reader* by Albert Einstein, 1956

1 **ANALYZING INDIVIDUALS** Why does Einstein feel guilty about the use of the atomic bomb?

_____

_____

2 **ANALYZING POINTS OF VIEW** What does Einstein fear about the way nations and people view the atomic bomb?

_____

_____

_____

3 **HISTORY** How does Einstein justify the development of the atomic bomb for use in World War II?

_____

_____

_____

4 **IDENTIFYING PERSPECTIVES** Who were the "trustees" of the atomic bomb during the 1950s (when this essay was written)? Does Einstein have complete trust in these trustees?

_____

_____

_____

_____

5 **EXPLAINING ISSUES** What does Einstein mean when he writes, "The war is won, but the peace is not"? What issues that we still deal with today was he concerned about?

_____

_____

_____

_____

_____

ESSENTIAL QUESTIONS

Why does conflict develop?

Why is history important?

How do governments change?

How does technology change the way people live?

How do new ideas change the way people live?

1 Think About It

Review the Supporting Questions you developed at the beginning of this chapter and the evidence you gathered in this chapter. Were you able to answer each Supporting Question? If there was not enough evidence to answer your Supporting Questions, what additional evidence do you need to consider?

_____

_____

_____

_____

_____

2 Organize Your Evidence

Use the chart below to help you understand how different events led to changes in society, government, and people's everyday lives. List these events or conditions and the changes they led to.

CAUSE Conditions or Events	EFFECT or CHANGE In government, everyday life, and so on.
Conflict:	
Ideas:	
Technology:	

❸ Talk About It

Work with a small group and use the chart to guide a discussion of those events and conditions that led to change. Discuss the different kinds of change that certain types of events or conditions lead to. Take notes as you discuss these ideas and identify evidence you might still need to gather.

_____

_____

_____

_____

❹ Write About It

Relate the historical conditions and events you read about to similar occurrences or changes in your own life or in modern life in general. Choose one or two of these life-changing conditions or events. Describe how they caused important changes in society today. You might want to gather more evidence about a particular condition or event that you will write about.

_____

_____

_____

_____

❺ Connect to the Essential Questions

You and your classmates might have ideas about changes that could be made to establish and protect the rights and responsibilities of everyone at your school. Work with a small group to write an outline for a school constitution that expresses the rights and responsibilities you believe should be expected for and of everyone. Make sure that your constitution addresses all the groups in the school: students, teachers, administrators, support staff, and those in charge of extracurricular activities (such as sports or theater). When your group has completed its outline, compare it to the outlines from other groups. Work together to create a more formal and complete outline that everyone can agree on.

TAKING ACTION

MAKE CONNECTIONS Society and technology are changing quickly today, just as they were in the early 1800s. For example, consider technology that is being developed now, such as self-driving cars and the ability to perform medical procedures remotely.

Technology has positive and negative effects. A positive effect is that the world's people can communicate with each other faster than ever before. A negative effect might be that people can lose their jobs due to automation.

DIRECTIONS: Select one significant new technological advancement. Conduct research to learn details about the technology. Then make a list of the benefits and drawbacks related to the technology. Use your list to write a letter to the editor of your local newspaper presenting details about the technology. Take a position about whether you think the technology will help or hurt your community using your list of benefits and drawbacks to support your argument. In addition, identify ways that residents of your area can prepare for the arrival of this technology.

_____

_____

_____

_____

_____

_____

_____

_____